REVOLUTIONARY
SPIRIT

A post-punk
exorcism

PAUL SIMPSON

JAW
BONE

*She didn't live to see it, but this book
is dedicated to my mother, Doris.
Probably just as well.
She'd have been appalled.*

**REVOLUTIONARY SPIRIT
A POST-PUNK EXORCISM
PAUL SIMPSON**

A Jawbone book
First edition 2023
Published in the UK and the USA by
Jawbone Press
Office G1
141–157 Acre Lane
London SW2 5UA
England
www.jawbonepress.com

ISBN 978-1-911036-83-8

Printed by Short Run Press, Exeter

1 2 3 4 5 27 26 25 24 23

CONTENTS

PROLOGUE

Not only was 'Revolutionary Spirit' by far the
best single that we put out at Zoo, but The Wild
Swans captured that 'young man's idealistic
vision' thing better than any other bunch of
English young men since the Brotherhood
first put paint to canvas back in the 1850s.

BILL DRUMMOND

Make another failure like that...
and you'll be immortal.

HONORÉ DE BALZAC, A DAUGHTER OF EVE

It fades in. The bass is inaudible, and for reasons unknown even to the band, the single has been recorded in mono. There's no seven-inch available, and the cover art looks like the design on an airline sickbag.

'It's a bit *Robin Hood*,' sniffs Julian Cope.

'I prefer the B-side,' drawls Ian McCulloch.

John Peel literally plays it to death.

Great, or at least *significant* records are often loved because of their imperfections, not despite them. If they connect on a physical or emotional level, all is forgiven. If they capture some spirit of the age within their spiral, they pass into sonic Valhalla.

By 1980, punk rock had done its demolition work, and we, along with some friends in the north of England, were shaping a new musical landscape; a literate antidote to bleakness and cynicism. In questing for aural arcadia, The Wild Swans tripped over our own ambition and fell, and I fell the hardest.

Waking up in my fifties, the last swan on the lake, I discover that in the Philippines, 6,703 miles away from my hometown of Liverpool, The Wild Swans are superstars, and I am considered a rock god. You couldn't make this shit up, and mercifully I don't have to.

Some bands are loved because of their imperfections, not despite them. It fades in.

PART ONE

A THING THAT DEVOURS
2011

I

A TASTE OF PARADISE

SEPTEMBER 2011. MANILA. Typical of my luck, The Wild Swans have landed in the Philippines during a Category 4 super typhoon: 90-to-150mph winds, monsoon rains, supersaturated earth. Freak waves have decimated Manila's sea defences, cutting power to homes and submerging entire neighbourhoods.

Observing the carnage through the floor-to-ceiling glass walls of my twenty-sixth-floor hotel room, I'm experiencing a tropical depression of my own right now and praying this trip isn't going to turn out to be my rock'n'roll *Götterdämmerung*—a career-ending clusterfuck of misfortune. Psychically fragile at the best of times, I'm paranoid that the concerts we've flown six thousand miles to play—the largest in the band's thirty-year history—are about to be cancelled due to a State of Emergency being declared. If our insurer invokes the *force majeure* 'act of god' clause, my Filipino tour promotor Jesse Cambossa Sr. and I will be in financial peril. With the little savings I had back home gone on recording our last album and on tour merchandise, I can't help but entertain the idea that perhaps this trip, like this group, was cursed from the start.

Naively, I'd imagined we'd be arriving here to tropical sunshine and ultramarine waters—all that *A Taste Of Paradise* 1970s television commercial crap—but the views through the Airbus cabin windows as we circled Manila Bay this morning were something closer to Pendle in fog. Now, just hours after landing, the skies over Metro Manila are an apocalyptic purple-black; shredded palm leaves and corrugated roof panels swirl overhead, debris in a cosmic Dyson. On the pinnacle of the nearby Mission Revival church, an illuminated Perspex crucifix rocks on its mount before short-circuiting in a fountain of incandescent sparks. This is End Times drama on a scale I've never encountered before, and I once saw Yes in concert.

High over P. Burgos Street, a five-metre satellite dish shears off a rooftop and Frisbees thirty storeys down, gouging a trench in the tarmac before screaming to a halt like a crashed UFO. Just as I'm thinking how dreamlike and hallucinatory all this is, I catch sight of the naked Filipina waving to me from the balcony of the residential tower block opposite. She's not in distress, she's washing her hair in the storm. Welcome to Manila.

This is the second severe tropical cyclone to hit the Philippine islands in the past fortnight. According to the hotel receptionist, nine people have died this morning—not from falling debris but as a result of venomous sea snakes escaping into the flooded streets. The television news channels are broadcasting footage of citizens wading waist-deep through floodwaters, stumbling over rubble while carrying frightened children and pets on their shoulders. The chewing-gum-spotted pavements of my Liverpool hometown have never felt so far away.

As if all this isn't distressing enough, a coup is underway. Not within the military or Philippine government, but within the ranks of The Wild Swans.

In two days we are booked to perform live on the popular daytime television variety show *Eat Bulaga*, with the first of two enormo-concerts to follow. Rehearsal rooms have been booked for us, but they are far across town, and we'd need a submarine to get there. Individually experienced as this line-up of the band is, we haven't seen each other since our UK tour ended three months ago, and we desperately need to bond and rehearse. It's my name on the contracts and I'm feeling ill with the weight of responsibility, but all my friends want to talk about right now is their split of the merchandise; one jet-lagged firebrand is even threatening not to play.

It's only day one of nine here, but it already feels as if things are beginning to unravel. I should have known, should have expected some Joseph Conrad *Heart Of Darkness* shit. Liverpudlians can't travel nearly seven thousand miles away from the perfumed Ganges of the North and expect to stay sane.

My antenna for trouble first began to twitch on the fourteen-hour-long connecting flight from Schiphol this morning, when the KLM air hostess, Marijke, sashayed down the aisles of the plane, displaying a notice to passengers.

THERE IS A MANDATORY DEATH SENTENCE FOR ANY PASSENGER
ATTEMPTING TO IMPORT DRUGS INTO THE PHILIPPINE ISLANDS.

'*Mandatory death sentence?*' I repeat. 'That's a little extreme, isn't it?'

Turning in my seat to locate my fellow band members, I improvise an *Oh no! I'm being handcuffed* mime, only to be met by ashen faces.

Oh! Perfect! We'll be fashioning shivs from toothbrush handles, and exchanging fellatio for tobacco, by nightfall.

II
POP NECROPOLIS

Eat Bulaga translates in the Filipino Tagalog language to 'eat surprise'. Well, the surprise for the millions watching us live on the show this coming Wednesday will be witnessing their 'new wave' favourites The Wild Swans standing mute as Milli Vanilli because we haven't practised a note. Ah well, with one national disaster underway, another one won't break the bank. Oh wait, that's right: it will. The TV slot is essential in promoting our concerts here, and if it or they are cancelled due to the typhoon, I'll be travelling home to Britain if not poor then certainly broke—and I'm too old for broke.

Niche bands discovering that they are superstars in some far-flung territory of the world is the stuff of satire and heavy metal rockumentaries, and I am half expecting some twat in a baseball cap and aviator shades to jump out of my hotel wardrobe and shout, 'Cut! Okay, let's take that again. Tarquin, I need more smoke and lightning! Paul, darling, can you actually start crying this time?'

It was fellow Liverpudlian musicians China Crisis who, in 2007, first alerted me to my level of fame out here, and I honestly thought they were taking the piss. While not unknown in the UK, The Wild Swans are somewhat trapped in amber as an early 80s 'John Peel' band that didn't quite fulfil their potential, and in the US as college-radio favourites that by rights should have been huge. I'm not complaining. A classic debut single on a credible record label and a loyal fan base is not to be sniffed at. Thousands of bands would love to be in my position, but after thirty years of being the bridesmaid, sometimes you wonder why you keep going.

It's not just The Wild Swans who are megastars out here, it's also Care, my short-lived collaboration with Ian 'Lightning Seeds' Broudie. It wasn't until Jesse's niece messaged me on his behalf earlier this year, inviting me to come out to the islands to play these dates, that the penny finally dropped.

Speaking of pennies, with my complete back catalogue out of print right now, money is tighter than ever. I need these shows to take place. Royalties from our recently released album, *The Coldest Winter For A Hundred Years*, could take years to filter through, and because I financed it myself, I can't even be sure I'll break even.

—

In 1990, I'd just crawled out from a hole in the ground, a pop necropolis of 80s nearly men. You know the types: those minor stars of the UK's post-punk independent music scene whose releases on once fashionable record labels like Fast, Rough Trade, Postcard, Factory, and Zoo brought their juvenile creators fame, credibility, and a temporary passport to the majors. For every Aztec Camera, Associates, and Orange Juice that successfully made the leap from fanzine to *Smash Hits* cover stars, there was a Manicured Noise, a Josef K, and a Blue Orchids that didn't. Fame was never the objective, of course. Recognition was. While the careers of my stablemates Julian Cope and Ian McCulloch skyrocketed when they traded up from Bill Drummond and Dave Balfe's Zoo Records to Phonogram and Warner Bros, my own attempts with The Wild Swans spectacularly failed to ignite.

Despite some success in Germany and North America, just eighteen months and two albums after signing to Seymour Stein's prestigious Sire Records, The Wild Swans' once-incandescent flame guttered and died. Without a recording contract and the support of a manager, my self-confidence shrank in equal proportion to my funds. As weeks of inactivity turned into years, my fragile grasp on reality began to warp like the neck of my unplayed guitar. By 1990, the character once cited as 'Best Dressed Man' in the *NME* was haunting the streets of Merseyside like a glamorous tramp in worn-out £200 shoes.

The way I saw it, only two courses of action were open to me. I could swallow my pride, bury my creative urges, and try to secure civilian employment. Or I could continue to follow my star and ride out the remainder of Margaret Thatcher's terrible Reich surviving on unemployment benefit, and the stretched-thin patience of my partner, until the world finally woke up to my 'terrible genius'. In my head, I was post-punk aristocracy. Haunted by stories of former bandmates and musician acquaintances reduced to driving taxis and ferrying human-transplant organs between hospitals to pay the rent, I chose to emulate the lifestyle of my literary heroes and embrace the way of the beatnik *flâneur*.

Incapable of work, I planned to turn all my anger and frustration into fantastical novels and film scripts. I kidded myself that skipping lunch and dressing in dead men's suits from charity shops was romantic and character-building but, in reality, all it built was good cheekbones and resentment.

Delirium from hunger, grief, and alcohol may have inspired Baudelaire and Knut Hamsun to create their masterpieces, but with no real outlet for my creativity, and still hurting from what I saw as the betrayal of a sacred bond by my former bandmates, I spent the first half of the 1990s in the foetal position, hiding from the world, a faint photocopy of the man I was. With Madchester, grunge, then Britpop spreading through the country like a rapidly mutating virus, I bunkered down in newly rented rooms on the banks of the River Mersey, avoiding tax demands and praying for missing royalties and a holy war on what I saw as a morally bankrupt music business.

At my lowest point, sedated on antidepressants, I was unable to pick up the handset of a ringing telephone, let alone a musical instrument. Instead, I busied myself with what I saw as manifesting my great and secret work: nailing tree bark to the walls and creating surreal children's stories that never left my desk.

Losing both my record and publishing deals in the Christmas of 1990 came as a shock. I'd been living in a bubble for so long that I hadn't realised that I had acquired a reputation. In 1979, I'd left the band most likely to, The Teardrop Explodes, to work in a city-centre tearoom. In 1984, I'd walked out of Care, my collaboration with Ian Broudie, after a hit single. And as far as the world was concerned, The Wild Swans had had their moment and blown it. Twice. What I had viewed as perfectionism in myself was interpreted by the industry as a self-destructive streak.

So, what now? I couldn't just 'get a job' because (a) I wasn't qualified, (b) I didn't want one, and (c) I hadn't completed the mission yet. I'd had a glimpse into the magical orchard, and I wasn't prepared to sell my life's time or the time of my life to strangers. I know. I know! Why should I be exempt? Am I really so arrogant and egocentric to believe that the laws and rules of society don't apply to me? Well, yes. I've known that from childhood. As every one of my school reports stated, *Paul is a dreamer. Needs to wake up.* Lack of security is the price I pay for personal freedom. If you choose to stay in the amusement park long after everyone else has gone home, as I did, you can't complain when things become a little scary.

When Sauron's terrible A&R gaze shifted from Liverpool to Madchester, I wasn't prepared to get baggy or die trying, so why didn't I flight-case my musical ambitions forever then and retrain, get a Cert Ed teaching qualification like so many of my musical peers? I could be running a department by now. Why? Because FEAR KILLS MAGIC. Because, if Arthur Rimbaud were alive now, he wouldn't be pressure washing his driveway in a pastel-coloured polo shirt. A steady job for life with a pension plan? Fuck that! Blake's angels are *still* in the treetops. Someone has to disappoint the expectations of loved ones; someone has to take selfish and wildly irresponsible stabs at magnificence!

Fucking Nietzsche. 'Live dangerously,' he says. I signed up for the free trial in 1979, and I've been trying to cancel my subscription ever since.

III
CHARM OF THE ABUSER

The Wild Swans haven't been an actual 'band'—as in a Beatles-style band of brothers, writing, and working together full-time to manifest a shared vision—since that ugly day in the summer of 1982 when, following a particularly heavy bout of depression, I returned from a fortnight's respite in Holland to discover my own band had been burgled from me. While I'd been in the Rijksmuseum, marvelling at Jan Asselijn's seventeenth-century masterpiece *The Threatened Swan*, the young maestro of the group had not only deceived my bandmates into believing that I had quit my own band but had also installed a replacement singer I had recently—and to his complete derision—pointed out as my only competition in Liverpool, his intention being for them to carry on using my band name of The Wild Swans and our co-written songs.

Innocent as he was in the overthrow, the new vocalist singing my strange Blakean lyrics was never going to fly. Emptying the Wild Swans bank account and rebranding under the name The Lotus Eaters, they took my wartime haircut and baggy trousers/sepia tone aesthetic, and one particularly significant piece of sonic opium I'd written with them, to the very A&R man and record label intent on signing The Wild Swans.

Too humiliated to tell friends and family what had happened, I retreated into myself, a spectre even to my long-suffering girlfriend. In the sultry summer of 1983, every shop I entered and every car that passed me in the street was playing their My Little Pony song about photographing flowers. The musical chorus of this hit record of theirs was entirely constructed from the chords I'd written for a Wild Swans song entitled 'Opium', recorded for a BBC Radio 1 session for David 'Kid' Jensen fourteen months earlier, having begun life in the basement of The Teardrop Explodes' rehearsal room in Prospect Vale, Kensington, when I welded those very chords onto a verse pattern written by my best friend, keyboard player Ged Quinn, with temporary bassist David 'Yorkie' Palmer (later of Space) and Justin Stavely on drums.

I'm not completely deluded, of course. I know my version of the song would never have been a hit. My voice was too strained, my melody and lyrics, about twisting tourniquets and binding wounds, too dark and niche for daytime radio, but listening to my own bastardised music coming back at me from the TV and radio . . . did they honestly think I wouldn't notice? The last time I had looked, my fellow The Wild Swans and I weren't trying to write yacht rock, we were aiming for post-punk glory, Blakean reach exceeding scally grasp. Their new version could be sung by housewives and pre-schoolers. To my poison-filled ears, the song's soft-rock-for-the-school-run cheerfulness was as caustic as lye. Just another rock'n'roll rip-off story—every band has one. But already damaged, that summer it broke me.

Fast-forward eighteen months to 1985, and after resigning from Care, my short-lived musical collaboration with future Lightning Seed Ian Broudie, I reformed The Wild Swans, taking my brilliant writing partners back. Why? Because I was told The Lotus Eaters had just split up (*quelle surprise*, this also turned out to be a lie) and because it was so ridiculously easy. Just plug in and go, the old gear in the old rehearsal room just a two-minute walk from my flat on Hope Street. More importantly because, in that moment, I believed that completing the original mission of The Wild Swans was more important than any still-bleeding wounds of mine. I could suppress the massive insult to me if together we were going to once more reach to touch the mythic.

Within months, a BBC radio session with fellow scouser, long-time supporter, and friend of the band Janice Long resulted in the offer of a fixed two-album deal from A&R legend Seymour Stein at Sire, the holy grail of record labels. But by 1986, the political and musical climate had changed in the UK, and, somewhere in the band's reformation, we forgot to be remarkable. It happens. Major-label thinking is like a virus—it starts with a heavy suggestion from on high that you dump your brilliant UK manager for *American representation*; you should work with X, not Y. X is hot right now. Before the ink on the contract has dried, you've forgotten your mission statement and adapted your timeless sound to make it current. You've forgotten what made you unique and why you started the band in the first place.

Fast-forward two more years to 1988, and, despairing at the latest predictable betrayal of my last remaining co-writer, I abandoned the notion of an English electric brotherhood forever. Shakespeare, Turner, Keats, Blake, punk rock, the Kibbo Kift—everything that had informed the band's vision, all corrupted. If my own bandmate didn't care about what The Wild Swans represented, why should I?

In 1988, determined to steer the ship alone, I began to write solo, drafting in the best possible musicians at my disposal as and when required. Not an ideal situation when you are traumatised and can't afford to pay anyone. Out of my mind, I delivered a second album so madly at odds with the Wild Swans brand name it went unreleased in the UK for eighteen years. Trauma replayed often enough becomes hardwired, and, as a result, I am damaged to this day—mentally fragmented by the charm of the abuser.

—

The current manifestation of The Wild Swans includes San Francisco-born Enrique Maymi, guitarist with notorious psychedelic dysfunctionals The Brian Jonestown Massacre. Ricky is by turns sweet, troubled, and brilliant. Having had one uncle in both the Grateful Dead and The Tubes and another in cult glam-rock legends Zolar X, music runs in his DNA. Unusually for a guitarist, Ricky is all about what best serves the song rather than simply investing in his own guitar parts. Resembling *Swordfishtrombones*-era Tom Waits, half-Columbian Ricky's motto of 'not too tight, not too loose' says it all. Investing his performances with everything he's got, Ricky will elevate even the thinnest musical idea he's asked to contribute to into something muscular, dynamic, and nuanced. Any musician with an effects pedal can sound psychedelic, but having chosen to live and operate in the invisible margins between the straight world and its hallucinatory reverse, Enrique *is* psychedelic.

Introduced to me in 2009 via Echo & The Bunnymen's co-manager, Peasey Gordon, Wild Swans fan Ricky and I arranged to meet at the Jonestown Massacre's upcoming Liverpool show. Finding him outside the venue deep in hyped-up conversation with my early 80s bong-buddy neighbour and fellow musician Mike Mooney, I beamed. Of course these two would be friends! Likewise, in that magic moment, it made perfect sense to Ricky and me to invite Mike to be involved in the recording of a new Wild Swans album.

A joyously dishevelled free spirit, Mike is the closest Liverpool has to a Jimmy Page-style guitar rock god. While you can't absolutely guarantee that he will turn up to the recording session you've booked, you can guarantee that if he does, he'll be channelling the highest possible magic. Mike is the gold leaf in your colour palette; the tiniest amount adds permanent lustre to the finished work. He and I first met in the July of 1981, during the second of the nine nights of righteous civil disturbances that constituted the Toxteth Uprising in Liverpool. While leaning out of my bedsit window on Rodney Street, nervously watching the glow from the flames of the burning Rialto Ballroom building nearby, I spotted two young men heading haplessly in the direction of the violence in an attempt to return to their homes beyond the police lines in Princes Park. With no way of knowing where or when the inner-city turbulence would stop, I invited the excited strangers up to my first-floor bedsit for a cup of tea. As we watched nurses from the Royal Liverpool Hospital running beneath my windows, arms loaded with bags of plasma to restock the waiting ambulances, Mike, his best friend Paul Green, and I bonded over the unfolding drama. Incredibly, despite having been a member of the touring bands for Echo & The Bunnymen, The Psychedelic Furs, Julian Cope, and Spiritualized, outside of his hometown, Mike is virtually unknown. Restless when told what to play, if given the freedom to improvise he will bend musical space for you. At our last Liverpool show at the University, his ten-minute-long improvised guitar abstraction during the encore left visible scorch marks on the stage. As frontman, marooned up there without even a tambourine to hit, all I could do was stand back, smiling, surrendering awestruck as Mike's shamanic quest for the infinite stole the show.

Playing keyboards for me in this line-up is smiling wunderkind Richard Turvey. Sharp, funny, and the most technically proficient musician in the band, Stoke-on-Trent-born Rich speaks his mind. When he is engineering and co-producing songs that will become *The Coldest Winter For A Hundred Years*, I tell him I want part of the track we are working on to swirl like the end section of 'Out Of The Blue' from Roxy Music's 1974 album *Country*

Life. He looks at me like I'm taking Swahili. 'Mate, I'm only twenty-three. I don't know what the fuck you're on about.'

I can't help but laugh. He's right. I'm fifty-one. The world has changed significantly since I was last in a twenty-four-track recording studio. It's like some septuagenarian asking me to replicate Al Bowley's vocal technique on a 78rpm shellac I've never heard. When I was Rich's age, rock'n'roll could still just about be contained in one's grasp, but for his generation, culture has atomised. He can't be expected to know every song ever recorded, to have seen every movie—and, with Google and a smartphone, he doesn't need to. Blunt as he is, I know he likes and respects what I am trying to do with this record, and I like the way he's pushing back at the tired sensibilities of the old gods. As if to prove it, after the recording session he offers to join the band on keyboards. An exceptional musician, engineer, and producer, Rich also co-manages Liverpool's biggest and best recording studios, so, of course, I accept.

In late 2010, Steve 'Billy Biscuits' Beswick, the incredible drummer on our *Coldest Winter* album, suffered a stroke. Despite his herculean attempts at speed-healing, the entire band are unwilling to further risk his health so close to the attack. Rich has recommended Stuart Mann, a former student friend of his, for our forthcoming UK tour. Stuart, the frostiest young drummer since Television's Billy Ficca, learned our entire live set, beat-perfect, simply by listening to a CD-R of the tracks during a seven-hour drive from Cornwall. Stuart is handsome, dry, and Cary Grant-level charming. He's also training to be a GP, which could come in handy if we can't get this merchandise-split business sorted and things get ugly.

Unbelievably, playing bass for me on this trip is Les Pattinson, a co-founder of Echo & The Bunnymen. Les and I started infant school together back in 1963; we've been through measles, moon landings, mopeds, girlfriends, punk, marriages, births, deaths, and divorce together. When I phoned him, asking him to play on both my new album and its UK promotional tour earlier this year, Les had been in self-imposed musical retirement for over a decade, so I wasn't expecting him to say yes. Calm, metronome tight, and *Man In A Suitcase* stylish, Les is, like his old bandmate Will Sergeant, that rarest of things, an honest and moral man, and I, along with several thousand Filipino fans, can't believe our luck that he's here. At our first rehearsal, watching him blow dust and spider webs from the back of the famous Ampeg bass rig he used on the first five Bunnymen albums was almost too exciting for Ricky to bear.

Yep, it's a killer band, and I may have to go on a murder spree if we can't sort this money thing out. Meanwhile, the typhoon rages on. The ancient Tagalog deities are angry and demanding a sacrifice. Something significant is required, and, with no one else volunteering, I think it might have to be me.

—

If I'm not handling this typhoon business well, it's hardly surprising. It's been a difficult few years. Eighteen months ago, somewhere in the jungles of Sri Lanka, I contracted a virus—a waterborne parasite that sapped my strength and gave me killer headaches, night sweats, and breathing problems. These malaria-like symptoms never completely leave me, but they can be subdued with exercise. Sadly, the tidal nature of the accompanying brain fog and its by-product of mild amnesia can easily give rise to depression, so I am not ideally placed for cyclones, cancelled gigs, and insurrection. Beneath all of this lays a deeper base layer of grief. While I was mixing *The Coldest Winter For A Hundred Years*, my mother died. It wasn't a complete surprise; she'd been on a physical slow fade for years. Diagnosed with early-stage vascular dementia, she wasn't ill so much as exhausted from a long life. Destabilised by the death of my father from prostate cancer in 2002, and unable to bear the indignities that come with old age, she just buckled and slipped away one afternoon in a temporary nursing home while my sister, Valerie, held her hand. Stuck on the school run in heavy traffic, I arrived just moments too late. All I could do was sit by the bedside and hold my mother's still young-looking fingers as the heat passed out of them. This remarkable new-age-before-it-was-a-thing woman who made me toy shields from discarded oil-barrel lids and fixed the broken barrels of my toy guns in the blue flames of the gas cooker before my tears had dried; this perfect foil and human shield against my disciplinarian father. With her passing, an irreplaceable presence in my life has gone.

'What are the guns for, Jesse?'

I've just noticed that the drivers of our SUVs are carrying firearms.

'Bit over the top, isn't it?' I suggest.

Jesse turns to me and asks me solemnly, 'Do you want to be kidnapped, Paul?'

Miraculously, despite the flooding, Jesse has found us an emergency rehearsal space nearby. It's a tiny recording studio; there's no air conditioning or flushing toilet in there, but at least we can plug into some amps and try to access the muscle memory of playing the set from last year's UK tour. We also have to work a Care song into the live set. If The Wild Swans being huge out here isn't already strange enough for me to grasp, Care are just as huge. Jesse insisted I do at least one Care song in our set or the Filipino fans will feel let down. I resisted at first, but Ricky persuaded me it could work. Care never played live, so it feels bizarre to be singing our twenty-seven-year-old song 'Whatever Possessed You' for the first time ever, so far from where it was conceived, but he's right, it sounds really good, and the closest to The Wild Swans in sound.

At eighty-three percent humidity, it feels like we're breathing opiated syrup, and after three hours of rehearsing, we all have killer headaches from dehydration and need to go back to the aircon of the hotel to lay down. Despite the many physical and emotional obstacles, we've had a good rehearsal, and because the flooding in Makati has eased a little, we have a longer one booked for tomorrow in a professional rehearsal space. It feels like the horrible debilitating tension of the morning has eased a little. Stu and Richard are clearly buzzing to be on such an exotic adventure, and, despite the jet lag, once back at the hotel none of us wants to go to bed. Jesse has forbidden us to leave the hotel without our security guys, so, faking our goodnights to them, the band all cram into a hotel lift. Once inside, instead of ascending to our rooms, we press the down button and escape through the staff exit out onto P. Burgos Street, where, unchaperoned, we enter the nearest bar. Once inside, we are delighted to discover the sort of dimly lit, strung-with-fairy-lights bagnio Tom Waits might immortalise in song. Because of the typhoon, the place is almost deserted of horny Western tourists. As we order a round of Red Horse beers, Ricky leans in close and whispers to me.

'Tell her to leave the caps on the bottles.'

'How come?' I ask.

'We don't want to get our drinks spiked.'

Years of international touring experience with the Jonestown Massacre means Ricky has come up against pretty much everything that can possibly go wrong for a rock band abroad. He's right to be wary—this is the red-light zone, after all—and, just thirty minutes later, Richard 'Baby Swan' Turvey, our curly-haired keyboard player, is acting very out of character. He's decided that the two dozen identically underdressed girls half-heartedly dancing on the thrust stage need to up their game. Telling the scary-looking, heavily muscled Mamasan of the bar that her girls look bored, he absolutely demands some upbeat music and a distinct shift in the girl's laissez-faire attitude. What on earth has come over him?

Berating her girls, the manager selects a CD of classic 70s funk and soul and gets every girl in the place up and in line. With Richard at their head, he leads them in a vast conga-style line of improvised shape-pulling around the club. Clearly, Rich has been subduing his inner club demon for years while hiding some serious choreography chops. Witnessing cherub-faced Richard leading a two-dozen-strong line of barely dressed Filipinas in an improvised dance routine to 'September' by Earth, Wind & Fire is just too funny. Rick James on angel dust couldn't bring the funk like this, and we are incontinent with laughter. This is brilliant—just what we needed to decompress. What we haven't realised yet is that Richard's second drink has been spiked. He's completely off his tits. Mooneye is laughing so hard he hasn't noticed the pair of stealth Filipinas that have silently appeared like sexy landmines up on his lap. Les, meanwhile, is not having any of it. He's been feeling massively uncomfortable since we arrived, and now he's up and preparing to leave.

'What's up?' I shout over the music.

'I'm going back to the hotel,' he says. 'I can't be here, Paul—I'm a married man.'

'Me too,' I reply. 'But we're not sex tourists. We're only having a drink.'

He's right, though, this is all a bit sketchy, and even by just drinking here we are contributing to this lovely country's pimp economy. We leave, intending to find a normal bar, but our hotel is smack in the heart of Makati's red-light district; there is no normal. I'm not ready for the Ladyboy bar *Mixed-Nuts*, dwarf boxing at *Ringside Bar*, and *High Heels*, *Plumpers*, *Honkers*, *Blimpers*, and *Boingers*, all look like variations on where we've just left.

Over breakfast the next morning, I learn that Stu and Rich stayed out partying until past 4am, and Ricky and Mike had been pulled in by the local police. Loose tobacco isn't a thing out here, and roll-up cigarettes are unknown. The local cops thought these two *Putis* were blatantly smoking weed in the street, and it took some fast talking to persuade them otherwise.

IV
SLOW POISON

Overnight, the flood waters around Metro Manila have retreated just enough for the band to reach the rehearsal room complex across town in Pio del Pilar. The city may be quiet right now, but the danger is far from over. Typhoon *Pedring* has finally passed by and is heading for China, but its sibling, *Quiel*, is currently gathering strength over the Philippine Sea and is forecasted to make landfall just north of here on Friday, just in time for our gig.

The Wild Swans have not played together in over three months, and thanks to the floods we have already lost two of the three daylong rehearsals we need to get in shape for the shows. While the boys restring their guitars and become acquainted with the hired drum kit, keyboards, and amplifiers, Jesse and his driver, Jonel, accompany me to three of Manila's most popular radio stations to conduct live interviews.

Sir Paul, what are your first impressions of the Philippines?
Do you agree that the 1980s were the best decade for pop music?
Do you find Filipinas beautiful?
So, what can your fans expect from your concerts here?
Have you tried our national dish, Adobo, yet?
Will you be including any songs by The Care at your gigs?
Is it true that Sir Les Pattinson of Echo & The Bunnymens is playing bass with you?
Sir Paul, what is the name of your horse?

The horse question comes up a lot out here. Of course, I don't own a horse, but back in the early noughties, when I was without a record deal and money was tight, I once joked on social media that I'd been patrolling my private estate on horseback, and the irony, lost in translation, stuck. During the final interview of the morning, the radio station switchboard receives a request from a listener, politely asking if I can talk to her husband, a lifelong fan of the band who has tickets for Saturday's show but cannot now make it as he has been admitted to hospital. Jesse arranges for her to phone back when I'm off air, and she is seated at her husband's bedside. We are en route to the practice rooms when the lady calls back politely informing me that she is now holding her mobile phone to her husband's ear. Presuming his arms must be incapacitated by bandages, I go into affable 'pop star' mode.

'Hello P—! I am so sorry to hear that you are unwell and that you are going to miss our concert on Saturday. Oh, man, what a drag! Your wife E— tells me that you are our biggest fan in the Philippines. I am so flattered. So, what on earth happened, and how are you feeling now?'

No response.

'Hello? Can you hear me?'

Gesturing to Jesse that there is no one there, I suggest that maybe we hang up, and call back. But wait . . . if I close my eyes and concentrate hard, I can just make out the shallowest of breathing and the faintest possible wordless attempts to respond. This is when I know, I just KNOW, that this isn't some broken-bone 'get well soon' thing at all but the strained exertions of a dying man. I've never been in this situation before, and I don't know how to handle it. Faced with silence at the end of the phone, I hear myself saying trite things like, *Thank you for supporting me and The Wild Swans for all these years, I hope you'll be feeling better soon. We'll come back to play in the Philippines again soon, maybe next year, and then we can meet in person, and I can sign all of your Wild Swans and Care records.*

I'm talking, talking, talking; kidding myself and kidding this poor man that I don't know what is happening. His wife and family love him so much that they are sacrificing a little of their precious remaining time with him to enable this moment to happen. I don't know what I am saying now, or for how long, but I talk quietly into the man's ear without pausing, until, when it intuitively feels right, I say 'God bless' and conclude the call.

God bless? Where did that come from? How odd. That was something my late father used to say when ending phone calls.

Arriving at the Infinitif entertainment complex, I am undone. The last thing I feel like doing after such a raw experience is rehearsing. I need to be alone to think about what just happened and examine why am I so rocked by it. I mean, I'm not Sting or Bono; I don't have audiences with the Dalai Lama or the Pope; I've never even been asked to sign a fan's plaster cast before. Things like this just don't happen to people like me, and I desperately want to understand.

Filipinos have a more translucent relationship with death than us Brits, and because the majority are devout Christians and believe in the concept of personal salvation, they don't quite share our ridiculous black-lacquered, Victorian fear of it. So, maybe that phone call wasn't such an unusual occurrence after all; simply a wife spotting an opportunity to do something nice for her beloved, without feeling the need to flag up the gravity of it to me in advance. Comforted as I am by this thought, I can't afford to examine it now because I can hear the boys tuning up next door.

Ideally, band practices are a bonding experience—at minimum, a good laugh—but walking into this soundproofed and windowless space right now feels like I'm gate-crashing a Stasi disciplinary meeting. There's more discord than harmony in here, and the very atmosphere appears to have taken on weight. There's mutiny afoot, some dispute over splitting the merch money. Rich and Stu are exchanging embarrassed looks, Mike is pretending to fix his guitar pedals, and Ricky, all out of American Spirit, is pacing the room like a jonesing bear.

Only Les, my oldest friend, spots the blight upon me and takes me outside to ask me what is wrong. How can I explain how a phone call has punctured me, amplifying the sense of dislocation I feel and forcing me to question the validity of what I am doing with my life? I mean, is being an entertainer really how I have chosen to spend my one brief flash in eternity? I'm not even good at it. I am convinced fate had other plans for me, but back in 1960, hearing 'Theme From A Summer Place' by The Percy Faith Strings sent me into a puree-dribbling swoon, and the die was cast.

For someone with the disposition of a rescue greyhound, even the shortest of UK tours brings a risk of psychosis. European outings double that risk, and Far Eastern tours, as I am just discovering, practically guarantee it. Back in the December of 1981, on the opening show of The Wild Swans' first ever tour, supporting my pals the Bunnymen, I walked onto the stage of the Oxford New Theatre only to overhear a girl standing at the front shout, 'Eeeew! He looks like he's dead,' and just like that, before I'd even strapped on my guitar, I wilted; my will draining out faster than blood from a stab wound.

A few nights later, in Liverpool, heckled by impatient young Bunnyfans during our as-yet-unreleased song 'Revolutionary Spirit', I soldiered on until a burning box of Swan Vestas was thrown at my face. Too humiliated to continue, I unplugged my guitar and slunk offstage, mid-set, only to be berated in the dressing room by my ex-bandmate Ian McCulloch for being unprofessional.

During the second incarnation of The Wild Swans, while touring with The Mighty Lemon Drops, some musical illiterate in the crowd started a chant of 'The Smiths! The Smiths!' and I was instantly brought so low that my soul tried to leave my body. We predated his favourite group by eighteen months. Maybe it was just our gravity-defying quiffs and our vintage 50s shirts that caused the confusion? Whatever it was, I felt dispirited, and it not only ruined the gig, it killed something in playing live for me forever. Vowing thereafter only to tour once a decade felt legitimate in my late twenties; but now, in my fifties, I'm nearly out of runway.

—

The tragic thing about this high noon over merch money is that it is all down to a misunderstanding. A private email to Jesse from my great friend, PR specialist and temporary manager Mitch Poole, has been intercepted by an inexperienced assistant, and, for reasons known only to herself, she has shown it to a member of the band.

The email—a simple instruction to 'look after Paul'—wasn't Mitch pulling some duplicitous stunt to syphon off my bandmate's dollars in order to fund some spiralling drugs habit of mine but simply a reminder to Jesse that I am still feeling a little fragile after the recent death of my mother, and that this temporary incarnation of The Wild Swans are already being well paid for what is in effect just two gigs and a nine-day holiday in the tropics, so to please remember just whose band it is.

Getting the wrong end of the stick and thinking he's being ripped off, this badly jet-lagged group member has called a band meeting and infected the entire group with his angry paranoia. As a result, I am now no longer their bandmate but some heartless Northern mill owner splashing them with mud as I speed past them in my Bentley on my way to take tea with the queen. And just like that, I've been sucked back into the black tar whirlpool of depression I've only recently crawled out of.

In 2005, I went to see my GP about a shoulder problem. After giving what I thought was a near forensic if lengthy description of my symptoms, she stunned me with her prognosis of major depressive disorder and wrote me a prescription for anti-depressants. I'd been emotionally rollercoasting since junior school, so I honestly thought falling into bottomless caverns of despair without warning was just my personality type, you know, like a horoscope trait: 'Geminis are creative, have an affinity with animals, and are regularly incapacitated by fathomless grief. Lucky colour: yellow.'

The vague sense of disappointment I feel with this consensus reality we call 'life' can be traced back to the early 1960s, when my mother took my sister and me to visit the famous Christmas grotto located on the top floor of Liverpool's Blackler's department store. The price of admission to this tinsel-and-glitter wonderland included a mystery gift presented by Father Christmas himself. *Bit small*, I thought, before ripping a hole in its gaudy wrapping paper and holding it up to my eye as if I were peering into the mouth of a cave. *Oh, wonder of wonders!* Nearly peeing my tartan trousers with excitement, I shredded the paper to reveal an Eastern-style dagger sporting three twinkling gems embedded in its gilded handle. The ultra-vivid colours of the fake jewels, the exotic curve of the blade, the glint of the golden plastic—this was a beauty hitherto unknown to me. That potent hit to my pleasure receptors is a magical thrill that I have been chasing and failing to locate ever since, and why 'My Childhood' by Jacques Brel is a towering work of art.

'Paul.'

There is an assumption that if you are a rock musician, you love rock'n'roll. Not me, I hate the stuff. I love its essence and its 60s blossoming. I adore its 70s excesses and punk revisions, but the casual use of the words *iconic*, *classic*, and *psychedelic*; the terms *riff* and *lick*; album reviews using star ratings; seminal punk singles used on TV adverts; The Rock and Roll Hall of Fame; they all make a little sick rise in my throat. Surely an 'industry'-created hall of fame is the very antithesis of rock'n'roll? When exactly was the counterculture sold to musical property developers, and who declared them to be arbiters of taste anyway? Isn't being labelled a *heritage* act just being wheeled into the nicest bedroom in the hospice, the one closest to the morgue? Pop culture has grown so vast and has become so pixilated that young people now cannot contain it all in their arms in the same way that my generation could; and although we oldies can forgive minor indiscretions, like *vinyls* being used as a plural and records *dropping* rather than being released, seeing Ramones and Sex Pistols merchandise on sale in Primark makes us want to go on a firebombing spree. As for *jamming*, I'd rather swallow Nitromors. The entire genre of jazz aside, the only good thing that ever came from a jam session was Bonne Maman's raspberry conserve. Most of all, I detest the term *rock'n'roll*—a name as limiting to the infinite plasticity of the medium as Bakelite. Oh, and the fetishizing of musical equipment. I mean, what does it matter if one owns a 1959 Crapsonic in Varicose Blue and plays it through a vintage Fuck-o-Plex 2000 tape delay, and an original Tweed-fronted Twonk Corporation valve-amp, if it's only ever going to be used to play lukewarm blues clichés and cod-60s drugs music? Psychedelia is a cul-de-sac. Turn right at beauty, hang a left at mysticism, and hit the accelerator hard.

Once, the night before my instrumental project Skyray played an Ochre Records electronica all-dayer festival in Gloucester, I spent hours dropping several shades of blue and silver glitter onto the wet-with-yacht-varnish surface of an entry-level Ibinetz bass guitar I'd somehow inherited from my time working with Ian Broudie in Care. Once dry, the bass looked reborn, as if Roger Dean had airbrushed it for a *Progressive Rock* float on an aquatic-themed Gay Pride march. Impressed from a distance, Pete 'Sonic Boom' Kember of Spacemen 3 looked offended when seeing it up close, telling me that I needed to swap the headstock for that of a Fender Precision pronto. Yep, I'll definitely be doing that. Right after I buy myself a racehorse. Julian Cope, also in attendance that night, rang me the next morning to invite Skyray to support him at a Southbank Festival he was curating, and then casually added that he was so taken with my cosmic sparkling bass that he was sending his complete guitar collection to be glittered by 'professionals'.

'Paul!'

And please! Can we all stop banging on about The Beach Boys, The Stooges, The Velvet Underground, Love, Can, and The 13th Floor Elevators? Because we know! Of course, we do. *Kick Out The Jams? Nuggets? In A Silent Way?* We know. We all shared similar childhoods and adolescence, we all loved *Noggin The Nog, The Singing Ringing Tree, Rowan & Martin's Laugh-In,* and *The Monkees.* We all ate Fig Rolls and collected Beatles bubblegum trading cards, and we all missed a party because we caught measles. Everyone fell in a clump of nettles, kissed in a bus shelter, pretended to be drunk after cider ice lollies, and had a white-out at their first spliff at that weird kid's party. 'Ace Of Spades' never gets tired, and Elizabeth Fraser could sing 'Wombling Free' and raise the vibrationary rate of the entire planet. If we don't own the original vinyl, we have the 80s reissue or the 90s CD remaster, the noughties boxed-set with the collected B-sides and outtakes. We have the Ebbetts Japanese mono files on our laptops and the newly-mastered-at-half-speed 180gm double vinyl. It's a given that Nick Drake's music is beautiful, and that Ziggy Modelistes' groove on 'Sissy Strut' is fucking ridiculous, that Ernie Isley is underrated, and Nina Simone, Jeff Buckley, and Prince Rogers Nelson are rather good; but all of these brilliant, luminous artists are packed together tight and dead as tinned anchovies in the Venn diagram of 'received' Western musical good taste. Other brands are available. Warning! The wild improvisational vocal flights of Qawwali singers and the soul-transfusion of Sufi devotional music are gateway drugs that can lead to open-mindedness and the giddy highs of the ninety-nine names of Allah. Careful now! Listening to Indonesian folk, the classical music of the country previously known as Persia, or the spiritual palette-cleanser of Sviridov's 'Three Choruses From *Tsar Feodor Ioannovich*' may overwhelm you with their beauty, cause drowsiness when driving, and risk possession by angels. The second half of the twentieth century was a musical golden age, and we were blessed to have experienced it in real time; but everyone wanking over the same hundred 'classic' albums gets a bit *zzzz* after fifty years.

'Paul.'

I'm always amazed when people I know and like tell me they don't like, or can't listen to, a particular musical genre. Invariably it's jazz, progressive rock, folk, or reggae. To me, that's like willingly narrowing the spectrum of light that one's eyes can perceive. There are no bad musical genres, just good and bad examples in each. If I hear one more 'ex-punk' proclaim that 'we' didn't fight the punk wars in order to listen to noodling dinosaurs like Yes or Gentle Giant? Firstly, there is no *we*. You probably weren't there anyway, and if you were, you didn't have your bayonet fixed but hid in the club toilets, tucking your flares into your socks. The founder of Eric's in Liverpool, Roger Eagle, was a man of sublime musical taste, and he loved Weather Report—and, in particular, their *Live In Japan* double album. I know this because I caught him hiding it, along with the rest of his jazz fusion albums, beneath the suspended tiled ceiling above his club's ticket office. It's no secret that Kurt Cobain's Nirvana took their quiet/loud template from King Crimson, and the intrepid and bass-less Van der Graaf Generator are the most uncompromising band of all time, not Throbbing Gristle. Just ask Sex Pistol and Peter Hammill fan John Lydon. Listening to VdGG's version of 'Gog' recorded live at Bangor University in 1975, while on MDMA (me, not them) is an experience only ever topped by listening to Magma offshoot Weidorje while on ketamine. Still not convinced? Check out that early photograph of Ian Curtis wearing a Nektar T-shirt. No division, only joy.

'PAAAUUL!'

We frontmen love to adopt the mask and cloak of the shaman, but we rarely earn our place closest to the communal fire by bringing anything of real value back to the tribe. Urging one's audience to get stoned and get their rocks off are statements as useful and transformative as 'Bird's Eye potato waffles are waffle-y versatile.' If Madonna had substituted *'Everybody, leave your bodies here'* for *'Everybody, get up and dance with me'* on the chorus of her debut single, rather than being just MTV-era famous she'd be immortal now. If my old mucker Julian Cope had sung *'Until the gods that diverged are restored'* on the hook of his 1981 hit 'Reward', those trumpets could have toppled the fourth wall of reality. If, rather than *'Push pineapple up a tree'*, Black Lace had sung *'Oh death, I shall smite thee'*, I'd be in a psychiatric hospital now. In its highest expression, rock'n'roll trawls the collective unconscious, decodes, translates, and delivers up to the surface, in a concentrated, symbolic form—the ineffable. The greatest and most potent examples propel society, further culture, and manifest the future *NOW*. Sadly, the majority of rock and pop music, including the bulk of my and my peers' output, is as potent as Action Man's missing genitals. If we writer/musicians are not being co-creators with the absolute, we are simply pollutants, clogging the ethers with musical landfill. Art is MAGICK, literal Magick, and, as such, should EVOKE, PROVOKE, and ILLUMINATE. Why were Magic Wands rebranded as Licorice Flyers? Where is Rimbaud's Hotel Splendide? When *did* the enchantment drain from the world?

'PAAAAAUL! For fuck's sake, mate! Are we rehearsing or not?'

Rich Turvey's Yorkshire accent could pierce Kevlar.

'Sorry. I was miles away.'

—

Last year, when these Philippines dates were first mooted, former WXB radio-station manager and DJ turned concert promoter Jesse Cambossa Sr. emailed me suggesting I come out to the islands as a solo artist, using one of several Wild Swans tribute acts in Manila as my backing band. I dismissed the idea out of hand as being too *Carol Decker on a Saga cruise*, but perhaps I should have listened. Granted, I might have felt a tad Limahl, but at least the band would be pre-rehearsed, and I wouldn't feel like I am being squeezed like Colgate. Slow poison like this money squabbling is the sort of divide-and-conquer bullshit with rainbow sprinkles I thought I'd exposed and eradicated back in 1988, when, disgusted with the latest chicanery of a bandmate ping-ponging between my group and its flowery facsimile, I chose to pilot The Wild Swans alone. And yet, fearful of how coming here solo might appear to fans back in the UK, and desperately wanting to do these shows with dignity, I brought the full live band from the *Coldest Winter* tour over on this tropical trip. Six of us splitting the not-insubstantial fee, and now, as I've just been told, the sales from my Skyray CDs and even the promo T-shirts I had made and have yet to pay the manufacturer for. The Wild Swans is a brand that I've preserved and protected alone for almost thirty years.

To my mind, that über-simple, stylised swan logo on the 'Revolutionary Spirit' record cover, and on these T-shirts, isn't just a logo—it's the symbol of a post-punk ideal, signifying a striving to reach beyond one's grasp, and an unfashionably uncynical and particularly Northern English strain of positivity. Since pianist and co-founder Ged Quinn left the band to pursue his art career, and original and brilliant guitarist Jeremy Kelly returned to The Lotus Eaters, that linear swan graphic has become my personal sigil. I'm not going to just snap it into equal chunks like a bar of fucking chocolate.

I'm not talking about money. There's rarely any money on the musician's side of the mixing desk—not anymore, and certainly not at my level. This isn't a career. I'm not trying to have 'hits' and failing, I'm just having a go and trying to make the best records I can under the constraints I live with. Does anyone honestly believe that Martin Bramah, Vic Goddard, Davey Henderson, Lawrence, Chris Thompson, or . . . you fill in the indie blanks . . . ever enters the recording studio with the sole object of making money? There is none. They continue, they go on, they endure because they are visionaries. And as such, they are compelled to complete the mission.

I'm slowly beginning to understand why John Martyn's status plummeted from *sacred* to *sacred monster* in the public consciousness, and why Van Morrison is consistently portrayed in the media as a cantankerous bastard. I mean, how can artists that work in the metaphysical ever hope to refine themselves enough to become musical vessels to channel light if people keep mistaking them for mere songsmiths? One can't float '*magnificently into the mystic*' through sewage. Ah well, as somebody once said, *the brighter the flame, the more enormous the darkness.*

—

The negative electricity I'm sensing as I walk into the rehearsal room needs grounding fast, before something ugly, possibly irreversible happens. So, we agree to just plug in and do what we came here to do today. We rehearse, playing the entire set through three times and working in the Care single 'Whatever Possessed You' as an encore. Weirdly, for a duo that never played live and only released three singles, Care are hugely famous out here. God is having a laugh with me. I mean, why make the only two bands I have ever fronted massive stars in a distant territory where bootlegging is rife and the bulk of radio play isn't logged? There is some biblical, shepherd's rod-of-tender chastening lesson here for me somewhere. If only I could work it out.

The band sound incredible. Really. Just a few hours into our rehearsal, the mood in the room has changed, the dark radiation of bad will toward me for the past twenty-four hours finally lifted. These brilliant musicians I'm beyond lucky to have with me on this trip, have synchronised into the same killer unit that they were toward the end of our *Coldest Winter* UK tour just three months ago. Even my voice sounds okay. I knew the boys would pull it off, but the latter is a surprise to us all. Those ridiculous scales and singing exercises I practised for months before we flew out here really worked in expanding my lung capacity, after the virus I picked up in Sri Lanka two years ago turned them into party blowers. However, the mortification of being caught descending the stairs in my underpants while singing scales of 'Chester Cheetah chewed a chunk of cheap cheddar cheese' by the snickering electricians my wife had let in to service the central heating while I was sleeping still keeps me awake at night.

I rarely practise because I am aware that singing isn't the job that I came to Earth to do. I have the vanity for it but not the temperament. In the mid-1980s, I reacted to my A&R man at Arista Records, Simon Potts, suggesting that I take singing lessons, as if he'd recommended that I neuter myself using his office paper shredder. When the rest of my own band agreed with him, I bristled, asking the room if they thought 'Love Will Tear Us Apart' would sound better if Ian Curtis had taken singing lessons, knowing full well that Ian's untutored and unvarnished Macclesfield timbre, set against the ambition-over-ability of the band, is precisely where that sublime and devastating song's alchemical gold is.

Network GMA-7's hugely popular noontime magazine programme *Eat Bulaga* airs widely across southeast Asia and follows much the same blueprint as ITV's *This Morning* in Britain. At least it would if the hosts of *This Morning* presented the show while abstract on psilocybin. The closest thing to *Eat Bulaga* in the UK would have been *Tizwas* with a bingo game included. Watching on monitors from backstage, the band's collective mouths hang open. It's rainbow-coloured unicorn anarchy out there. Once on camera, we're faced with so many presenters we don't know who to address.

The first thing any visiting rock musicians to the islands have to learn is that Filipino audiences are here to party, and that's it. Bands adopting an emotionally detached, cooler-than-thou, indie-goth stance will die here, and the faintest whiff of an inflated ego from the frontman will stink up this television studio faster than a split durian fruit—the aroma of which is so bad that it is been banned from being carried on public transport here.

I've just noticed that Ricky, Stu, and Rich are all wearing spectacles. Wow! They look like The Zombies or The Feelies. It's a cool look, and I'm jealous because I've left my reading glasses back at the hotel. At the TV station's request, we play 'Bringing Home The Ashes'—the mk2 Wild Swans' most popular song out here—and, as we do, the studio audience sings along, swaying in unison. If they only knew that the chorus lyrics of the song concern a nightmare I'd once had about carrying the ashes of my parents in golden urns and accidentally spilling the contents over myself.

Not having performed on live television in twenty-five years, I'm a little nervous, but I sing in tune, and the boys play well. Afterwards, when I am introduced to our fellow guest, the glamourous actress and singer Julia Clarete, I kiss her hand, and the audience whoops and cheers as if it were a marriage proposal. Just as we are packing up to leave the studio, Ricky asks the station manager about the viewing figures for the show.

'Oh, not sure exactly—I'll check, but about twenty-two million.'

I'm so glad we didn't know that an hour ago.

—

After a ninety-minute flight, Jesse, his three assistants—Sandee, Kai, and Giselle—and the band all check into our hotel on the island of Cebu. We have an hour-long press conference at 2pm before being driven over to the venue of tonight's gig to meet the owners and our local promoter—the wonderfully named Federico V. Peñaflorida III—before our soundcheck at five. Teetering on the tasteful side of Las Vegas velvet and marble, the Waterfront Cebu City Hotel, Grand Ballroom & Casino is titanic in scale, and about as un-rock'n'roll as it gets. CBGB it's not.

We will be playing in the Grand Ballroom, and grand it is. I have just spotted the huge, cordoned-off VIP area, with massive circular dining tables and ice buckets for champagne at their centre, in front of the vast stage. This place looks more like the venue for the Oscars ceremony rather than a rock gig. The bulk of the actual paying audience is roped off in the back. Trying to connect with the audience on any significant level tonight is going to take some doing.

Quick, pass me one of those Moet buckets. I'm going to throw up.

—

Back at the hotel, and as if to signify the before-and-after impact our TV appearance has had on the islands, a complimentary monster fruit basket has appeared in my room that wasn't there when I left two hours ago. All the usual tropical suspects are represented, plus starfruit, custard apples, aratilis, rambutan, longan, and some Venusian sex-toy-like things I don't recognise. The Wild Swans' stock has just gone up.

In between the soundcheck and the gig, the entire band meets on the sixteenth floor for a swim in the rooftop pool.

'Jesus Christ!' says Stu. 'Look up there!'

A man in a boiler suit is hanging by one hand from the wrong side of a hotel balcony on the apartment block opposite. Holding a paintbrush in his free hand, he's not had an accident, he's simply touching up the ironwork on the balcony. No ropes but a drop of hundreds of feet to certain death if he slips.

'Fucking hell!'

Under-rehearsed for our first ever enormo-gig, with another Category 4 superstorm heading our way, I know how he feels.

—

Backstage at the venue now, we're changing into our stage clothes while self-medicating on Jack Daniels and the strong, local Red Horse beer. Back in the UK, I'd given a lot of thought to how this, the third and newest incarnation of The Wild Swans, should present ourselves live. Too old to get away with the Spanish Civil War look of jodhpurs and brown leather jackets that our first incarnation set out in in 1981, or the 'Ace Café' rocker' look our wonderful rockabilly roadies Martyn Muscatelli and Phil Hines inspired in our second, I landed upon a compromise more suited to the three members of the band with the highest mileage on the clock: a budget version of Roxy Music's 1979 comeback to promote their *Manifesto* album. Sporting tailored suits and leather jackets, with not an ostrich feather in sight, they looked a little conservative, but Bryan Ferry knew that the band had to reflect the now cooling aftereffects of the firestorm of punk rock. Even David Bowie realised that he had to shut the lid on the dressing-up box once he hit thirty. He knew that, for him, just wearing jeans and a leather jacket for the cover shoot of *"Heroes"* was a powerful statement in itself.

Okay, we are not Roxy Music, and we are not going to get any panties thrown up onto the stage by fans tonight, but these slim suits work in an elegant *dignified men of a certain age* way. To ease and sex up the sense of sartorial sell-out I'm feeling, I'm wearing a pair of Spanish leather boots beneath my tapered trousers so viciously pointed that they could kick the pimento out of an olive. Winklepickers must be unknown on the island of Cebu, as tonight's promoter, Federico, is standing transfixed, staring at my feet, hypnotised.

It's 8:45pm, and tonight's support band, Dead Pop Stars, have just concluded their set of new-wave covers. Backstage, we check ourselves out in the lightbulb-framed mirrors that line the huge communal dressing room. We joke nervously and begin to pace. Every performer knows this stomach-tightening, *do I have time for a pee?* adrenalin surge that comes in the final fifteen minutes before showtime, just as they know that this same crippling stage fright will drop away like a cloak falling from their shoulders the nanosecond they walk beneath the spotlight.

Jesse informs us that our intro music, the opening theme from the 1965 French/German TV series *The Adventures Of Robinson Crusoe*, is now playing in the venue, and that we should assemble in the wings, stage left. Vain as ballerinas, Ricky, Stu, Mike, Rich, Les, and I check our reflections one last time before draining our shot glasses and following Jesse and Federico's torch beams along the dim, labyrinthine corridors that lead to the stage. As we pause for a moment in the wings, the Grand

Ballroom looks transformed. What at soundcheck resembled Liberace's sequin-strewn farewell concert at Caesar's Palace now looks like the mirror-lined, jewel-encrusted interior of Elton John's brain while she's being injected with $20,000 worth of a celebrity-grade hallucinogenic liquidised diamonds.

Oh, God. I'm tripping from jetlag. I shoot a nervous *Will everything be okay?* glance over to Mike Mooney. He says nothing, just smiles. That same *life is magical, nothing is real, so why worry?* smile he first disarmed me with at eighteen years old.

We'll be okay. Of course we will. From now on, everything will be okay, forever and ever and ever.

PART TWO

MY BOYISH DAYS
1960–1969

I
BOMBING THE GERMANS

1960. HUYTON, LIVERPOOL. In an effort to get me off the potty and peeing into the grown-up toilet, my dad, home on leave after a nine-month voyage with the merchant navy, jettisons his cigarette stubs into the toilet bowl and instructs me to *bomb the Germans*.

Being a toddler, I have no reference points for either bombs or Germans, but intuitively I get the gist. What I don't know is that cigarette filters float, and no matter how strongly I pee or how accurate my aim is, the fascists won't die.

Born just thirteen years after the end of the conflict my dad served in, I'm too young to know that World War II is still so fresh in my fathers' memory that he can't move on, and, consequently, any toys he buys me are military. Mum berates him for bringing home for me a present of cast-iron model toys of a Centurion tank and an anti-tank field gun for my second birthday.

'Oh, Roy! He's too young for those!'

Roy disagrees. Loading a wooden match into the barrel of the anti-tank gun, he pulls back the spring-loaded catch and shoots it across the sitting room, where it lands in the fire grate and ignites.

'He's never too young to learn about Nazis, Doris.'

II
ELECTRICITY

1962. AUGHTON. LANCASHIRE. I'm standing wondering why the back is off our first ever Radio Rentals black-and-white, two-channels-only television set. My father is away on one of his six-month-long voyages; Mum is in the garden hanging out the washing while my sister Val is playing with her Fuzzy Felt. We've just moved from the two-up, two-down terraced house where I was born in Kingsway, Huyton, into a two-up, two-down semidetached house on an under-construction housing estate in the greenbelt between Maghull and Ormskirk in Lancashire. It's only twelve miles from Huyton but light years away in quality of life: no local shops or kids to play with but clean air, albeit with the tang of manure. It's all fields and farms around here, and when Mum opens the cooker door, she finds a rat trapped inside.

Before fetching a replacement for the burnt-out valve for the TV, my lovely uncle Ken bends down and warns me not to go anywhere near the back of the set as I could be electrocuted, even killed. I'm three and a half, so I have no idea what electrocuted means, but the moment he is out of sight I toddle over and stick my little fingers deep inside the open cabinet. I mean, how could a television set *possibly* hurt me?

Thrown across the room, I black out. My mum and Ken are distraught. 'Can you hear me, Paul?'

Seconds later, when I wake up, sit up, and ask for a biscuit, they finally exhale. Mum has only just got over my last brush with the reaper: just before the house move, I was hospitalised after eating a pair of solid fuel firelighters.

Fast-forward a few years, and while playing on the building site opposite the house I fall on a drainage pipe, breaking it and gouging a three-inch-long *trench* in my leg. Blood is pumping out, but for whatever reason Mum doesn't think it serious enough for the local doctor, let alone the hospital, resulting in me living with six inches of numb nerve damage in my left thigh. You could stick a fork in it and I wouldn't notice.

As soon as I'm old enough to hold a screwdriver, I disappear into the den I've made behind the living room sofa and begin to dismantle my father's precious Bakelite longwave radio—the one that had accompanied him in his ship's cabin on many a voyage. I enjoy the effects my efforts have as I scrape the screwdriver's steel tip against the strange-looking components inside. Fascinated by the sheer weight of the heavy blue battery, I gingerly put the tip of my tongue onto the cold, chromed terminals.

Woah! That hurts.

I do it again and again just to make sure.

III

DOGGY DADDY

1963. Saturday morning and Mum is in the kitchen scraping burnt toast into the sink while Val is sprawled on the sitting room carpet, playing with her talking doll. For some reason it can only say distressing things like 'Where's my doggy?' and 'Daddy's gone away!' I'm fascinated by the tape mechanism hidden inside the creepy thing's back, and when Val leaves the room for a moment, I tug hard on the doll's pull string again and again until the tape inside stretches, lowers in register, and goes out of phase, making it sound like the abode of demons:

Doggy-daddy-gone-waaay! Doggy-Daddy-gone-waaay!

My actual daddy, Roy, is home on shore leave after a nine-month-long voyage and sitting in 'his' chair in front of the coal fire, his cigarette smouldering in the terracotta ashtray that I like so much—the one he brought back from Lagos on his last trip. I like it because, when I put my fingers inside it, I can feel the finger marks of the person that made it.

Staring off into space, Dad barely registers me as I climb up onto his knee and rub my face against his morning stubble. It hurts my cheeks, but in a good way. I'm intoxicated by the unfamiliar smells of Vitalis hair oil, Kensitas filter tips, and last night's McEwans Export bitter. *My dad's home!*

He tolerates me for just a few seconds before ordering me to get down. Presuming that he's joking, I laugh and try to rub my face on his again. Shouting at me, he pushes me to the floor.

Lying there on the carpet at his feet, I'm unharmed but hurting. What on earth have I done, and why doesn't he want to play with me? Daddy has indeed gone away.

—

Sunday morning and brilliant sunshine streams in through the gaps in the Venetian blinds of my parents' bedroom. I've stealthily crawled up under their quilted pink nylon bedcovers and slid in to nestle between them both. I'm excited and comforted by the novelty of having both parents at home.

Dad immediately jumps out of bed as if he's been electrocuted and disappears downstairs on the pretext of making a pot of tea. He's the same if I try to sit next to him on the sofa. He's got serious body-boundary issues, but I don't understand this; I just think that maybe he doesn't like me very much.

As the years pass go by, Dad becomes increasingly tyrannical and at times deliberately cruel. Frustrated by my inability to gain weight, he harangues me with, 'Do you know why you are so thin? It's because you've got a tapeworm in your stomach, and it's eating all of your food.'

I'm so horrified at this little mind bomb he's planted that I can't move. 'What's a tapeworm?' I whimper, close to tears. My father coldly tells me about the mile-long parasitic worm that he claims is squatting in my intestines. I can't believe it! A worm, inside me? I'm just a skinny child. My dad was the same at my age, and I've seen a photo to prove it.

I know there's no tapeworm inside me really, but I'm disturbed by the way my own father is deliberately trying to frighten his little boy. I love my dad, and I know that underneath all the anger and bitterness he's not a bad person and he loves us. He provides for my sister and me; we get cool toys on our birthdays, and at Christmas. But we don't get what we really want: a hug, a kiss, or even the occasional pat on the head. Not once, not ever. If we bring home a drawing or a painting we've made in school, it's not good enough—nothing is ever good enough.

Thank God we've been blessed with a groovy mum. Even at my young age, I know she's a one-off. Other kids' mums just can't compete with her trendy clothes and arty ways. If Doris—or 'Doe', as she prefers to be called—isn't standing in a field full of sunflowers with her paintbox, she's practising meditation. When I come home, tired and cold from playing outside on the building site with my plastic tommy gun broken in half, tears welling in my eyes, she sits me down on the kitchen worktop, and, like a multi-armed Shiva, pulls off my balaclava and stuffs a jam sandwich in my mouth while welding together the two halves of my machine-gun barrel in the blue-flamed jet of our gas cooker. In three minutes, I'm back outside, saving the world from the scourge of the Nazis.

In the early 1950s, my mum was one of the only female members of the Liverpool Rifle Club, and I love it when she shows me the pierced targets and medals that she won at the shooting range at Altcar army-training camp. When she meticulously paints the profile of a Native American tribal chief on the lid of a discarded tar barrel then fashions it into a shield for me, I can't believe it. It's beautiful. Today, she's run up a pair of Batman masks from a length of PVC bought on Ormskirk market on her treadle-powered sewing machine.

My big sister, Val, insists that if we are really going to catch baddies, I have to play the part of Batman's sidekick, Robin. Robin is rubbish, so I agree to a compromise: I'll answer to the *name* of Robin, but only if I'm allowed to wear a full Batman mask like hers.

With ripped bed sheets serving as cloaks, Val and I wait in the darkness of the Batcave, a tiny box room at the top of the stairs that is still plastered with black-and-white photographs of The Beatles and Freddie & The

Dreamers cut from the *Liverpool Echo* years before. For the sixth time in a row, my weary mother, standing in for Commissioner Gordon, waits at the bottom of the stairs and, on our signal, half-heartedly shouts up, 'Batman, Robin. Come quickly. There's a cat stuck up a tree at the bottom of the road.'

Bursting through the box room door, we leap down the stairs two at a time, tearing past my mother, through the sitting room, and out of the kitchen door, running full tilt across the road and down the hill, only stopping when we reach the 'big tree' twenty yards away.

To mask the anti-climax of there being no baddies to *SOCK!* or cats to rescue, Val strokes her chin and says, 'Robin, I've got an idea.'

'What?' I ask breathlessly, my eyes wide on thrill overload.

Val looks around for inspiration. Finding none, she shouts, 'Let's go back to the Batcave and do it again.'

By the late 60s, Mum is dressing like Ann-Margret in purple flared trouser suits, white fun-fur jackets, and red leather zip-up boots. One afternoon, Val and I come home from school to find that she has transformed our drab lounge with a flaming orange vinyl three-piece suite, dark turquoise cushions, and a vivid purple carpet, her own trippy, five-feet-tall oil paintings of giant poppy heads hanging from the walls.

IV
FLOWERS OF SULPHUR

BLEAK MIDWINTER, 1967. I'm hiding beneath a two-hundred-year-old bridge that spans the Burscough-to-Halsall stretch of the Leeds–Liverpool canal. My feet are blistered, my skin goose-fleshed and marbled blue with cold. Every weekday for the past fortnight, I have walked six miles through housing estates and along B roads and the frozen furrows of agricultural farmland to conceal myself here. Apart from a bowl of Weetabix at breakfast, I have had nothing to eat for over seven hours, and my stomach is cramping. At nine years old, I should be carefree—reading, drawing, playing with my Hot Wheels cars, watching *The Monkees*—not experiencing a full-blown existential crisis.

I've chosen this secluded spot to conceal myself in because it offers cover from the rain and has a fantastic echo, and, best of all, the arched underside of the bridge glitters with stalactites of saltpetre—an ingredient, I've recently discovered, of gunpowder. If only I could reach high enough to scrape some off, I'd mix it with my mum's sketching charcoal, iron filings from my Merit chemistry set, and the mysterious *flowers of sulphur* in her bathroom cabinet and blow myself out of this terrifying world.

Something less tangible than bullying or physical abuse is the cause of my truancy from school, and any actual danger I am in is from myself. For the past three weeks I have been plagued by dark thoughts—thoughts too strange to share. Although I can think it, I don't yet have the vocabulary to articulate the dramatic shift in consciousness that I believe has occurred in me. All I can do is freefall within it while waiting for gravity to be restored.

A fortnight ago, my universe was finite and had some semblance of order. Christmas, summer holidays, and birthdays punctuated the interminable school terms; toys, television, and my bicycle defined my life; but recently the veil of innocence has been torn from me in an event so unexpected, and traumatic, it has destabilised me to the point of mutism. In fact, right now I must appear to my bewildered mother to be little more than a barely sentient cabbage. I have got it into my head that somehow, through some hideous cosmic accident, my soul—my consciousness—is no longer located within my body but hovering just outside it, trying to escape. I'm scared that if I don't at least try to psychically glue the two back together using sheer force of will, prayer, or some *Tales Of The Arabian Nights* incantation, they will fly apart forever like repelling magnets. Bereft of its animating spirit, I am scared my body will die, possibly right here on this isolated canal towpath, leaving my soul to drift like mist across the turnip fields of West Lancashire.

I don't know whether it's the subliminal influence of the leaden crucifixion hymns I'm forced to sing at the two-hundred-year-old rural church school I attend, or from absorbing my mother's Besant and Blavatsky books by osmosis, but the gulf I feel between my physical and spiritual forms tortures me. It's all I can think about, night and day. Alone, friendless, and unprotected, all I want is to go back in time to before the fracture in me occurred. I want my innocence back. I want to go home.

What hasn't occurred to me yet is that this separation theory I am obsessing about isn't the whole event but a double whammy of hormonal depression meeting abstract thought. Too young to recognise either, this soul-split idea has taken centre stage in my head and is temporarily blocking out the sun. Attempting to comfort myself, I rock back and forth as if shuckling at the Western Wall. I don't know why I'm doing it, but making this swaying motion while repeating a whispered mantra of *You're really here, you're really here* temporarily comforts me, anchoring 'me' to my body and my body to the earth.

Without a watch, I have to gauge the light quality to intuit when it's somewhere close to 4pm and safe to walk home without arousing my mother's suspicions. But the sky hasn't darkened sufficiently yet, so, for at least another hour, I'm the coldest, loneliest child on Earth. I may still occupy the shape of a schoolboy, but that shape contains a boiling universe, and the grief I feel for my lost innocence wears me like a child-skin suit.

—

NARROW CROFT ROAD, AUGHTON. Late on a Thursday afternoon in the third week of my truancy, I am confronted by my mother, demanding to know why I've been skipping school; and, more importantly, where. The headmaster telephoned her just after I left home this morning, enquiring as to my whereabouts. Tomorrow morning, I have to return to school for an informal interrogation.

Instantly confessing to my mother as to where I've been hiding, I go silent on the question of *why*. If I can't explain how I am feeling to my mother, the only genuinely open-minded adult I know, how can I possibly explain it to Mr Noble, that combover-sporting propagator of a consensus reality that instinctively repels me? Thankfully, my dad isn't around right now to further tighten the vice. Cheated out of the luxury of a real childhood himself, he wouldn't entertain this apparent lunacy of mine for one second.

If Dad were home, he would just punish me for causing him and the family problems, but he left for a three-week business trip to Canada a couple of months ago and has failed to return. After finding a risqué Polaroid photograph of a woman in lingerie hidden in his sock drawer, I suspect some kind of infidelity may be involved. Terrifying as the thought of facing my headmaster tomorrow morning is, I am strangely relieved that my three weeks of skipping school are over, because I'm exhausted from upholding the deceit.

—

On Friday morning, as my mother and I are shown into the school office, the headmaster tousles my hair. What fresh hell is this? Like Hitler petting his German shepherd for the newsreels, he's not fooling anyone— particularly my mother, who is wringing her hands like she's beneath the cross at Golgotha. In response to Mr Noble's question as to why I've been playing truant, my mind goes into freefall. What I want to say is, *Well, sir, I've been obsessing about how weird it is to be alive, how 'I'—whatever that is—is trapped in this damp cave of flesh we call a body, so school didn't seem quite so urgent*, but instead I offer up the first thing that comes to mind.

'I don't like school dinners, sir.'

Pathetic. Of course, he doesn't believe me, but because it is an easy get-out for him, he pretends to. What he desperately doesn't want at this moment is my mother accusing him of putting her child at risk by not spotting my truancy for an unbelievable three weeks. Immediately suggesting that I simply 'nip' home at lunchtimes from now on, he extends his hand for me to shake. He clearly considers the matter dealt with.

Mum is saying nothing, but I know she's fuming. Doris is a free spirit; she doesn't want me cooling her jets by returning home for lunch each weekday, preventing her from attending her spiritualist church, oil-painting the soon-to-be-demolished streets of old Liverpool, or whatever other mysterious adventures a middle-aged, 'new-age' woman goes on. Food is just energy to my mother, an unwanted but necessary interruption to her day. If she could swallow a one-a-day food pill, she would.

Mum is disgusted with the headmaster's games and her face is showing it, but he has already given us fifteen minutes of his morning and he wants us out. Mum doesn't budge.

Seeing he's got a live one, Mr Noble reverts to his real self and goes for the jugular.

'Tell me, Mrs Simpson,' he asks. 'Do you think your son is a genius?'

Oh, God! Where did that come from? *Say nothing, Mum.* I'm dying here. *Please say nothing.*

'Yes,' she answers. 'I do.'

Uh-oh! Smirking for England, Mr Noble shows us the door. Mum has never been really angry with me before, but as we leave the school grounds together, she's incandescent with rage and can barely look at me. She's guarding a secret, but I'm not going to find out about it for some time. Twenty-five years, to be precise.

—

Back at school on Monday, it's almost business as usual. Facing some light interrogation from friends as to my protracted absence, I fob them off with the catch-all excuse of 'tummy ache'. Today, temporarily liberated from my recent trauma, I'm playing a favourite game of mine that is centred around the two-ounce bag of Midget Gems secreted in the pocket of my school pants. Midget Gems are long-lasting, fruit-flavour gelatine sweets. The game is to pretend that the sweets contain compressed oxygen and that only by keeping one lodged in the corner of my mouth without chewing am I able to breathe normally. It's not much of a game, but it stops me from dying of boredom during lessons.

So addicted am I to this game, and so seriously do I abide by my own rules that, overexcited and finishing the bag too soon, I find myself in danger of turning blue. Sneaking over the playground wall, I run to the nearby Alker's tobacconist for emergency supplies. The bell above the door nearly flies off as I burst through the door. Slamming my coppers down, I manically point at the jar until the breath explodes out of my lungs. With a sweet in my mouth, the colour returns to my cheeks. I'm halfway over the low wall that borders the playground when I'm grabbed by my shirt collar and hauled over and frog-marched before the headmaster. Already considered to be trouble, I am made an example of in front of my classmates by being caned upon both hands. It hurts.

A week later, I'm caned again, for the same thing. This time I'm hit with what is known as a yardstick—a three-foot-long, half-inch-thick ruler for the teacher's use on a blackboard. The yardstick is too big and too heavy to be effectively wielded, so it doesn't really hurt, but it looks very impressive to my watching friends and classmates. Finally, I have been noticed by my beautiful classmate Susan Myers. She's a goddess in my eyes, and as such, when I can, I leave offerings of ha'penny bits and 'Penny Arrow' chew bars inside her desk.

—

MARCH 27, 1967. BLACKPOOL APOLLO. We never camp out, light fires, or make animal traps; we never play with sheath knives or do any of that cool stuff they use on the propaganda posters they use to lure us in; and I'm only putting off leaving because it's 'Bob-a-Job' week next month, when I can earn some money by washing neighbours' cars in order to buy myself their Corgi and Dinky toy versions. I have no idea what tonight has to do with the Cub Scout movement but, along with fourteen other boys, I've travelled by coach up to Blackpool Apollo to watch something called a 'variety show'. I've only been a member of Cubs for a couple of months, and apart from the night that some bloke in a bush hat brought in a bat-eared fox, I've been bored stiff.

Clueless as to who any of the acts on the bill are, we're all just excited to be out after dark. When the house lights dim, an enormous bag containing a shaken-up mixture of Fruit Salads, Black Jacks, Refreshers, Tooty Frooties, Fruit Gums, Fruit Pastilles, Liquorice Pipes, Anglo bubble gum, Beech Nut chewing gum, and sherbet Flying Saucers get passed along the row.

'Shhh!' an adult whispers. 'It's starting.'

First up is the compere, a comedian called Ray Cameron. The adults are laughing, but we can't tell if he's funny or not as we don't understand a word he says.

After ten minutes—just enough time for the sugar to kick in—he introduces a drippy-looking bunch called The Settlers who perform a folky pop thing called 'Major To Minor'. They may resemble missionaries, but it's pretty good, actually. The Robb Storme Group are next. We like them. Sonny Childe & The TNT troop on. There are thousands of them, all playing saxophones. God! What a racket. No thanks. We are all a little disappointed when a group called The Small Faces come on because, despite loving their frilly shirts and waistcoats, and the jokey messing-about onstage, their faces are of a completely normal size.

The singer looks drunk. Taking the microphone, he informs us, 'This is a new song, it's called "Itchycoo Park".'

The boy next to me whispers 'Itchy Poo Park', and the kid we call Tommy explodes with laughter. More shushing from the adults. After six songs, the chirpy cockney singer introduces a guest vocalist named 'Pee-Pee', and Tommy goes back into hysterics—until he sees her, that is. It's not Pee-Pee Arnold, as in a kid who smells of wee, but P.P. Arnold, as in a gorgeous woman in mini-skirt and go-go boots who sings and dances, and I can't take my eyes off her. I may only be eight and a half years old, but I know what I like when I see it. I've already got a thing for Sandie Shaw, and I feel weird in my stomach when the camera does a close-up of her feet.

Next up are the twins, Paul and Barry Ryan. I recognize these two—I've seen them on TV. Paul is wearing a tight white polo neck, black slacks, pointed shoes, and a medallion. Barry is his negative in black top and white slacks. I'm loving these two.

After the Ryans, we are surprised to see that on top of the bill is a blind man in sunglasses with what looks like an entire bottle of Silvikrin in his hair. He sings spooky songs in a wobbly American accent. The words are like little films about how women keep leaving him. 'Crying', 'Only The Lonely', 'It's Over'. Song after song. I'm not surprised they keep leaving him, he needs to cheer up a bit. Roy Orbison? Roy Snorbison, more like.

—

SEPTEMBER 1967. CHERRY TREE ESTATE, AUGHTON, LANCASHIRE. My friend David North has two things I covet. One is a calliper of leather and chrome strapped onto his left leg that causes him to limp like Dr Don Blake, the human host for Thor, the Norse God of Thunder, as seen in my new *Fantastic* and *Terrific* comics. The other is his long-haired older brother, Peter, who just about tolerates David and me hanging out with him while listening to his records.

Two singles Peter plays endlessly on his portable record player fascinate me: 'Green Tambourine' by The Lemon Pipers (oh, those swirly whirlpool echoes!), and 'Mr Tambourine Man' by Bob Dylan. Sitting cross-legged on the carpet of Peter's bedroom, listening intently, barely moving for fear of being kicked out of this very cool scene, I'm checking out Peter and his long-haired friends in their pointy-collared, shirts, matching neckerchiefs, and elastic-sided Chelsea boots. I'm saying nothing but taking in EVERYTHING, desperately trying to break their secret teenage code. If I can decipher these song lyrics about tambourines and jingle-jangle mornings, maybe I'll be groovy too.

Thunderbirds toys, Spirographs, Twister, and Kerplunk are being advertised everywhere right now, but when my birthday comes around in June, I ask my mum for a fitted pointy-collared shirt. When it arrives, it has saffron, brown, and maroon stripes. It's fantastic! Particularly when worn with my old washed-out tan corduroy Wranglers.

My hair has finally grown out of its disastrous village-idiot phase too. Last year, to save money, my mum cut my hair around an actual Tupperware bowl. Maybe I wriggled or she had a twitch, but the result was I looked like a medieval farm boy, and I was so ashamed I wouldn't leave the house.

I want to look like I'm in The Monkees, and this shirt is a great start. All I need now are the Chelsea boots, but they cost an eye-watering seventy-five shillings and eleven pence, so I can't have them, even for Christmas. They don't make them in children's sizes anyway. It's not fair. I'm going to have to wait years.

—

Weekends and school holidays, rain or shine, I'm outside climbing trees in either my Wranglers or my 'Tesco-Tearaways', worn with black Woolworths baseball boots. 'Tearaways' are super-cheap, heavily starched supermarket own-brand denims so thin once washed that they never last beyond the summer. Today, I'm playing in the partially built houses on the ever-expanding Cherry Tree estate I live on. When a roofer switches on his transistor radio, a song blasts out that's so exhilarating that I stop what I'm doing and stand to attention, concentrating hard. I have no idea what this music is, but the singer just declared that he has magic in his eyes.

Magic? In his eyes? Wow! Did I mishear that? And then he sings a strange repetitive bit about how he can *see for miles, and miles, and miles, and miles, and miles.* The guitars sound like crashing cars! The drum kit is exploding! It's beyond genius.

I don't know why, but this song makes me feel something new. Like I've eaten too much sugar and want to chase Susan Myers, that blonde girl I like from school, behind the back of the bus stop.

I'm impatient for the DJ to tell me the name of this incredible group, but at the same time, I never want this song to end. The what? The Hoo? Oh! The Who! Mind-meltingly exhilarating as this song is, they won't get far with a rubbish name like that.

This is the first time that a song has stopped me in my tracks since my dad brought home 'Love Me Do' by The Beatles and I couldn't help but dance around the room with my mum and sister. From this day on, I start paying more attention to the radio.

While not in the same league as 'I Can See For Miles', 'Kites' by Simon Dupree & The Big Sound resonates with me, triggering something. I don't know why, but this softer, dreamier-sounding song feels connected to my recent truancy in some way. Again, I can't express it, but I sense that the song is a Trojan Horse and that secreted within it is a hidden layer of meaning. For now, the song's secret evades me, and I mentally archive it alongside 'Strawberry Fields Forever' by The Beatles, 'Everyone's Gone To The Moon' by Jonathan King, 'Hole In My Shoe' by Traffic, '(Excerpt from) A Teenage Opera' by Keith West, and 'Nights In White Satin' by The Moody Blues in the 'weird pop songs I like but don't quite understand' category.

V
DON'T MENTION THE WAR

DECEMBER 1967. When asked what I'd like for my Christmas present this year, I reply, 'That's easy! The German Stormtrooper uniform for my Action Man.'

Dad is incensed. He may dress in the very slightly progressive '60s dad' fashions of the day, but in his head, it's forever 1943; and, as such, I wake on the morning of the 25th to unwrap the allied Australian 'Jungle Fighter' uniform instead. Bursting blood vessels trying not to appear disappointed, I thank my parents, but oh! There's no iconic helmet, jackboots, or Schmeisser Maschinenpistole; instead, there's a tailored safari jacket and matching shorts in sandy-coloured twill. Granted, there are some cool weapons, but shorts? Action Man's knees are riveted at the knees! Integral to the allied campaigns in the Southwest Pacific or not, once dressed my

Action Man looks to my young eyes like a robot Kenneth Williams having a hissy fit with a flame thrower.

Like many of his generation, my father never talks about the war. If pressed, he'll answer with, 'What's to be said? It happened.'

When my Scottish grandfather, Andrew 'Jock' Simpson, died while my dad and his younger brother Derek were still in short trousers, they were sent away to be raised in the Swanley Home For Little Boys in Kent. The name alone makes me feel sad, but as we grow it helps my sister and me to better understand the lack of affection shown us and make some sense of his anger. Asked by my mother as to how he felt when he was beaten after being caught stealing a potato from the school kitchens and trying to cook it in the basement furnace, he replies, 'What do you mean, how did I *feel*? I just got on with it.'

He'll never answer direct questions about his early childhood, the boys' home, or his apprenticeship from the age of fourteen in the merchant navy. When war broke out in 1939, he was already at sea. On very rare occasions he will surprise us all by volunteering a jaw-dropping story from his life to a visiting stranger. Our eyes go wide hearing him tell visitors about how, in November of 1937, on shore leave in Shanghai, he heard the ship's horn and raced to the harbour, only just making it before they raised the anchors, enabling them to sail just hours before occupation by invading Japanese army. How, on the high seas somewhere off the coast of Africa, his best friend fell from an observation platform, smashing his head on a deck hatch and killing him outright, and how they had had to keep his body in the ship's freezer along with the food until they reached the nearest port and he could be buried; or how, during the war, a German U-boat had sunk the sister ship to his in an unprotected two-vessel convoy. Just hours out of harbour, the massive chains securing a steam engine to the deck of his ship worked loose, threatening to capsize them and necessitating a hasty return to port, thereby saving his (and my) life.

The one and only story he actively volunteers to me personally is a joke. Watching him shave one morning, I notice a large, circular scar on his upper arm. He tells me it is where he was hit by a bullet from a German Stuka fighter plane as it strafed the deck of his ship.

Oh my God! This is the coolest thing I have ever heard in my life. My school friend Christopher Matthews is going to freak! This might even top the deerskin-covered German army backpack his dad brought home with him from Dunkirk and lets Christopher use as his school bag.

Just as my young brain is about to explode with excitement, my dad confesses that he's lying.

'Aeroplane fighter bullets are the size of cucumbers,' he tells me. 'They would have torn my arm clean off.'

'I'll tell you the truth,' he says. 'Somewhere in the tropics, a spider laid eggs in my arm. Weeks later, the puncture wound had ballooned into a huge boil, the ship's medic lanced it . . .' He pauses for effect. 'And hundreds of tiny spiders poured out.'

OH, GOD! This might be an even better story!

Five minutes later, as I prod his scar looking for spiders, he tells me that this story isn't true either. The scar is from a smallpox injection. What a swizz.

My favourite true story of his is a gentle one. In the late 1950s, having finally made the rank of captain, he was charged with transporting, as well as the usual cargos of timber and fruit, a pair of beautiful freshwater intertidal, clawless otters—the pets of a wealthy South African couple who were relocating to America. So enamoured was my dad with these creatures that shortly into the voyage, feeling sorry for them, he had a large freshwater storage tank converted into an on-deck play pool for them. Soon they were *his* pets, running around playing in his cabin and exploring the decks of the ship like a pair of dogs.

Discovering this warm, human side to my ultra-repressed, disciplinarian, semi-detached, can't-do-anything-to-please-him father is the story I like the best, and the one I decide I will pass on to my children, should I ever have them.

VI

TELEKINESIS

1968. ORMSKIRK COUNTY LIBRARY, LANCASHIRE. I approach the counter with a Pop Art primer, a book of Japanese prints, and *How To Draw Anything*. The librarian refuses to stamp them. In her opinion, these books are too old for me, and she directs me back to the children's section, which I've long since exhausted. From the Reverend Awdry's *Thomas The Tank Engine* series at one end all the way to the Norse myths at the other, there's nothing left to interest me there. I feel humiliated and flush red with embarrassment. Too intimidated to argue, I just sit and wait for my mum to return from shopping at the local market to collect me. When she does, she is so disgusted at the librarian's myopic attitude that she loudly instructs me to go back and choose a fourth book from the adult section and says she will check all of them out for me using her ticket.

Miraculously, just when my mind is most porous and in need of it, I chance upon *The Secret Life Of Salvador Dalí*—the book that changes everything forever. This weighty hardback isn't a collection of the artist's paintings—those I can take or leave—but a memoir of his formative years, and I am hooked from the opening paragraph:

> *At the age of six I wanted to be a cook. At seven I wanted to be Napoleon. And my ambition has been growing steadily since.*

Leafing through at random, I land upon a story of the young Salvador, so jealous of the attention his parents are bestowing on his younger brother that he attempts to decapitate him by wedging his grandfather's sword at head height at the bottom of a children's slide in his local park. *Whaaat?* The teenage Dalí outrages the occupants of his hometown of Figueres, first by growing his hair long and then by having it bobbed like a girl. *Woah!* Believing it to be a cockroach burrowing into him, a half-asleep Dalí cuts a large mole from his back and nearly bleeds to death. *Oh my God! This is solid gold!*

I had no idea that adults could still think as children—still play, act crazy, and actually, well, enjoy life. For me, the best part of this magical book is reading about how, as a young boy, Salvador simply *decided* to live a remarkable life. Like a magical seed blowing into a suburban garden, this book plants itself deep in my consciousness and blossoms into abstract thought. I renew it monthly for the next two years.

—

2015. OXFAM, BOLD STREET, LIVERPOOL. I already own the paperback reissue of Dalí's remarkable memoir, of course, but four decades after discovering it, I spot an identical dust-jacketed hardback copy displayed in the window of a local charity shop. Excitedly, I enter just in time to see a customer reach in and remove it from the window. After glancing inside at the price written in pencil, he tucks it under his arm and continues browsing. I cannot believe my bad fortune, and the more I think about it, the more furious I become at this cosmic injustice. Clearly intended for me, this rare object, layered with memory and meaning for me only, has found its way into a shop I regularly frequent. Fuck this guy! He doesn't even look excited about it.

Channelling a Cold War Russian psychic, I concentrate all of my will into a pencil-thin beam that I locate deep into this guy's consciousness and visualise him returning the book to the shelf.

Put it down.

He's queuing to pay for it, with one customer in front.

Put it down.

The veins in my temples are near to bursting with the potency of telekinetic energy I am expending. If I have to die in my attempt to make this fucker obey my will, so be it.

PUT. IT. DOWN!

This is when I see the man hesitate, about-face, and lay the book—my book—down on top of the nearest bookshelf and exit the shop.

VII

STICKS OF ORANGE DYNAMITE

AUGUST 1968. Christine Russell is the youngest and prettiest of three sisters who have just moved here with their parents from their native New Zealand. I've fallen madly in love with her, and I let her know it by scrawling it in chalk across the curb outside her parents' house. She succumbs to my attention, and we become inseparable. I drive her poor parents crazy by ringing their doorbell every night while they are in the middle of their evening meal to ask, 'Is Christine playing out?'

It's the summer of 1968, and we're playing in her back garden. The sun is out. I'm sucking an orange-flavoured Sea Jet ice lolly while Christine, in black Speedo costume and Woolworths elastic-fronted pumps, jumps through lawn-sprinkler rainbows. I've never seen anything so beautiful. Afterwards, sitting wrapped in warm towels in her mother's outhouse laundry, we breathe in the dry, OMO-perfumed air while whispering over the hum of the washer-dryer.

The months pass blissfully until Christine and I fall out one day when playing with some of the other kids from the housing estate. During a game of *Catch a girl, kiss a girl*, my mettle fails. Once I've caught Christine, I'm too shy to kiss her, but I'm terrified one of the other boys will. She thinks I don't want to kiss her and is upset. I kick a stone and sulk. I can't explain.

We stop speaking and I wander home, too proud to back down.

Now, as an act of totally unjustified revenge, I'm pretending to have a crush on Susan, Christine's older, more athletic sister. One afternoon I spot her in our local park talking with my sister. I join them and start showing off by hanging upside down by my knees from the monkey bars. I'm not a very convincing monkey, and I wake up back at my parent's house with two black eyes, a grotesquely swollen face, and a lump on my forehead that will never completely disappear. A week later, when the swelling subsides but not the bruises, I return to school, where an insensitive teacher christens me 'Shiner'. For a while, it sticks.

Of course, I'm still wildly in love with Christine, and I'm devastated when a *For Sale* notice appears outside her house. I so want to, but I still can't bring myself to ring the doorbell. Then, soon after, the lovely Christine and her sisters are gone forever.

My school friend Les Pattinson has moved even closer, just a few streets away. Les is nuts about cars—everywhere in his bedroom there are pictures, models, and drawings of them. If we're not out on our pushbikes, we're sitting in his bedroom, playing with his Scalextric rip-off racing set. We try to make the game more exciting by putting Sellotape on the fat back tires so the car's wheels spin and skid off dramatically on the hairier corners.

Les has some fantastic toys that I covet, like the 1/25-scale plastic MPC model Monkeemobile. Mind you, I'm the sort that refuses to play with the little orange sticks of dynamite that come with the frogman's outfit as they're hopelessly out of scale with Action Man's fingers.

Les's mum, Laura, is friendly and cool, and she takes it upon herself to teach me to swim. No namby-pambying around with rubber rings in the shallow end for her, though: Laura insists that I face my fear and jump straight in at the twelve-foot end of Crosby swimming baths. I'm not convinced but, feeling bullied, I leap in. After swallowing a bit of chlorine and kiddie piss, I rise to the surface furiously, treading water like a terrier, and the fear has miraculously gone. After a few more visits, I'm only happy when I'm out of my depth.

Les's dad, Frank, virtually lives in his garage and is always covered in motor oil or its nemesis, Swarfega. Forever in the process of fixing something intricate, he is, unlike my dad, friendly rather than domineering. I'm amazed at the easy way he talks to Les, treating him with respect. I honestly didn't know that a boy and his dad could be friends, and I walk home wondering what that must feel like.

One afternoon, as we sit talking in the grass near his house, Les and I are joined by some other boys from the estate and are invited to hang out. These guys are a bit wild but friendly, and then, all of a sudden, Les and I realise that we've been press-ganged. The gang's leaders are the

Campbell brothers, two curly-haired southerners new to the area. Our turf is the housing estate, but our base is a den in a disused quarry that, unfortunately for us, borders another gang's turf. Spoken of in hushed tones, the Harris gang's exploits are legendary. The most feared of all their members is Phil Bickerstaff. If we get wind that he is out on manoeuvres, we lie low in the Campbells' parents' garage. One day we get caught on what the Harrises consider their territory and are gathered like sheep into a ring of thugs while Mike Campbell, being the older of the brothers, steps forward and takes a ritual beating-up from Bickerstaff.

The younger of the two brothers, Phil Campbell (or 'Bruno'), is a dead ringer for Mickey Dolenz in *Circus Boy*. He and I hit it off straight away. We've both got the same sense of humour, but we also recognise a darker side to each other's personalities. Bruno, our gang-mate Gary Dempsey, and I take it hard when Tramp, a local stray mongrel and gang mascot, is killed by a truck speeding along nearby Northway, the dual carriageway linking Liverpool and Preston. We stand at the side of the blood-spotted tarmac with our heads reverentially bowed in silence, like old soldiers at the Cenotaph.

Just as we're walking away, we hear a low drone from beyond the camber of the road. Squinting in the direction of the noise, our eyes go wide to see a huge army of Merseyside Scooter Boys tooled up and riding into the woolyback territories of Ormskirk or Southport, looking for a scrap. These guys are mobile skinheads rather than the increasingly rare mods, and hours later, as I'm falling asleep, I hear them returning in small, scattered groups, like shot-up Spitfires at the battle of Britain.

—

JUNE 1969. Our teacher sets the class a project based upon the imminent Apollo 11 moon landing, and Les and I collaborate on a control panel for a space rocket using sheets of cardboard, silver foil, bottle tops, buttons, and sweet wrappers. We really get into it, creating dozens of little switches and dials that turn on butterfly clips. The teacher loves it, and up it goes on the wall with the whole class *oohing* and *aahing*. Les and I can't believe it; much like Buzz Aldrin and Neil Armstrong, orbiting high above us, our popularity in school rockets. Unfortunately, it's too little, too late, as we're about to leave junior school forever, for secondary school and what my dad assures me will be the biggest shock of my young life.

—

SEPTEMBER 1969. After the summer holidays, I start at Deyes Lane Secondary Modern in Maghull. It's huge, but unlike its name, it's not modern, and I hate it from my first nanosecond there. I don't know the layout or the routines; I can't find the classrooms I'm supposed to be in. I buddy up with unsuitable people to whom I can't relate. On my first afternoon, I have a terrible stomach ache, and at break time I go and stand outside the headmaster's office. My sister, on her first week of the third year, sees me and tells me I can't be there. She doesn't use these words, but she explains that there's a hierarchy in place that I can't bypass by seeing the headmaster directly. I don't understand. How can the man in charge of the school not care about my pain?

For the first two terms, I'm miserable and lonely and consider myself a prisoner in a state-sponsored prison. The only thing I have keeping me together these first few terms is my music, my library books, and a newly launched series of magazines on a supernatural theme called *Man, Myth & Magic*.

By the second term of the second year, I've learnt the complicated official and unofficial school ropes, and I've made a few friends. I'm not the most popular kid in school, but I'm not the least popular either. Although I'm not in the same class as my junior-school pal Les, I still see him and hang out with him at breaktimes.

My new best friend in class is Trog, a tough blow-in from Yorkshire who has just arrived in town with a shaggy bowl haircut and a massive chip on his shoulder. I've agreed to go on a double date that he's hastily arranged with two girls in his class that I hardly know. He's promised me that I can have the pretty freckle-faced one and he'll settle for her plainer, olive-skinned friend. Trog's magnanimous gesture is not entirely altruistic, as he figures the plain girl is more likely to be what he calls 'dirty'.

After school, I just have time to go home and get washed and changed and splash on some Brut aftershave before I arrive at an address that one of the girls has scribbled onto a page torn from her school exercise book. Thinking we will take them to the local park, Trog and I are pleasantly surprised to be quickly ushered inside the house before the girl's neighbours catch a glimpse of us. The girls are now wearing make-up, and I'm thinking how strange we all look in our street clothes.

'Trog's girl' gets four mismatched glasses, and we all sit around in the dark listening to T. Rex's *Electric Warrior* album while nervously sipping the Woodpecker cider Trog and I chipped in to buy. After the cider has all gone, Trog, flushed with fermented confidence, reneges on our deal and waltzes off into one of the bedrooms with the pretty girl. I knew he'd try this, and for a few moments I sit fuming. Then, feeling bad, I turn to look at the other girl and I'm struck by the dignified way she's handling this awkward situation. It makes me look at her properly for the first time since I arrived. With the curtains drawn, in the orange glow of a three-bar electric fire, she looks delicate, almost beautiful. It's the 'almost' bit that makes me want to kiss her. I'm no David Cassidy myself.

Taking her hand, I draw her to me. She kisses me as if we've been lovers forever, and, in a flash, I realise just how desensitised by Trog I've become to what's important. This girl is fantastic, and the intimacy we share for the next hour is magical.

As Trog and I walk away from the house, he apologises to me for swapping partners and proceeds to brag about what a result he had—how she had rubbed his cock through his pants. I just keep quiet, knowing who out of the pair of us had the better deal.

PART THREE

| LUCIFER'S CHILDHOOD
| 1971–1976

I

THE DEMIGODS

1971. In their filthy denims, studded leather jackets, Belstaffs, and sheepskin-lined motorcycle boots, The Aces—greasy-haired rockers from the nearby council estate—are demigods in our eyes. Hanging around their Castrol-stained turf on Rothwell Drive, my friends and I stand around, chewing Anglo Bubblys, watching nervously as they adjust the points on their motorcycles with their tattooed hands until one of us gets up the courage to talk to them.

Their bikes—Bantams, Tiger Cubs, Bonnevilles, and Commandos—are all British, they tell us. This is important, apparently. Kawasakis are tolerated, but as a rule, Japanese bikes are considered 'crap'; the only thing worse than having one is to own a scooter. The Aces wouldn't be seen dead riding one of those 'hairdryers'. Nodding our heads in agreement, we haven't got a clue what they're talking about; to our young minds, owning *any* motorbike (or a scooter) is unbelievably cool, irrespective of the brand and country of manufacture.

Wiping their hands on Swarfega-soaked rags, the Aces start showing off for us, doing wheelies and time trials around the housing estate. Suitably awed, we give them the thumbs up; thereafter, if they see us perched on our gang bench by the old quarry, blowing on our hands to keep warm at night, they'll rev their engines until even distant curtains start to twitch. Releasing clutch levers in unison, they accelerate into a blur of chrome until, drawing parallel to us, they lower their steel-tipped boot heels onto the road surface, and we gasp as cascades of sparks fly up like Silver Fountains on Bonfire Night.

One evening, to our incredulity, the Aces offer us pillion rides to Southport's Pleasureland funfair—eleven miles there and eleven back!

It's already 8:15. Mum will go hairless if I'm not back by ten. But I can't not do this.

Once we're free of the dual carriageway's xanthous-coloured lighting, the darkness swallows us and I cling on, tracing our route by headlight beam. Turnpike Road, Fir Tree Lane, on and on past Prescott's Farm, through pigsty stink and rotting sprout-stalk-smelling arable fields in the direction of Halsall, Shirdley Hill, and the coast. Helmetless and underdressed in our piss-thin anoraks and market-stall parkas, we're excited and terrified in equal measure as the wind pulls at our hair roots and turns our knuckles blue. Hypnotised by the strobing of white-painted estate fencing, I'm lost in a waking dream of Saturday afternoon biker films—*The Leather Boys* and *The Damned*—and my New English Library pulp paperbacks, *The Bikers* and Peter Cave's *Chopper*. I am free. Free from school, my dad, gang hierarchy, and, most importantly, free of the tyranny of my own loneliness, cowardice, and insecurity. When the Triumph I'm riding pillion on swerves sickeningly to avoid a pair of wild rabbits on the road, my gut contracts, the film snaps upon its spool, and the spell is broken.

Chopper was dead before the back wheel stopped spinning.

Just as my friends and I have convinced ourselves that, young and bike-less as we are, this wild ride is a secret initiation into the Aces gang—some unspoken covenant between us—their leader raises a leather gauntlet, signalling the pack to slow and come to a halt. Under red brake-light illumination, he instructs us 'kids' to dismount, 'just for a moment', so they can turn their heavy machines around on the narrow country lane.

Climbing off, bowlegged and freezing, my unquestioning friends gather together, talking excitedly, while I, drunk on the twin perfumes of hot engine metal and the methane rising from cow slurry on the surrounding fields, gaze upward. The Aces don't turn their bikes around; instead, they rev their throttles in concert until the enormity of their volume threatens to swallow the whole of creation. In a sky spat with numberless stars, I spot the millisecond streak of a meteorite, and something in the surgical cold, the howling wolfpack roar of the motorcycle engines, and the twinkling black glitter overhead aligns in me to make some ritual magic.

I don't need to look down to know they've gone. I can hear them whooping in the distance like a Sioux war party as my uncomprehending friends watch their taillights recede to pinpricks, their already distant engines rumbling in Doppler effect over the Saracen's Head canal bridge as they head for the coast and Pleasureland.

On the five-mile walk home, out of frustration, Gaz Dempsey and the Campbell brothers kick rotten cabbage heads angrily down the unlit lanes. I'm not angry. I've tuned out their griping, because tonight, despite scorching the inside of my right leg on the Triumph's exhaust pipe, I, however briefly, tasted magic. Right now, I'm silently reciting a litany of names to myself, listing off as many of the names of Pleasureland's fairground rides and attractions as I can remember. The Wildcat. The Cyclone. The Galloping Horses. The Ghost Train. The Helter-Skelter. The Sky Boats. The Rapids. Noah's Ark. The Whip. The Waltzers. The Crazy Cottage. The River Caves. The Astroglide. Aladdin's Cave. The Haunted Inn.

And, oh yes, the oldest of the lot, the now-dilapidated House Of Nonsense, with its hand-painted sign over the entrance doors:

WHERE JOY REIGNS SUPREME.

—

1972. I'm leaning against the school wall one lunchtime, eating Midget Gems with my classmate Melvyn. We're feeling like real dudes in our flared-from-the-bum school keks and our half-assed regional salon feather-cut hair, checking out the girls as they return from the sweet shop in the local shopping arcade, the Square. I'm listening to a radio blaring from a parked car's radio. The song is 'John, I'm Only Dancing' by David Bowie, the 'Starman' guy. What's going on? This is even better!

Within a week, I have the girls in my class bringing me posters torn from their *Jackie* magazines of this wild-haired freak in the metallic-blue bomber jacket and knee-length lace-up boots. What is that strange chorus lyric supposed to mean? Who is John? Another kid in my class tells me Bowie is a Queer. What's queer? Really? Wow. Weird.

Things are changing fast. Bored of the herd instinct that's prevalent in school, David Bowie becomes my new obsession. He's made it cool to be skinny. Like magic, girls who have hitherto never paid me any attention start to take me seriously. Months later, to show allegiance to my alien leader, I have my straggly hair razored in a bland approximation of the Ziggy cut in a newly opened 'unisex' hairdressers above an electrical retailer in Ormskirk.

I'm feeling pretty self-conscious as I stand waiting for the bus home. A gang of Smoothie girls in cheap Crombie overcoats hanging out beneath the clock tower smile across at me, giggling.

Yes! I think. *I've finally arrived!*

Egged on by her friends, the bravest one sidles over to me and says, in a broad Lancashire accent, 'Me and me mates reckon you don't arf look like Rud Stuwut.'

Shit, Shit, Shit! Fucking hairdressers. I hate Rod Stewart.

For us boys living in Northern England in 1972, looking like anything other than a Smoothie, a Trog, or a Greaser is tantamount to mincing around in a ballet tutu. Looking weird can get you battered. Bowie is a wild card. I have to tread carefully, yet I am desperate to up my game. To externalise my inward shift from the safe toward the intrepid, I buy a pair of lattice-fronted, stacked-heel shoes from a classmate, Stephen Topping, for three quid. He has to walk home from school in his socks, three inches shorter than when he'd arrived, and I walk home with aching calves.

—

One balmy evening, Melvyn loses an eye while launching a homemade arrow into the sky. When he comes back to school six months later with a permanently watering glass eye, we all pretend not to notice. Such is his standing in school, no one dares to take the piss.

I'm sitting near the back of the chemistry lab, trying to avoid being gassed or set on fire by class maniacs Stephen Topping and 'Woolly' Wolstenholm. I'm listening to Radio 1 on a palm-sized battery-powered radio hidden in the inside breast pocket of my blazer. There's a wire running up my sleeve, the earpiece hidden from view by my cupped hand. I'm lost in a complicated fantasy involving Alison Wright, the girl with the shortest skirt and highest platform soles in school. Suddenly I'm zapped back into reality by the strangest, most exciting music I've heard up until this point in my young life. I can't quite believe what I'm hearing. Just as I'm beginning to get my head around its simple complexity the record finishes abruptly on an unaccompanied vocal.

'*What's her name? Virginia Plain.*'

I'm speechless, looking wildly about the room for someone, anyone, with whom I can share this epiphany. But no one else has heard it. My heart is beating faster than it was, and no other record the DJ plays can match the pop thrill of those few moments. Roxy Music, Bowie. Roxy Music, Bowie.

—

As an experiment, the school begins holding discos in the gym at lunchtime. Us boys don't dance, of course; we lean against the wall bars, trying to act cool, passing judgment on each track as it's played. 'Ride A White Swan'? Ace! 'Paper Plane'? Mmmmm. 'Silver Machine'? Ace! Chicory Tip? Shit!

For me, it's a chance to gawp at Wrighty or Susan Townsley as they dance in a group with their mates. I'm now secretly in love with Susan, but unfortunately, if she thinks about me at all, she thinks I'm a dickhead. With my head full of music, it's now that I send off for the Bell Musical Instruments catalogue and marvel over all black-and-white photographs of Burns Rapier electric guitars. I also start buying the weekly music papers and, when I can afford it, *Songwords*, the magazine with all the lyrics to songs in the Top 10.

On the first of April 1972, Gaz Dempsey drags me down to see Hawkwind at the Stadium, an old boxing venue at the back of Dale Street in Liverpool. The place seems huge to me, and, looking around, I'm aware that we are the youngest kids in here by several years. It smells strange—an interesting mixture of wet military greatcoat, patchouli oil, and what I later come to recognise as marijuana. Status Quo open the show, and although they're not really my teenage thing, I can't argue with how effective their linear three-chord hard rock is. I'm just amazed that whoever runs this place has let us school kids in tonight.

Hawkwind take to the stage in total darkness to an eerie synthesizer drone interspersed with squelps and burbles. All Gaz and I can see are the tiny red lights of their amplifiers. A voice swamped in echo and reverb crackles through the PA system, '*Space is infinite, it is dark / Space is neutral, it is cold.*' I'm so excited I nearly piss myself. It doesn't matter that I don't know any of the songs the band are playing apart from 'Silver Machine'; I just love the sheer spectacle of it all. This is the coolest thing I can imagine it's possible for two schoolboys to be doing right now, and then, just as I'm thinking that it can't get any better than this, it does. A naked woman, Stacia, freaky-dances her way between the band members and over to our side of the stage. I see Gaz standing with his mouth open, watching Liquid Len's oil wheels sliding across the woman's pendulous breasts. They're swaying just ten feet from our faces.

All this trying to behave like an adult has become too hard an act for me to maintain. I nudge Gaz, and a smile spreads across his face; we both start to giggle, and soon we're both crying with laughter and freaky-dancing. Later that night, lying in the darkness of my bedroom, unable to sleep due to a high-pitched ringing in my ears, Liquid Len's oil wheels slide across the insides of my eyelids while I tent the sheets as a spectral Stacia gyrates at the foot of my bed.

II
NO BLEEDING

1972. LANCASHIRE. It begins with a mounting compulsion to drag the point of my steel school drawing compass down my arm until it hurts, eventually breaking the skin until tiny bubbles of blood appear, and it ends a year later with me being caught by my sister gouging bloody runways down the length of my forearms. The term 'self-harm' has yet to be coined so, as such, I honestly believe it is something unique to me. Being exposed and admonished by my sibling like this is powerful magic. Her firm threat to inform my mother makes me feel deeply ashamed. The thought of my self-vandalism causing my mum pain is enough to make me instantly and permanently stop, yet cutting myself is how I cope with my loneliness and sense of isolation, so I'm angry at my sister's well-intentioned intervention. Angry because it was a private act that served a necessary function for me. The pain and the sight of my own blood took me out of my head and reconnected me to my body. I don't know if it's a cry for help or not—at fourteen years old, I don't think in those terms—but controlling the level of pain I inflict upon myself is how I keep sane. What am I going to do now?

—

NOVEMBER 1973. Spotting Les Pattinson's shy classmate Will Sergeant standing alone in the school yard one lunchtime, I nod hello and join him. We're both carrying albums under our arms. I've got *No Pussyfooting*, Brian Eno's first post-Roxy Music album, and Will is holding *Atom Heart*

Mother by Pink Floyd. I've come via the Smoothie, glam-rock route, while Will has come from rocker, Trog roots, but that is irrelevant as we are open minded and hungry enough to experiment. We swap albums for the night and find enough in common in the records to cement our friendship. Visiting his council house in Melling for the first time, I'm pissed off to find he's already got more albums than I have, and all heavier in content: Tull, Zeppelin, Floyd, The Groundhogs. Will is funny and refreshingly direct; he loves Bowie and the Velvets and, most importantly, he makes a great cup of tea.

III
IS THERE SOMEONE INSIDE YOU?

MARCH 1974. THE ALBANY CINEMA, MAGHULL. It's now, at the age of fifteen and a half, that I do something stupid—something that I will regret for years to come. I go alone to my local cinema to watch *The Exorcist*. I've been following the evening news reports, interviewing outraged clergymen who, fearful for the souls of the nation, are picketing cinema queues, even small, regional theatres, imploring them not to go in. This must be quite some film.

The Exorcist is an X certificate, which in the UK means you have to be a minimum of eighteen years old to see it, but as usual at the Abbey, vetting is lax, and I'm not questioned when buying my ticket. After a week of the film being screened, the priests have gone home and the cinema is only a quarter full. I'm expecting Peter Cushing levels of cartoon gore; *Vault Of Horror*, Amicus Productions-type shlock. What I am not ready for is child possession, Babylonian demons, levitation, and a girl masturbating herself with a crucifix.

The concept of demonic possession is entirely new to me, and the most horrific thing I can imagine. As a result, it triggers the recollection of being less than a year old and waking in the darkness of a cinema to the nightmarish image of the ghostly Banshee in the 1959 Disney film *Darby O'Gill & The Little People*. Not knowing where I was and having no frame of reference for the concept of cinema, I thought the ghostly images on the screen were real. Add to that the memory of that oh-so-weird soul-separation period I endured at nine years old, and I come out of the cinema doubly traumatised and unable to sleep properly for the next twelve months.

IV
THE RADIATION SUIT

SEPTEMBER 1974. In her flared loon pants, wedge-heeled shoes, sequined butterfly T-shirt, and Afghan coat, Karen Bone turns heads in the student canteen at the Hugh Baird College in Bootle, where out of total desperation I've begun a two-year course in advertising and exhibition design, a subject I have no interest in whatsoever. When, several months into the first term, Karen sends me a Valentine's Day card, I can't believe my luck. As a lanky sixteen-year-old virgin, I'd go out with a shire horse if it showed me any interest, let alone this almond-eyed rock goddess. The best-looking girl in the entire college wants to be my girlfriend! There is a god.

Until now, my idea of a good time has been riding my second-hand Vespino 'Rally' moped to Formby beach, going to the Albany to see kung-fu and horror films, and attending the occasional gig at the boxing venue the Stadium: The Sensational Alex Harvey Band, Cockney Rebel, Camel, Be-Bop Deluxe. Sometimes I take a risk and see bands I've never heard, like Fanny, fronted by Filipino sisters Jean and June Millington.

As an introverted ex-Tamla Motown smoothie turned Bowie and Roxy Music obsessive with one foot still in progressive rock, sartorially speaking, I'm a little confused right now. I don't know what image I am projecting to the world, but it isn't pretty. Saying that, second-year art-student golden boy John Montgomery aside, compared to most of the boys at college, I'm a dude, in that at least I'm trying to dress with some degree of originality. This is, after all, the era of the huge pointy-collared fitted shirt printed with repeating Art Deco patterns, 1920s flappers, and Model-T Fords.

Under Karen's influence, out go my high-waisted Oxford bags and platform shoes, and in come the latest side-fastening, flared-from-the-bum denims from Silly Billies, Liverpool's premier boutique and head shop. In my cap-sleeve T-shirt and *Starsky & Hutch* cardigan, I'm aiming for Robert Plant but probably look closer to a member of Pilot, Jigsaw, or—God help me—Smokie. Stylistically, I'm going retrograde, but Karen is my pole star now, and if she wants me to wear a frogman's outfit to go on a date, I'll happily don a snorkel.

A glamorous hippie in a sea of Huyton scallies, Karen has appeared in my life right on hormonal cue. I've had a few snogs on the school bus, and a disturbed girl once grabbed my cock while we were crossing the channel on a school trip, but I've never been actively desired before.

On Saturdays I meet Karen from her job at the Saxone shoe shop in the St. Johns shopping precinct and we head straight to the Moonstone, the subterranean longhairs' pub situated just twenty yards away. It's a twilight grotto peopled with counterculture wreckage: hippies, Trogs, and metalheads. Hawkwind's mystical-sounding 'Seven By Seven' is a permanent fixture on the jukebox, and all is right with the world.

On Valentine's Day, at Karen's suggestion, we go to a Berni Inn steakhouse for the £5 fixed price menu of steak and chips with Irish coffee as dessert. I've never been to a restaurant before, five quid is a fortune to me, and I'm so mortified that I'll make a fool of myself in such posh surroundings that I don't enjoy a minute of it.

'Wine list, sir?' Er, no thank you. Oh great, not only have I inherited my semidetached dad's bizarre inferiority/superiority complex, but I've also got his repression and fear of embarrassment.

As the months go by, my hair grows out of its feathery side-parted soul-boy wedge and into centre-parted hard rock territory. With my long nose and wide nostrils, this isn't a good look. I'm wearing the painted

Pronto Das clay beads that Karen has made for me around my neck and daubing myself with the cloying stench of patchouli oil. Worse still, I replace my cream-coloured platform soles with those instruments of Satan, slip-on clogs. They're not called slip-ons for nothing, and several times I accidentally slalom down the college stairs between floors and land sprawled at the feet of a dozen or so applauding, boiler-suited yobs queuing for engineering class.

Strangely, Karen is gravitating more toward what was my taste in music and fashion; she's losing interest in all things progressive rock and is dressing more like the models from the covers of my Roxy Music albums. We fall madly in love, and our special record is the same as every other courting couple's in January 1975: Minnie Riperton's 'Loving You'.

I lose my virginity to Karen on a single bed in a terraced house in Huyton while her mother is out at work. The incredible thing is that her parent's home backs onto the very house I was born in, number 62 Kingsway. We think it's kismet—a sure sign that we are made for each other. I can't believe it: I'm sixteen and I'm finally having sex, even if it is mostly among the ferns and bracken of my local woods.

On my seventeenth birthday, we go to Blackpool on the train, eat fish and chips on the seafront, and hang out at the fairground until five o'clock, when it's time to watch Ken Russell's film version of The Who's rock opera, *Tommy*, at the local cinema. In a shorefront boutique, Karen buys me a 'genuine' Mexican turquoise pendant to hang around my skinny neck, but when I get caught in the rain on the journey home, the turquoise genuinely rubs off on my fingers.

Back in Bootle, I've just been turned on to my first joint by cherub-faced class joker Carl Cookson. I don't get a hit, I just become paranoid and sit in class unable to speak, waiting for the effects to wear off. It's now that I notice John Montgomery's crepe-soled, customised shoes. He's modelled them after the Mary Jane shoes Steve Harley sports on the cover of Cockney Rebel's *Human Menagerie* album. It looks like he's cut away the shoes' tongues entirely and added silver piping. I'm beyond impressed, but sadly, having none of John's patience or dexterity, I ruin a perfectly good pair of shoes trying something similar.

—

One weekend, Karen and I attend a party thrown by Yvonne Gilbert, one of the more flamboyant and liberal-minded of the college lecturers at the Hugh Baird. We are the youngest guests by far, and I'm in awe of the clothing worn by some of the late arrivals: Hawaiian shirts, evening suits, fox fur. It's local band Deaf School, who have recently won *Melody Maker*'s 'Rock And Folk' competition. Enrico Cadillac? Betty Bright? Eric Shark? Even their names sound like they should be written in neon. They may not be famous yet but, my God, they dress as if they are. Somewhere within me, a lightbulb switches on.

After supplying her guests with wine, Yvonne disappears, leaving the party to look after itself. While Karen is busy talking to our uber-stylish lecturer, Pete Asbury, I down several glasses of wine and smoke a joint that I've been passed by a tall, raven-haired woman with a strong Texan accent. At least eight years my senior, she is wearing a Biba-style dress cut on the bias with 1940s-style platform heels. The more wine I drink, the more this exotic American starts to resemble Ann Bancroft in *The Graduate*. As she leans her back against the wall next to me, I slide my hand along the wall and place it between the cheeks of her bottom. Purring like a cat, she pushes herself back against me, wriggling, before yoinking me, stumbling, into a bedroom on the ground floor.

'Look what I've got!' she whispers into the darkness. I wonder who she's talking to? Hearing the sound of a cigarette being lit in the darkness behind me, I glance back over my shoulder to see party hostess Yvonne illuminated in the flare from a lighted matchstick.

'Don't mind me,' she laughs.

I'm so shocked I step down off the bed and all hell breaks loose. A huge Samoyed bitch that has been sleeping unseen under the bed leaps up, barking hysterically. Convinced that I am harming her mistress, the dog lunges at my groin, but its claws slide on the polished floorboards. It lunges, snarling, missing my genitals but sinking its teeth into my thigh. Instantly sober, I waddle for the door, the women's laughter tinkling in my ears, and my orange nylon Y-fronts around my knees.

'Where have you been?!' asks Karen with a raised eyebrow as I return to the party, dishevelled and breathing hard.

'I've been playing with that dog.'

'What dog?'

'The Texan woman's dog.'

Karen looks confused. 'What Texan woman? How drunk are you?'

'The tall one,' I say. 'The one with the cool shoes.'

'She's not Texan. She's not even American! She's a Geordie.'

—

Karen works hard at college and is a far more talented artist and draughtsperson than I am. I'm not the only one to have noticed this, and the tutors soon make it obvious that they consider me a bad influence. I receive an official warning: the tutors consider Karen—along with John Montgomery—one of their top students, and I am to stop distracting her from her work. My attendance record will have to be 100 percent from now on, and if the standard of my work doesn't dramatically improve within the next few weeks, I will be asked to leave.

This shot across the bow does the trick, and Karen and I immediately stop our weekday assignations in Karen's parent's house. Instead, we snatch our love during lunch and break times in a locked cubicle of the girls' toilet, just yards away from the staff room.

In the April of 1975, we see Genesis perform *The Lamb Lies Down On Broadway* live at the Liverpool Empire. Although I consider their new double album a horribly cynical move to break America, and lyrically about as far away from what appealed to me about the band as it could be, the show is wildly entertaining. During 'Slipperman', Peter Gabriel appears dressed in a rubber suit of boils, and as the song progresses, the testicles slowly begin to inflate until they're the size of Space Hoppers. Only when the band encore with 'The Knife', from *Trespass*, do I realise that I'm watching a band whose best-before date has already expired. This early live favourite of theirs sounds so urgent, so dangerous, that it reveals the last two hours to be imaginative but wildly overinflated pomp.

When Gabriel leaves shortly after the tour, I'm not surprised. He, along with Peter Hammill of Van der Graaf Generator, has always been ahead of the game. They've both smelt a change in the wind. I feel a bit sorry for the remaining members of Genesis, though. There's no way they can carry on without him. I mean, who would sing? The drummer?

Part of my final college examination is the design and construction of two mocked-up window displays in an empty room on the uppermost floor. Students are randomly allocated a product to promote. Some poor bastards are presented with packets of Flash detergent or toilet tissue; I'm offered a popular range of orange-scented cosmetics called Aqua Manda and a Harrods department store clothing range that I call *Country Life* after the Roxy album of the same name. My display features a male mannequin wearing a three-piece tweed suit, trilby, and brogues, frozen in the act of crossing a wooden stile in a window frame dressed with an assortment of rapidly wilting ivy, shrubs, and vegetation, hastily gathered from the local park. I've carved the words *Country Life* into the wood.

For authenticity, the college principle, 'Evil' Mr Price, has kindly loaned me an antique shotgun, and, on the eve of the examination, he also surprises me with an actual brace of ducks that he's shot especially for the occasion. Unfortunately, at the eleventh hour, the outside examiners postpone their visit to the college for an entire week due to illness. Not familiar with the concept of hanging poultry, I stuff the duck and drake into a binbag and stash them, out of sight, in a hollow beneath my display stand. Seven days later, the entire top floor of the college smells like a morgue, and when I reach my hand into the bag to retrieve the ducks, a putrefying miasma of beaks, bones, and maggots crawls out to meet me.

Despite this fiasco, I surprise myself and my course tutors by finishing the course with distinctions. Not that these paper certificates count for much; the only thing I have really learned in these past two years at college is that I definitely don't want to go into either advertising or exhibition design.

—

Karen looks beautiful tonight as the mirror ball plays across her eyes in our favourite pub, the Moonstone. Onstage, our favourite local band, Skyfall, are doing their proggy, sub-Jethro Tull/Genesis thing. We are so happy, sitting here holding hands and drinking lager. We know deep in our hearts that our love will last forever. It doesn't.

One spring lunchtime, while sitting on a park bench near to college, Karen informs me without warning or explanation that it's over. We are finished. It hits me like a death in the family. I am d-e-s-t-r-o-y-e-d.

Unable to handle the pain and humiliation of this rejection, I turn into a teenage Oliver Reed and try to drink the hurt away. My being dumped perfectly coincides with my parents going to London for a long weekend to visit my elderly grandmother. This is a miraculous piece of good timing as my parents never go anywhere together, ever, and it will save me the embarrassment of having to answer Mum's probing questions regarding the split. She's as fond of Karen as I am, and she won't accept a shoulder shrug from me as adequate explanation. Mum has left me some money for food and a little extra behind the clock in case of an emergency. I'm so upset by recent events that I have no appetite whatsoever, and I'm thinking, *If your first heartbreak isn't an emergency then what is?* I begin drinking at noon the next day, starting in the Moonstone, where Karen and I spent so many happy nights priming the jukebox with 10ps worth of 'Black Dog', 'Fireball', and 'Twilight Alehouse'.

Hours pass until, anaesthetised by alcohol, I drag myself the twenty yards or so to that subterranean pit of human degradation, the Sportsman bar, where I set up camp against a plaster pillar, watching a stripper with orange-peel thighs and sticking plasters on her heels, while I wait for local boogie band Supercharge to come on. Swallowing pint after pint, I'm having difficulty focusing on anything. When Karen appears on the staircase in front of me, I think she's a mirage brought on by the drink and the tears in my eyes. That is until I see that she isn't alone. Standing behind her is my replacement, a wholly unremarkable boy with ordinary clothes, 'bevvying' keks, and hair cut by Liverpool city council.

Spotting me, Karen's face drains of colour. She about-turns and runs up the stairs. Downing my pint in one, I give chase, shouting threats, obscenities, and early Roxy Music lyrics until love's young dream escapes me by jumping onto a well-timed bus back to Huyton. I stagger drunkenly through the city centre, a crippled yacht in a storm, still trying to make sense of what just happened. Swearing at passers-by, I rail at the moon for daring to illuminate my misery.

The following weekend, still on a drinking jag, I find myself in the North Star on Button Street, a smoke-filled, traditional Liverpool old man's pub, all mahogany bar and brewery advertising mirrors. John Montgomery is with me. He always carried a flame for Karen himself, and he has it in his head that I burgled her from him. We'll probably never agree on it—and, whatever the truth, he has no reason to be civil toward me now—but when I drunkenly pour out my heart to him, he's genuinely sympathetic. Despite being pretty drunk himself, he can see the dangerous state I'm in, and he volunteers to escort me to Exchange station for the train back to suburbia.

I've been drinking for nine hours now, and I can't believe it's still only mid-evening. Crossing Dale Street we're passed by two other pissheads, one of whom takes exception to our clothes and aims a drunken swing at John. Moments later, when John asks why I didn't help him, I tell him I was taking off my watch. I don't know why, as I don't wear a watch.

I say goodnight to John and stumble blindly in what I hope is the direction of the Maghull train. I pass out in my seat, waking only at Kirkdale to vomit on my shoes, then pass out again until I'm shaken awake by an angry guard and ejected from the train. It's twenty-five past midnight, and I've been travelling back and forth on the Northern Line between Liverpool and Ormskirk for three and a half hours. I'm back where I started, at Exchange fucking station.

Struggling between nausea and tears, I shelter in the shuttered doorway of the Private sex shop on Moorfields to weigh up my options. Do I wander the streets all night or find a sheet of corrugated iron on some waste ground to cower shivering under until the first train at 6:20am? Or do I ring the only person I know who can possibly help?

Finding the one unvandalized telephone box for miles, I ring the beautiful girl with the ugly name. Thirty-five minutes later, I'm slumped in the back seat of a warm car with my head cradled on Karen's shoulder. Her father, who I've never met before, isn't exactly sympathetic.

'Karen, open the window! Don't let him be sick on those seats!'

I can't talk. I'm too wretched. Arriving at the little house I've spent so many happy hours in, I'm on autopilot as I climb the stairs, making straight for Karen's bedroom, but then I'm steered by unseen hands into the sparsely furnished box room where I wake in shame at 9am with Algol, demon of alcohol, clawing up at me from the abyss. A month later, when I finally summon up the courage to phone Karen to arrange a time to pick up the forty or so vinyl albums of mine that are still in her charge, she takes a deep breath before telling me they were all stolen in a recent burglary. Just like that, half of my entire record collection is wiped out. *Killer, Axe Victim, Machine Head, Fragile, Close To The Edge, Trespass, Nursery Cryme, Electric Warrior, Pin-Ups, Fear, For Your Pleasure, Transformer*—all gone. I think I'm even more upset by this news than by her infidelity.

—

In an attempt to at least outwardly divest myself of Karen, I have my long hair cut short. It's time to bin all this satellite hippie shit, too. My college friend Joe Piet steals clothes to order from Cape, the ultra-fashionable boutique he works in on Saturdays, and where he assures me there are spyholes drilled in the walls of the changing rooms. Freed from Karen's retrograde influence—and thanks to Joe's sticky fingers—I go through a sartorial transformation: vintage green candy-stripe American ambulance driver's shirt, worn with a North American zip-fronted blue ice skater jumper of my sisters; baggy, 1930s-style pleated, burgundy-coloured trousers; and some stupidly expensive Bryan Ferry-style brogues I'd spotted in the window of the Jonathan Silver boutique on Seymour Street.

In November, Joe tells me about a shop on London Road that is stacked to the gills with deadstock 1960s Merseybeat-era clothes. Apparently, the elderly owners have struggled since the death of Beatlemania and are now so desperate for a sale they can be bargained down on anything in the shop. When I make the effort to visit this palace of wonders for myself, the first thing I notice as I open the door is the eye-watering stink of ammonia. The source of the smell is a huge, aged, pink-eyed breed of water dog that is lying on a pile of matted fur and piss-soaked blankets at the rear of the shop. Beautiful glass-fronted mahogany cabinets displaying unsold shirts from the 50s and 60s line the shop's damp and peeling plaster walls, while hanging from the ceiling, like cured hams in a deli, are dozens upon dozens of pairs of original elastic-sided Beatle boots.

The couple who own this peculiar shop are so wildly dishevelled that they resemble Quentin Blake illustrations. The wife—a *Struwwelpeter*-headed lady wearing long johns under her dress, an apron, and two cardigans—asks me politely what they can do for me. When I point to a particularly fab example of Cuban-heel winklepicker boots and ask if it would be all right to try them on, I'm told that they're too high up for 'Jack' to reach. He's got a bad back, you see.

Seeing a perfectly serviceable ladder on wheels nearby, I suggest they let me climb up to get the shoes down.

'No, no,' grumbles Jack, clearly irritated by my request. 'I'll get them down if you're sure you really want them. Do you really want them?' he demands.

'Erm, well, I don't even know if they'll fit me yet,' I say.

This is clearly the wrong answer, and Jack shakes his head, mumbling.

Effortlessly climbing the ladder, he grabs the nearest footwear to hand. Before I can point out that he's got the wrong pair, he's back down again, wheezing theatrically.

'There! Are you happy now?' he snaps, handing me a pair of dove-grey Italian leather winklepicker shoes a half-size too small.

I feel like screaming, but in no circumstances can Jack be persuaded back up the ladder. After getting this far, I think I may as well try for one of those cool shirts in the cabinet, but again it's like I've asked if I can have sex with their dog. I don't get to see a selection of styles or colours; Mrs Jack ignores my request for a size-fifteen collar and presents me with a stiff, white, tailored affair in a sixteen. The shirt has a cool metal tie bolt that passes through two small holes in its rounded collars. It's not brilliant but it is weird, in an Italian mod, skinny-tie way. I hate mods but I am into weird at the moment.

Mrs Jack wants three quid for the shirt and six for the shoes. I'm shocked and I tell her I don't have that much money—and I'm not lying, I don't. My college informant implied that I could kit myself out with a whole new wardrobe for the price of a Fray Bentos pie, but I now realise that he's been wildly exaggerating. Finally, a deal is struck: the shirt I can have for two quid, but the shoes they can't let go for less than four as they are 'good ones'.

—

It's lunchtime in the Jutland, the revamped pub sandwiched between Bootle Strand shopping centre and my college. I'm in a terrible mood due to my sore feet and the reception my retro outfit is receiving. *Bastards!* I think. You'll all be wearing winklepickers and drainees next year. Actually, thinking about it, this is Bootle. They'll be sporting bevvying keks and shit moustaches come the millennium—and that's just the little girls.

Limping back to college, my eyes fix on a poster that's just appeared on the side of a bus shelter. It's a huge monochrome photograph of an androgynous-looking woman in a crisp white shirt and black tailored jacket. I stop and scan it, taking in every detail: the wild hair, the thin black tie, the metal lapel badge of a horse. At first, I think it's advertising a photography exhibition in Liverpool, but no: it's promoting a rock album called *Horses*. The beautiful woman's name is Patti Smith, and some powerful witch magick in her expression compels me to head to the nearest record shop and blow my week's entire spends of £2.79 on her record.

Back home at six o'clock, my mother frowns and I get a tingling in my belly at Patti's shock-tactic opening line, '*Jesus died for somebody's sins but not mine*'. 'Free Money', 'Break It Up' . . . what is this dangerous and oh-so potent art music?

This is late 1975, when everyone who thinks they've got their finger on the pulse is raving about Bruce Springsteen's just-released *Born To Run*. I bought that too, on the strength of the press reviews and the monster-budget advertising campaign. 'Finally, the world is ready for Bruce Springsteen,' proclaimed the strapline. Well, it's good. Really good, in fact, but it's also just a little bit phony.

Phony is fine—Bowie, my lodestone, is often phony, but knowingly so. Phony attempting to pass itself off as authentic is criminal. Springsteen's lyrics, although beautifully detailed and atmospheric—all fire hydrant summers and tailfin cars—are hard to relate to while queueing outside Lam's on Hawthorn Road for sausage and curry sauce. The only car I've noticed today was a Hillman Avenger, and that one had been torched by joyriders. The only woman I've seen today is called Elsie, and she has a front tooth missing. Patti, meanwhile, is looking up at Saturn from the fire escape outside her New York loft.

—

That spring, I start seeing Ann Hedges, a pretty, blue-eyed sixth former who shares my train carriage home from college on weekday afternoons. On going to meet her mum and dad, I'm amazed at the tidiness of their home, the deep wool carpets, and the biscuits they serve alongside the Mellow Birds coffee I am offered. These are not the supermarket own-brand fig rolls, custard cremes, and ginger nuts I'm used to but something new and expensive called Dunkers—huge American-style things made with butter and chocolate chips. What's more, these crumbly wonders are kept in a wooden-lidded, ceramic 'cookie jar' decorated with sheaves of wheat.

Although Ann lives only two hundred yards from me—on the same housing estate—I suddenly feel like my family lives in a council skip with curtains. I'm just glad I polished my shoes.

I'm mad about Ann. When her mother gives her the money to buy some new school shoes, I go along, but when Ann returns home with a pair of stiletto heels that I've urged her to buy, her mother is understandably furious. It all ends predictably enough when I take her home tipsy; her parents understandably step in and put an end to it.

'We can still be friends,' Ann says sadly into the telephone.

'No, we can't,' I bark, as if I don't care. Inside I'm devastated, and my heart bursts open where the seam was weak.

V
GET OUT OF MY MIND, ALL OF YOU!

MARCH 18, 1976. LIVERPOOL. Sitting in the red-velveteen semi-darkness of the Odeon cinema on London Road, I have butterflies in my stomach. I'm not on a date. I've only recently been chucked, and my heart is still too raw and full of poison to think about girls. Too poor to buy popcorn or a drink, I'm fishing in my pocket linings for stray wine gums. Expecting a queue, I've arrived early, but after the trailers, the Kia-Ora advert, and the Pearl & Dean music, I take a quick last look around me.

I'm the only person in the entire cinema, and I can't understand it. This is the first ever screening of Nicolas Roeg's *The Man Who Fell To Earth*, featuring my north star—David Bowie. Bunking off from Hugh Baird College in Bootle for the afternoon, I've even dressed for the occasion in my burgundy pleated trousers (stolen to order from a shop called Cape), my candy-stripe ambulance driver's shirt, and £3.50 jelly-bean sandals. For the next one hundred and thirty-eight minutes, it's just me and my new best friend, Thomas Jerome Newton.

VI
MARINE MAGNETRONS

JULY 1976. In my three-piece pinstripe Jonathan Silver suit, chocolate brown shirt, metallic bronze tie, and two-tone brogues, I look like a dude, and Elio Caponi—the silver-haired Italian editor-in-chief who interviews me for the position of sales executive at *The Journal Of Commerce*—thinks so too. The meeting consists of endless questions about my tailor, where I buy my shoes, and where I get my hair cut.

'Yes, of course I can drive,' I hear myself lie.

Elio calls my bluff, requesting that I start work in a week's time. I make some wild excuses and we settle on five weeks. Mum, God bless her, allows me to kangaroo and swerve around the Cherry Tree housing estate for hours each afternoon in her just-resprayed Cortina. She sits in the passenger seat, slamming her foot down on invisible brake pedals, until I enrol with a local driving instructor she knows, who, when told of my predicament, absolutely guarantees that he'll have me pass my driving test in the time available. What I can't understand is why he gives me double—sometimes triple—lessons back-to-back, yet only charges me for one.

To show me how confident he is in his abilities to get me a driving licence, the instructor applies to the test centre immediately, asking to be informed of any last-minute cancellations. There are, and amazingly I pass the test by the skin of my teeth on the Friday before I begin my new job on the Monday. Now, passing one's test and being able to drive on a motorway are two different things, and on my first morning at work, I'm horrified to be given the keys to a Honda Civic and sent to the freight depot of Manchester Airport to pick up a parcel. I bang two parked cars just manoeuvring out of my space on the Dock Road.

I'm an advertising executive, apparently—at least that's what it says on the stack of business cards I've been furnished with—and as such I am shown to a large desk in a busy corner room of Tower Buildings that overlooks both Water Street and the Liver Buildings. I have two telephones and an assistant who, colleagues tell me, was also up for my job. Sulking, they refuse to give me one single contact to get me started. The lads on the sales team suggest I check out the drawer in the alphabetical filing cabinet marked with the letter *P*. When I do, I find it filled with hard-core pornography brought back from their sales trips. Apparently, it's a tradition. I smile, but inside I'm cringing. I'm never going to be one of the lads.

Elio puts me in sole charge of securing new clients for a book-format quarterly index of all new ships currently being built around the world. It's called *New Construction*. I like the title—it sounds like it could be a song by Be-Bop Deluxe. Because not one molecule in my body is remotely interested in selling advertising space, I'm completely rubbish at it. I spend an hour on the telephone talking in Pidgin English to a Mr Nakamura in an engineering works in Osaka before I work out that Japan is nine hours ahead of the UK, their head office is closed, and the night-time security guard is probably not authorised to issue company cheques for several thousand yen.

If I need to use the office photocopier, I have to pass through the noisy typing pool, where twenty girls wolf whistle, take turns feeling my bum, and laugh at my blushes. Lunch hours I spend hanging out in Probe Records in Button Street. I've followed Probe around town until it moved to the basement of the Silly Billies clothes shop at 51 Whitechapel, where, on a whim, I purchased a second-hand import copy of the Love compilation *Love Revisited* from a guy called Norman who looks uncannily like John Lennon. I've never heard of the band; I only bought it for its cover, a heavy card gatefold chessboard sleeve. Once home, I love 'Little

Red Book', but Love's sound is too wimpy for me right now, so I pass the album on to my mate Les Pattinson, along with copies of *The World Of David Bowie* and Leonard Nimoy's *Spock Sings*.

To look at them, the Probe Records staff are hippies to a man, but Geoff Davies, Norman Killon (the Lennon lookalike), and John Atherton are sweet, on the ball, and clued up to the interesting new records that are coming out of London, Jamaica, and New York. I've got money now, so I start experimenting with the pricey import section. The first things I buy are a copy of Patti Smith's 1974 'Hey Joe' / 'Piss Factory' single on the Mer label—I can't believe they have it—and a shrink-wrapped copy of the just-released album by a band called Television. Again, I don't know who they are, but the minimalism of the cover and the little spiral galaxy graphic on the back cover speaks of modern art, and that alone makes me buy it.

A pet hate of mine is people examining their vinyl purchases while on public transport, but today the pull is just too strong. Standing on the platform at Exchange station, waiting for the 6:05 home, I carefully slit open the import-only cellophane shrink-wrap on the heavy gauge American cardboard sleeve with my thumbnail and examine the rehearsal room shot on the inner sleeve. Absurdly minimal drum kit, Fender guitars and amps. The singer with the Prince Valliant haircut and the neck of a swan is called Tom Verlaine. Yeah, right! That's like me calling myself Paul Byron!

Back in the sacred space of my bedroom, static electricity crackles as I pull the inky vinyl from the inner bag. I've got a good feeling about this record, but I'm also nervous, in case it's a disappointment. It wouldn't be the first time, after all. 'See No Evil', 'Venus', and 'Friction' blow me away, but by the end of the title track, I'm stone in love. It's a total epiphany. I'm staggered by the scope, ambition, and beauty.

The brittle, crystalline guitars put me in mind of Richard Thompson's playing on the fantastic *I Want To See The Bright Lights Tonight* album that I bought on spec in a remainder bin for 50p last year. Returning to Probe's import section a few weeks later, I pick up the debut album by Blondie on Private Stock along with issue two of Legs McNeil's American *Punk* fanzine with Patti Smith and Television on the cover and an article on The Marbles inside. I stay up deep into the night drinking in this strange news from another planet. Patti is namechecking nineteenth-century French symbolist poets Arthur Rimbaud and Gerard Nerval, so I write down their names to check out later. Clearly, I'm not, but right now I feel like the only kid in England even aware of this alien culture.

Marquee Moon and *Horses* are the only two vinyl albums I ever have to replace when I wear out my original copies by playing the euphoric-sounding guitar solos on 'Break It Up' and 'Guiding Light' over, and over, and over again. Even Bowie's *Station To Station* didn't get the heavy rotation that my new best friends from the US receive.

Another import that pays off is The Modern Lovers' debut album on Beserkely, featuring the wonderful 'She Cracked' and 'Hospital'. The sleeve of this album alone weighs about a pound. I'm particularly intrigued by the song 'Astral Plane', because my Spiritualist churchgoing healer mum has been talking about my meeting her, post-death, on the astral plane since I was about eight years old. But life isn't perfect, and I make a few expensive mistakes, like the Split Enz album I play only once. Just as well Probe has a trade-in policy.

I finally make a big sale at work with a company called EEV Marine Magnetrons, but only because I doggedly pursue them, and not for the benefit of *The Journal Of Commerce* but simply because I want them to send me one of their promo T-shirts, thinking that Marine Magnetrons will make a good name for a band.

Around this time my sister, home from teacher training college in Poulton le Fylde, introduces me to a new hair product. It's called Sun-In, and it's a spray-in hair lightener 'with lemon'. It's virtually aerosol bleach. That shit is addictive, too, and before I know it, I'm no longer mousey but an unnatural blonde.

PART FOUR

YOUNG MANHOOD
1976–1979

I
THE NIGHT THE COMET HITS

DECEMBER 10, 1976. ERIC'S, MATTHEW STREET, LIVERPOOL. Just eight weeks ago, the Sex Pistols played upstairs here at the Revolution Club, but I missed it. All I knew about them at the time was the disturbing photo of them fighting with each other on the cover of that week's *Melody Maker*. Along with the Damned's 'New Rose', I've been playing their 'Anarchy In The UK' single to death this past fortnight, but information on these intimidating aliens is scarce. The term 'punk' hasn't landed in Britain yet, so this nameless, evolving-by-the-day scene is, for now at least, still plastic in my mind.

Tonight, my college friend Roy White's band—Berlin—are playing at the Revolution, supporting Slaughter & The Dogs. It's my first visit to the club, and although I don't know it yet, it's the night the comet hits. Channelling The Velvet Underground and *Ziggy*-era Bowie, Berlin and their flame-haired frontman, Roy, are shoestring glam, and I love it. They are, after all, playing the best of my record collection live.

Their short, exhilarating set over, I go to the toilets, where, to my mortification, I am joined by a stranger who stands uncomfortably close to me at the urinal and stares. He hates me and wants me to know it. He detests my too-neat hair, my pleated trousers, and my tasteful Bryan Ferry shoes. Terrified to meet his gaze, I stare ahead, pretending to read graffiti. As he leaves, I turn, taking in the zips, safety pins, and savagely chopped, dyed-black hair. His openly aggressive disdain has instantly rendered both me and my Bowie/Roxy, art-school sensibilities redundant. For the first time in my teenage life, I feel passé, and it hurts.

Although Slaughter & The Dogs are exciting onstage, they are not quite connecting with me; it's all a bit relentlessly one-note. *Oh, God.* I've just realised that their singer is the guy who was giving me grief in the toilets. But while I might not get Slaughter, I am starting to appreciate what's going on around me. It's exotic local night creatures Pete and Lynne Burns, Jayne Casey, Holly Johnson, and young Paul Rutherford—and the music DJ Norman Killon plays either side of the band's set—that inform me not only what this nascent scene is but, more importantly, what it's not.

I came down tonight with my sister's friend, Rio, who I've been seeing in secret for a while. A few years older than me, she's tall and slim and tonight is rocking a pair of tight-ass Oxford bags and the same sort of wedge heels and bubble perm as Angie Bowie. She's Bowie obsessed, and as such she takes to my friend Roy like a sexy limpet. Understandably confused, Roy looks worried that he's stealing my girl. What he hasn't figured out is that she's the adorable sweetness in a Venus flytrap.

At 2am, back in the suburbs, I take wallpaper scissors to my hair and a razor blade and a match to a plain white shirt I've purloined from my dad. Over breakfast, he asks me how I 'survived the plane crash'. I buy 'Spiral Scratch' and 'White Riot' as they are released and hide my pre-punk records under the bed.

Eric's and its bizarre inhabitants are my entire world now. Attending the club alone for the first few months, I always catch the last train home from the nearby Exchange Station. It's not too bad as the headlining bands are always on early, and only very occasionally do I have to leave during a band's set. Soon, Les Pattinson joins me; initially resistant to the aggressive simplicity of punk music, he is soon won over too.

II
NEVER RESIST A SENSATION

APRIL 1977. ERIC'S. There's a new face in Hell tonight, a new-wave Michael York so fizzing with spontaneous fission that he makes hyperactive club regular Pete Wylie appear introverted. We're a little suspicious of each other upon first meeting. Bespectacled trainee teacher Julian Cope has me pegged as an effeminate clotheshorse, the type who'd be kicked out of David Sylvian's Japan for looking too camp; I have him down as one of punk's part-timers, the sort who leaves home in a rugby shirt and attends the club twice as a *crazy* experiment before disappearing back to the safety of his Baker Gurvitz Army albums. But any doubts we have about each other evaporate when we start talking music.

While Julian concentrates on the positive aspects of this burgeoning scene, I vent spleen on what I think is diluting and polluting our teen revolution—namely, late-to-the-party former glam-rockers and prog-rock nearly men who, sniffing a change in the air, have rebranded overnight. Tiger Lilly become Ultravox, Jet become Radio Stars, Pegasus become The ID. Julian nods furiously in agreement. If he's still worried about the crappy old man's suit that I'm wearing and the studiously burned and distressed collar on the white shirt I've stolen from my dad's wardrobe, I'm more than a little alarmed by his custard-coloured T-shirt with its people's poet graffiti stencilling, *BOREDOM IS FOR STUDENTS* on the front and *I AM A PRODUCT OF URBAN SPRAWL* on the back.

Urban sprawl? Tamworth has a twelfth-century castle and a moat!

As I frown at his T-shirt, Julian pulls me up by flicking at the decomposing apple core and razor blade hanging in a tiny plastic bag safety-pinned to the lapel of my oh-so-carefully distressed suit jacket.

It's not just his perfect diction and Percy Punk clothes that give Julian away as an outsider. In subsequent visits to Eric's, he bounds up to us, his newly made friends, and engulfs us in massive hugs, which to repressed Lancashire icebergs like Les and me feels almost like sexual assault. Thing is, his wild over-enthusiasm is exactly the rocket fuel us poorly-educated, peripheral character stiffs need to help transform and propel this damp basement into a scene.

It's almost irrelevant what bands are playing at the club each week now; we would all come here anyway, just to bathe in each others' rays and reflect them back. For weeks now, I've been chatting to Julian's girlfriend, Kath Cherry, and her best friend, Hilary 'Hil' Steele, fellow students at Liverpool's C.F. Mott Teacher's Training College. The warmth and excitement these super-friendly girls display at this incredible club they've discovered is catching. Sporting long blonde plaits, Frye boots, and a fire-engine-red anorak with the word *GRIP* embroidered across the front in honour of her favourite group, The Stranglers, Hilary is a punk-rock Valkyrie. Without discussing it, without even flirting with each other, Hil and I fall into a relationship, and it only makes sense that we begin to hang out and socialise with Julian and Kath outside the club.

Staying over in Hilary's room at C.F. Mott drinking Earl Grey tea, eating Lyon's ginger cake, and listening to Bob Marley's just-released *Exodus*, I decide to adopt as my own the words I spot written on a scrap of paper pinned to Hillary's wall. *NEVER RESIST A SENSATION.* She accompanies me home after Eric's late one night and I introduce her to my dad over breakfast the following morning. There's no *Hello dear, pleased to meet you*, just a look of disgust and a loud, uncomprehending 'Bloody Hell!'

Hilary and I spend my nineteenth birthday in the freezing basement of the Old Bridewell, a former Victorian police station in the Kensington area of Liverpool, where the city's first authentic punk band, The Spitfire Boys, are rehearsing: Pete 'Budgie' Clarke on drums, Pete 'Griff' Griffiths on bass, and David 'Aladdin' Littler on guitar and shaved eyebrows. The star of the outfit is sixteen-year-old pretty-boy singer Paul Rutherford, who just oozes cool. I've dressed for the occasion in a pinstripe suit that I bought in a charity shop and have stencilled with the HM Prisons logo and a serial number over the breast pocket using white fabric paint. A blue-and-white-striped borstal shirt and a pair of genuine prison-issue work boots complete the sad picture.

My paternal grandmother, Florence Simpson, is unwell, and my folks have gone to visit her in London, so, unknown to them, I've got the keys to their car, which I've parked half a mile away from the rehearsal room on waste ground opposite the notorious 'Bullring' housing estate. Returning two hours later with our ears ringing from the music, Hilary and I are relieved to see the car is still there, but we can't get into it as the keys are locked inside. There they are, dangling in the ignition, taunting us. There's no way I'm going to smash the passenger side window, as Hilary suggests, so instead I flag down a passing police patrol car. When I can get the two constables inside to stop laughing at my suit, they half-heartedly try to get in using a piece of bent wire before quickly giving up and telling us they can't help.

'But it's a Ford Cortina!' I protest. 'Any twelve-year-old scally could get into it!'

'We suggest you find yourself one, then,' they deadpan.

Having no other options, I hail a black cab and take the hour-long round trip to my parents' house to retrieve the spare set of keys, praying all the way that my dad's old car will still be there when we get back. It is, thank God, but I can't get too excited as it's cost me the colossal sum of £15—all of the birthday money I got from my parents, sister, and grandmother combined, in fact—to pay for the cab. Happy Birthday.

—

Although the term *punk* hasn't yet taken hold in the UK—it's still 'the scene with no name'—my Eric's pals and I are buying every 45 that sounds, looks, and feels like it belongs to our tribe as soon as it is released. One has to be discerning, though, as for every three-minute rocket that sets our hair aflame and accelerates the scene, a lot of dullard pub rock is cynically being redressed in skinny ties and pointy shoes and stickered as 'new wave'.

By now, everything is moving so fast that the club DJs and regulars are bored by anything too on-the-nose punk. Every fourth record played by Eric's DJs Roger Eagle, Norman Killon, John Atherton, Henry Priestman, or John Campbell is a reggae import. Typically—in between records by Patti Smith, Jonnie Allen, The Modern Lovers, The Saints, The Sonics, Big Star, Flaming Groovies, Iggy Pop, and The Seeds—will come 'Croaking Lizard' 'No Bones For The Dogs' by Joe Gibbs & The Professionals, 'Two Sevens Clash' by Culture, 'Black Star Liner' by Fred Locks, and 'Disco Devil', Lee Perry's magnificent dub of Max Romeo's 'Chase The Devil'.

I'm slowly building up a small collection of Jamaican import singles, but at £1.50 a time it's an expensive business. With their badly printed labels and poor-quality recycled vinyl, it's a labour of love. It's not unusual to put one of these recycled vinyl singles on your record player only to have two or three identical paper labels fall off. When, after months of searching, a copy of Prince Far-I's whacked out to the-rings-of-Saturn reading of the sacred poems of the Old Testament—*Psalms For I* on the Carib Gems label—turns up in Probe, I scoop it up. That burning bush, *Methusael begat Lamech* stuff at infant school went deep.

Gradually more punk and new-wave singles are released, and it gets harder to sift the wheat from the chaff. This is the time of the second wave of punk, and a glut of major-label product gorges the market. Coloured vinyl and singles coming in three alternate sleeves with free button badges start hitting the shelves in Probe.

It's now that I discover that Probe have a 1974 Ork records pressing of Television's 'Little Johnny Jewel' seven-inch behind the counter. This record is so precious to me that I don't even keep it with my other records. It gets a cupboard drawer of its own.

—

Just as Les and I are alighting from a bus on London Road in Liverpool's city centre, three denim-clad, long-haired Rory Gallagher clones shout some abuse down to us from an open window on the top deck. We laugh openly and point up at these antediluvian fossils, who could be roadies for

Nutz. It's August 1977, for fuck's sake. They think they can hold back the new wave tsunami with Newcastle Brown empties and Status Quo jacket patches? Using universally recognised sign language, we tell them to fuck off back to the Bickershaw Festival they don't seem to know has ended.

Three hours later, after an uncharacteristically dud night at Eric's, Les and I decide to cut our losses and catch the last train home from Exchange station. I'm wearing an overlong raincoat over a pair of 48-waist combat trousers pulled into 28s using kilt pins and tucked into army boots, while Les is rocking a customised, vivid orange plastic jacket he's lifted from the boatyard where he works. By customised, I mean he's hacked it short with one slash of a Stanley knife.

A couple of minutes out of Exchange, as the train approaches Sandhills, the internal doors that divide one carriage from the next open, and the same three hairy wankers from the bus stumble into our carriage. They're drunk and heading straight for us.

I'm not overly concerned; our carriage is half full of straights heading home after a night at the Grafton, and who is going to mess with Les? He's a big bloke. They'd have to be mad, or drunk, or both, to start anything in a carriage this full of people. They're standing over us now, legs braced, fists curled in fighting stance. I'm nervously toying with what Ian McCulloch will later jokingly refer to as my 'gimlet': a wooden-handled corkscrew secreted in the pocket lining of my overcoat. On nights like this, when I have to use public transport, I'll always have something hidden about my person that can, in an emergency, be used as a weapon: a dividing compass or a cigarette lighter set on a four-inch flame; something half explainable, if I'm ever searched by the police.

The leader of the trio, an unshaven Trog with Ian Gillan hair, flicks his lit cigarette at my face. I bat it away with as much cool as I can fake. They're just bluffi—

Fuck! They're on us!

Francis Rossi pulls Les's jacket over his head from behind, completely immobilising him. *How the fuck?* Heavy blows start raining down on our heads and upper bodies. My heart is beating out of my chest. Les is struggling to extricate himself from the orange nylon tent he's found himself under, while I, for God only knows what reason, have entered some kind of dream state. It can only be the torrent of adrenaline pumping around my bloodstream, but I honestly can't feel a thing. Then it happens. Another passenger, neither Montague nor Capulet, intervenes.

'Hey, you chaps! Leave them boys alone. Stop all this senseless violence right now.' Or something along those lines.

Distracted for a moment, the cave troll who's clobbering me looks away, drunkenly trying to focus on the ballsy passenger trying to calm the storm. It's all I need. Clambering up onto my seat, I get behind him. Les, out of his orange prison now, is using some of the muscle he's earned working at the boatyard to clock Ian Gillan. Surreptitiously whipping out the corkscrew, I start lunging at the rocker's leather jacket. I must be hallucinating, because I could swear I can hear a pig squealing from somewhere nearby. One of the three attackers has lost his nerve and run down the aisle to hide. I was not expecting that. The gang leader has left his pals to face the punk music alone.

Now I'm standing up, wild-eyed and breathing hard. Looking around the carriage for the first time since the fight began, I see the horrified looks on the faces of the other passengers as they huddle into their seats, desperately trying to look invisible. Why are they looking at Les and me like that? We didn't start this. We're just trying to get home to some tea and toast and Open University, or whatever might still be on TV at half midnight.

I surreptitiously slip the corkscrew (now bent like a pretzel) back into my pocket lining. But wait. A golden opportunity has just presented itself to me. Les, standing with his back to the carriage doors on the non-opening side of the carriage, has the Francis Rossi clone in a Yale/Chubb-grade deadlock. The guy is drunk and humiliated but still wants to fight. Denied the use of his arms, he's pushing back with all his weight, trying to crush my pal into the plate glass carriage-door divide, while Les, completely on top of the situation, is barking short, sharp, SAS-style orders at his prisoner.

'Calm down! Stop struggling! Stop. It's over.'

It's brilliant. Rossi's legs are braced wide apart to keep his balance as the train lurches around the curves in the track. It's an open goal. Taking a run at Les's captive, I kick him in the balls. Goal! The crowd goes wild. He's going to need an ice pack on that in the morning. Against the odds, it's all going horribly wrong for the Trogs.

When the sliding doors open at Orrell Park, Rory Gallagher is off, but his companions suddenly find their guts and come back to meet us. Unfortunately for them, it's too little, too late. Buoyed by our success in repelling them so far, Les and I channel our inner Bodie and Doyle and manhandle our attackers off the train. These poor guys. It isn't even their stop. Not only have three older, stronger, hairier men lost a fight to two far younger punk rockers in front of an audience, but this being the last train of the night, they're going to have a long walk back to 1973. Once the carriage doors have closed behind them, it starts to rain, and one of them throws a rock through the window, showering an innocent passenger's hair and Chinese takeaway with safety glass. They're freaked out, most definitely, but thankfully none of the passengers are hurt.

As the train pulls out, heading for the next stop, The Old Roan, Les mixes us a pair of dry martinis while I whip out my Dupont lighter and spark up a Sobranie cocktail cigarette, flashing a smile at Miss Guatemala and Guadeloupe, who are heading our way in golden bikinis and heels. Well, that's what it feels like as Les and I breathlessly flop back down into our original seats, look each other in the eye, and explode with laughter.

'Fucking hell!'

—

Kath and Julian, missing in inaction since July, arrive straight off the train from Tamworth and, along with Hilary and me, stay the night at my parent's vacant-for-two-nights house. In lieu of anaesthetic, Kath uses an ice cube held against my earlobe before piercing it with a blunt, three-inch kilt pin.

Julian has insisted that she pierce my right lobe, the same as his. He has a theory that it will piss off more people this way. I've got a theory that it really fucking HURTS and the hole isn't straight. The next morning, we head for Southport Funfair, where Hillary takes our photographs next to the Waltzers, with Julian gurning like Norman Wisdom.

Again without talking about it, my relationship with Hilary naturally and mutually sputters out, and I start seeing a strange girl who lives with her foster parents in Thornton, near Crosby. Lynne is a pathological liar who's more interested in my Gat air pistol and sheath knife than she is in me. Because she's the only Asian woman attending Eric's at this point, Pete Burns nicknames her 'Mina' after a regular character on *Crossroads*, which makes her cry. Her ridiculously far-fetched stories are getting me down, but just as I'm thinking I'll break off our non-relationship, she beats me to it and disappears forever.

Six months later, I receive a censored letter on military stationery. She's volunteered for the Israeli Defence Force and is currently on manoeuvres at a secret location somewhere in the desert. She writes informing that she can now strip and polish a weapon in six seconds. Pity she never did the same for me.

—

Sitting on the yellowed Formica shelf beneath the strip-lit mirror surround in the girls' toilets in Eric's, I'm talking to Julian and his overly tall, overly eccentric college friend, Paul 'Smelly Elly' Ellerbeck. Les Pattinson and Pete Wylie are with us, and we're just talking about great new bands and what sessions Peelie played on his show last night when a submarine-deep voice with a cartoon Scouse accent thick as molasses enters the conversation.

'Way-o! 'Av yer seen the 'ed on that bouncer? It looks like it's made of soddin' granite. What a no-mark!'

It takes a moment for my brain to translate this near gibberish to *Hello all. Did any of you happen to notice the doorman's unique physiognomy? He's a loser.*

I'm staring into a pair of spectacle lenses so thick they magnify dust mites. At first I think they're being worn as some kind of punk affectation, like Pete's plastic lobster or the toilet seat he used to wear around his neck.

'Alright, Mac!' says Wylie.

I'm agog. This! This is the legendary Ian McCulloch? The bloke everyone has been banging on about for weeks? No way could I ever be friends with this guy. I mean, check him out—he's got the fashion sense of a halibut. I'm fascinated.

Leaning in close enough to do retinal surgery on me, Mac assesses and judges me on the spot.

'Good cheekbones,' he deadpans. 'But you'll look like Peter Cushing when yer old.' I think I've passed his audition.

Mac does this brilliant thing of talking as if he's famous. His brain is scalpel-sharp, and he's really funny. Within a few weeks, he and I are mates, and comfortable enough with each other to give each other nicknames. Within a year, we're in a band together.

Like his idol, David Bowie, Mac has adopted an alter-ego to channel through. He calls his character Benny Lomax. Benny is a degenerate Mel Torme, a sleazy jazzer on the cabaret circuit, a cigarette permanently burning between his fingers, an acid put-down always perched on his huge lips, ready to level any detractors or potential competition.

III

VARIOUS TIMES

NOVEMBER 1977. Like two committed but under-funded scientists, Will Sergeant and I have been rehearsing in secret for months. We call ourselves Industrial Domestic after a bank of tracks on an early BBC sound-effects record. Our musical arsenal consists of two electric guitars, a drum machine, a microphone, a transistor radio, and a tape echo. We jam around spooky riffing for hours over a reverb-drenched beat, only stopping to drink tea and watch regional TV's *So It Goes* with Tony Wilson. Swapping my entry-level electric guitar for his plastic drainpipe keks seems like a fair exchange, until I return two nights later to find he's taken a saw to it. What was lyre-shaped in a sunburst finish is now black and coffin-shaped.

Julian is fascinated by Industrial Domestic, and his enthusiasm for our non-band makes us feel good. In the June of 1978, I bring him to Will's dad's council house in Melling where, frustrated by our awkwardness, Copey suggests we jam a version of 'Satisfaction' to loosen up. More Residents than Rolling Stones, it's horrible, but that's okay. No one need ever hear it. Twenty-two years later, a recording of it surfaces on the third volume of Julian's *Floored Genius* compilation CD. Flawed yes, genius no. At the time of writing, I consider Industrial Domestic the greatest band I was ever a member of.

—

'We are The Fall-*uh*! Northern white crap that talks back-*uh*!'

The Fall are playing their first gig at Eric's. I'm with Mac and his orbiting satellite friend Dave Pickett, along with Julian, Will, Smelly Elly, and Les, and we go nuts. They are completely brilliant. I've finally found my literate, rebel music. 'Stepping Out', 'Last Orders', 'Psycho Mafia', and 'Repetition' blow us away. Their singer, Mark E. Smith, looks like he's just walked off the set of Ken Loach's *Kes*. One of my genuinely favourite things about this band is how keyboard player Una Baines's electric Pianet lines sound like they were written by Harry Corbett and played by Sooty.

I love the way The Fall don't follow any of the punk rules. There's no fashionably distressed clothes or cool hair—they look more like the sort of people who dish up fish suppers at your local chippy than a band. Mark's lyrics are brilliant, acerbic diatribes against ignorance, industrialisation, and Fascists. With his non-image and broad Manc accent, he's like some fiery Ned Ludd, inciting us punk workers to smash up the factory.

In June, Mac, Julian, and I catch a coach from the Pier Head to see our new favourite band at Leeds University. As the coach reaches the slip road to the motorway, Julian suddenly leaps up and asks the driver to stop and let him off. He's going to walk back to his girlfriend's room at C.F. Mott. WTF? Mac is incredulous at Ju's cop-out loss of nerve and passes instant judgment.

'Soddin' no-mark.'

We spark up a pair of Disc Bleurs, the maggot-smelling French throat strippers. 'He probably just wants a night with Kath,' I offer, but Mac is adamant.

'What a div.'

We're early for the gig, so we pass the time drinking tea in the nearest greasy-spoon café to the venue. Being skint, we nurse our mugs of tea, and ten minutes later, The Fall walk in, in all their scumbag glory. Remembering us from the shows at Eric's, Mark and his girlfriend-manager, Kay Carrol, are thrilled to see us. They can't believe that we regard them highly enough to have travelled all the way from Liverpool just to see them. We're their first ever out-of-town fans to do this, they tell us.

As Mac and I have got about fifty pence between us and are going to have to hitch back home after the gig tonight, Kay gets us into the gig for free, and when they see us on the slip road later, they pick us up in their transit van and offer us a lift back to Mark and Kay's flat in Prestwich. There are no seats in the back, so we perch on top of the band's gear. Every time we go around a bend, I fall into drummer Karl Burns' hi-hat stand and bruise my back.

Mac is pissed, and I suspect Mark is pissed and speeding, so when Mac makes an un-PC remark, Mark is on him like a ton of Victorian masonry. The conversation's getting heated, and I wish Mac would just shut up and let it drop. Mark is letting us stay at his place tonight, after all. Several months later, their argument is immortalised in the 'Present' section of The Fall's anti-Fascist song 'Various Times'. Later, Julian receives the same treatment in 'Music Scene', from the *Live At The Witch Trials* album, for naively claiming that it's impossible to buy dope in Liverpool.

IV

BY THEIR WORKS SHALL
YE KNOW THEM

I'm having an argument with some fake punks out shopping for fake punk records in Probe. They tell me they consider Eric's posey, and they prefer the Swinging Apple, Liverpool's only other punk club. I try to reason with them. For all their protestations, I can't help but think that there's one small point these sad chumps are missing: *THE BANDS ALL PLAY AT ERIC'S, THREE NIGHTS A WEEK!* If this was New York, these morons would be shunning CBGB's as being too cliquy.

'We don't need the bands, we've got the records,' they bleat. Yeah, and look what they're buying: Chelsea, Eater, and London singles.

You can't reason with sheep, but to show I'm open-minded I tell them I'll check out the Swinging Apple. I do, and I drag Julian, Will, and a posse of Eric's regulars down there with me. We stay for twenty-five minutes. It's pitiful. Dozens of chinless, safety-pin-sporting, felt-penned swastika-shirt-wearers pogoing to Sham 69 and records that wouldn't even get an airing at Eric's.

As the Wigan Casino is to Northern Soul, Eric's is to Northern Punk. Apple punk? You blew it. In later years, hundreds of people will claim to have been regulars at Eric's, but there are really only about thirty-five who'll remember the golden fibreglass sphinx head on the wall and who go every night the club is open for the first year, and not one of us has paid to get in.

Arriving late, I nod at the Brylcreem'd, Kray Twin lookalike doorman Reg or his ex-squaddie sidekick Pidge and we are ushered in. More often than not, the lovely Doreen Allen, manning the ticket desk, smiles and ushers me to go in quickly before the owner, Roger Eagle, sees us. Only if Roger is on the door and in a bad mood are we expected to pay.

It's easier to list the few UK and US punk and new-wave acts who don't play at Eric's during this period than those that do. We are completely spoilt by the quality and quantity of the bands and become blasé about watching groups that in just a few short years will be considered legendary: The Cramps with Bryan Gregory. The Heartbreakers with Johnny Thunders. Cherry Vanilla backed by The Police (wearing NY policemen's caps). Wayne (later Jayne) County & The Electric Chairs, whose show climaxes with the charming 'If You Don't Want To Fuck Me, Then Baby Fuck Off'. Bristol's sonic terrorists The Pop Group supporting Pere Ubu, whose frontman, David Thomas, clangs a massive lump of iron with a hammer all through their set. Iggy Pop being carried onstage under the arm of his huge security man. Talking Heads supporting The Ramones. The Modern Lovers. Warsaw morphing into Joy Division.

Meanwhile, life at home has reached crisis point. Dad and I have ceased all communication. It's time for me to go.

—

I find the bedsit through an advertisement in the back of the *Liverpool Echo*. Flat 3, 14 Rodney Street is one very large room occupying the first floor of a Victorian terrace that overlooks the churchyard of St Andrew's Scottish church. The room has three large sash windows that look down onto the street; there's a single bed, an armchair, a sofa, a table and chairs, a long sideboard, and a wardrobe. The room is painted an Art Deco eau-de-nil colour, and in one corner is a partitioned-off kitchen measuring three inches by five.

The rent is cheap: £7.50 per week. To my amazement, the landlord tells me I'm the only applicant; no one else wants to live in the city centre. What? Are they nuts? This place is paradise. No more buses, trains, or cadging lifts. I can walk to and from Eric's. I've also got Kirkland's and Plummer's wine bars, the Everyman Bistro, the Philharmonic pub, Probe Records, Penny Lane Records, the Atticus book shop, and the second-hand clothes shops Déjà vu, Oliver's, and 69A right on my doorstep.

Dropping me off with my boxes of records, kettle, and suitcase of clothes early the following Saturday morning, my mum bites her lip as she drives away. I feel terrible that I'm leaving her alone with my dad after nineteen years, but then most of the friction between them is due to me. I tell myself that maybe things will improve for her when I've gone.

I've only just finished unpacking my clothes and experimenting with moving the furniture around when Will Sergeant calls in, kindly loaning me his old Dansette record player. We spend a few hours drinking tea and listening to Kraftwerk, whose just-released *Man Machine* album I bought from Probe this morning, leaving me a bit short of funds for the week. Money is going to be tight for a while, and I shall have to supplement my £16-a-week dole money by stealing loo rolls and cleaning products from city-centre café toilets.

My 'kitchenette' comprises a Baby Belling countertop hotplate and grill and a cracked, half-size Belfast sink that belches up disgusting eggy smells every morning. There's an elderly gent living on the top floor who never leaves his room, and I am convinced he urinates in his sink as he never appears to use the shared toilet between floors. On occasion I find parcels wrapped in brown paper and string clogging up the toilet.

Julian totally flips when he comes around to see my bedsit for the first time. He knows this place is going to be a cool hang, right at the centre of the wheel—the perfect place to plan the revolution, and he's right: 14 Rodney Street becomes a drop-in centre and salon. With visitors calling by at all hours of the day and night, I'm never alone. People I barely know ring my doorbell late at night on their way home from clubs, hoping at best to keep the party going a little longer, or at minimum for a cup of tea and to debrief me on their night. Even if I'm in bed, I'm always up for an impromptu party.

The bedsit's previous tenant has thoughtfully left a stack of corner-shop porno mags in my wardrobe. Ju and I sift through about a hundred copies of *Razzle*, *Playbirds*, and *Whitehouse* until we find the issue with Gaye Advert in. Copey steals these mags and stuffs them up his shirt when I'm out of the room. He thinks I don't know, but he just loves these curvaceous fleshpots. He's too scared to ask, concerned that I will consider him uncool. God forbid.

Here I am at the hub of everything. I'm Hemingway, and Liverpool is my Paris.

—

We meet on the stairs one night at Eric's. A soberly dressed civil servant by day, by night working-class Catholic girl Karen K is a black mascara'd new-wave girl, all mohair jumper, skin-tight jeans, and pointy-toed stilettos. She's the first serious girlfriend I've had since my hippie chick Karen at college. At least I can't call out the wrong name.

Because of Karen K's religious upbringing, it takes me a while to wear down what I see as her prudish defences. On the night she finally agrees to sleep over, I forget to buy condoms and she says we can't do it. I've never been out with a Catholic girl before, and of course it's a big deal for her. We are happy for a while, but I'm a lousy boyfriend to her. I'm only nineteen, not yet ready to commit to a long-term relationship, but it takes me a year and a half to tell her that.

—

Copey's coaxed his bleached-blonde, grown-out punk hair into dreads like Green from Scritti Politti, and he's painted a likeness of Frank Zappa on the back of his biker's leather, aping Will Sergeant's hand-painted portrait of Lou Reed. My own chopped-blonde Joe Brown spikes grow out, and in an effort to look like Conrad Veidt in the still from *The Cabinet Of Dr Caligari* I keep on my mantel, I dye it black. It looks horrible. When I attempt to bleach it back to my natural colour, it goes carrot-coloured. More bleach. Paler carrot, but still horrible. If I bleach it again, it will turn into overcooked pasta and fall out.

Julian and I must look like a strange pair as we trudge around the city centre in search of a scene. We haven't twigged yet that we *are* the scene.

On weekday mornings, Julian swings over to my flat sometime before

10am for an early morning mug of tea and to enthuse about his latest record purchases from Chris Cutler's weirdo label, Recommended Records. At 11:30 we hit the food hall beneath Lewis's department store, where we are slowly working our way through the strange and frightening world of Eastern European smoked meats. We have an unspoken arrangement with the delicatessen staff there: if we turn up looking thin and unkempt, they will supply us with garlic sausage and broken pies. At 15p, the thin, foot-long, smoked Kabanos sausages are the cheapest foodstuff on display, and they're so peppered with fat we barely feel the cold.

The all-female counter staff sigh and tell us that we remind them of their sons before pointing to a pair of perfectly intact Melton Mowbray pies in the display cabinet.

'Those two are damaged, luv. You can have them both for 10p.'

Glancing left and right to check they are not being observed, they punch in the pie crusts before popping them into a bag for us. We'll eat anything on offer, even Boczek, the cured pork flank from Poland with tiny black hairs protruding from the thick outer layer of fat.

Our next port of call is the subterranean Penny Lane Records. We check out the import section first, cooing over the Residents and Chrome albums we can't yet afford, before hitting the back room of Probe and poring through the second-hand section. While Julian pulls out 60s obscurities he thinks I should hear by The Sonics and The Shadows Of Knight, I recover the near-mint copy of *The Zodiac: Cosmic Sounds* on Electra Records that I spotted and secreted in the wrong alphabetical section for him yesterday. Having grant and summer job money, Ju has more disposable income than I—and an arrangement with Probe boss Geoff Davies, who lets him put away dozens of albums at a time. My musical filters are far more uptight than Ju's, and while I can totally appreciate the raw proto-punk of The Monks and The Stooges, I'm really looking for the zeitgeist stuff—the sound in my head.

V

FAG SMOKE AND RAIN

SPRING 1978. Somewhere between the high and low art of Lou Reed, the sarky minimalism of The Fall, the punk experimentalism of Wire, and the burning giraffe of Captain Beefheart lies A Shallow Madness. Julian H. Cope on bass guitar is the live terminal, and Ian 'Mac' McCulloch on vocals is the neutral. Keeping us all grounded is Mac's dour best friend, drummer Dave Pickett—the earth terminal—while I am the foppish fuse, breaking the circuit when the temperature gets too hot.

Up until last week, using paintbrushes upon an upturned washing-up bowl, I was the drummer, but at Julian's suggestion I'm now playing keyboards. In my head, I'm the Brian Eno of the group, not its cheesy Alan Price; I honestly don't believe that I'm failing to play the keyboards properly so much as this second-hand 1960s electric organ I've just bought for £40 is failing to make the haunting synthesizer noises I hear on Roxy Music's '2HB' and Nico's 'You Forget To Answer'. I have zero desire to *play* this crappy instrument at all; I want to make supernatural howls and 'Mass Production'-style drones on it. When I do submit to memorising a few chord shapes from Julian, I choose to focus on the gloomiest-sounding combinations, but I prefer to play my own monotonous four and five-note riffs *à la* Una Baines.

We're an odd bunch with diverse tastes in music. Julian and Dave are Beefheart fans, but while I genuinely love the Straight label copy of *Trout Mask Replica* that Ju has recently gifted me, I cannot go there with the zany Frank Zappa jazz fusion he's also raving about. I mean, what was punk for if not to purge the scene of diminished sevenths, minor elevenths, long hair, and flares? Likewise, come July, Copey completely loses his shit when he hears 'The Electrician' from my copy of The Walker Brothers' brilliant *Shutout* EP and goes on a Scott solo album buying spree, yet he cannot entertain my Magazine *Still Life* album because he's affronted by John McGeoch's aloof pose on the back cover.

Ju and I adore Scritti Politi's *Skank Bloc Bologna* EP, Pere Ubu's *Modern Dance*, Suicide's debut album, and everything to date by San Francisco's The Residents. Not Mac, though—he's pretty much closed to anything but the holy trinity of Bowie, Lou, and Iggy. Because everything new that Julian and I play him is decreed either 'cherry on'—his slang term for embarrassing, i.e., having a red face—or 'think again!'—which translates as 'you are mistaken'—we give up trying.

Perhaps it's the Serge Gainsbourg-like perma-ciggy on his lip or the scouse braggadocio, but it's always just been assumed that Mac is going to be our frontman. We've never actually heard him sing, but he's certainly got the lips and the ego for it.

Our earliest rehearsal is a late-night session in my Rodney Street bedsit with Julian playing the organ, Dave keeping Neolithic time on the arm of my sofa with a knife and fork, and all of us singing along to Mac's made-up-on-the-spot song '(I Love) The Parisian Sound' and some McCulloch/Cope co-writes, 'Robert Mitchum' and 'Spacehopper'. Everyone but me thinks these are songs of hilarious genius; I'm just waiting for us to stop playing the punk Barron Knights and start working. I blame 'I'm Sticking With You' from The Velvet Underground's just-released *Etc.* bootleg compilation. I love that song too, but where is our darkness—our 'Venus In Furs', our 'Heroin'? Why can't we take ourselves seriously?

The following morning, my postman neighbour, Tommy, wakes me at dawn, banging loudly on my door and bawling me out for last night's noise.

'How do you bloody well like it!?'

I don't like it.

From the moment Pete Wylie proposes securing Mick Finkler as guitarist for our just-formed band, we like him. Sharp, funny, self-deprecating—the positive side of sarcastic—Mick owns and plays a Fender Telecaster, the same guitar as Richard Lloyd of Television, which is reason enough alone for us to welcome him into our magic circle. Okay, his curly black hair is a little long, but then so is that of his lookalike, Mick Jones of The Clash, these days. Our Mick is sporting a very non-rock'n'roll duffle coat, too, which he immediately apologises for, but we love it. It's very Subway Sect, very The Fall.

—

It's while suffering from a dose of the flu that I discover cough syrup—or, more accurately, the codeine suspended within it. One 150ml bottle buys me twelve hours of insulation. Long after I am recovered, I start buying it for kicks until, along with milk and rye bread and French ciggies, it's part of my core shopping. If you looked in the pockets of my tweed CC41 overcoat right now, along with the soft pack of Gauloises, comb, Pentel rollerball, notebook, and penknife, you'd find a half-empty bottle of Benylin. Small swigs during the day keep reality at a safe distance; knocking it back at night keeps the ghosts at bay. There's a second bottle on top of the coin-operated electricity meter that acts as a shelf at the side of my bed, so at night I can reach out and self-medicate while reading Henry Miller's *Tropic* trilogy, Genet's *Miracle Of The Rose*, Knut Hamsun's *Hunger*, and Hemingway's *A Moveable Feast*. Bizarrely, anything with haunted, horny, hallucinating, or hungry young men trying to stay warm in winter helps me to feel like I am not entirely wasting my life.

I love my circle of Eric's friends, and I love this bedsit of mine at the centre of Liverpool's counterculture hub, but I'm already nineteen years old. In three and a half months I'll be twenty, for fuck's sake! What am I doing with my life?

—

Returning from signing on at Benson Street Unemployment Benefit Office, I find a note pinned to my door.

Dear Paul, practising at Smelly Elly's, 138 Belmont Road. If you are going there catch a 15d, give the driver 16 pence and say, 'Put me off at Belmont Road, my man!' Bring your keyboard, we've got the amp and leads. Lots of love, Michael N. Finkler and Thug.

Who is Thug? I wonder. Julian? Possibly our intense and brooding, quiet-with-a-side-order-of-menace drummer, Dave. Prize-winning eccentric Smelly Elly is harder to define, so I won't try.

Back from visiting his parents in Tamworth, Ju strides into rehearsals carrying a fretless bass. In an attempt to make it look less Jaco Pastorius and more punk, he's sprayed it matt black, but Mick, Dave, and I are horrified. Who are we, The Mahavishnu Orchestra?! How is it that he even owns such an instrument?

Annoyed at our reaction, Ju straps it on as if it's a flamethrower. Adopting a power stance, nostrils flared, he stands silently glowering at us. It's a bit scary, but because we love him, and because it's the only bass guitar we have, we eventually decide to agree that our fretless bass is not the Ian Carr's Nucleus, Weather Report, Return To Forever muso instrument of the devil it first appeared to be but an ironic punk statement. It's 'post-cool'.

Our 'singer' is becoming a problem. Adore him as we do, Mac is always two hours late to rehearsals. When he does eventually show up, he has no lyrics written, and he flat-out refuses to sing. In his absence, we've cobbled together a set of five instrumentals, but no matter how many times we hone and repeat them, Norris Green's own Thin White Duke won't open his mouth. Some weeks he fails to show at all. When he moves into Smelly Elly's spare room, we are delighted. He can't possibly be late now! But somehow he is. When we challenge him, he gets moody and defensive: 'The songs are all sodding crap.'

Crap or not, we can't tread water like this forever. Tired of lugging the equipment on the bus to and from Wavertree each week only for Mac to keep us waiting, we decide to give him one last chance to get his act together. He assures us he's going to be there on time and have some lyrics written for our rehearsal next Saturday, and we believe him. A week later, he doesn't show. Arriving just as we are packing up to leave, he still hasn't written any lyrics. He won't even come and hang out with us in Reece's or the Armadillo Tea Rooms in town like he once did. He goes back to bed instead.

Julian has had enough. At his behest, we hold an impromptu vote outside Probe Records, where we unanimously agree that Mac has to go. This is particularly awkward for Dave and me, as we both socialise with Mac outside the band. He isn't just our bandmate, he's also our friend.

To my relief and to Mac's credit, he isn't mad with me about being sacked from the band—at least not openly—and we still hang out as usual in the coming months. Early on Saturday or Sunday evenings, his dad drops him at my bedsit, and we spend an hour getting ourselves gussied up to go to Checkmates or one of the Bowie and Roxy clubs. Occasionally, out of desperation, we hit the Gazebo, the Continental, or the Cabin in the hope of meeting girls. After closing time, we sometimes chance the Masquerade, Sadie's, or Jody's; being gay private members' clubs, they stay open an hour or two later. Dodgy Bowie clones that we are, we are rarely questioned regarding our eligibility to be there. Only the formidable Tony Sadie at the Royale Royal bar gives us the third degree. She tells us that she *knows* we're not gay, even if we don't, but because we're 'darlings' and we promise to buy drinks, she lets us in.

—

At our first band rehearsal without Mac, before we've even plugged in, Julian raises the question of who is going to replace him as our singer. Then, before we've had a chance to reply, he offers his services. With great tact and diplomacy Mick, Dave, and I shout out one of Mac's classic put-down lines: 'Think again!' Despite never having heard him sing, we're adamant that Julian is not frontman material. We don't discuss it with him or explain why, so he's frustrated and pacing the room while giving us the silent treatment. Surely Ju must know that a frontman needs addictions, demons; *at minimum*, some deep-rooted Oedipal complex? Over cups of tea, we have a rethink. Copey's got a point—the coolest people we know are already in this room, so who else is going to do it? I'm not even in the frame. Okay, okay. We're not convinced Julian is the lizard king—not just yet, anyway—but we agree that he'll do until one comes along.

After rehearsing, Julian returns to the damp flat he shares with Kath in

Prospect Vale, Kensington, where he's accosted by his fifteen-year-old near neighbour and questioned about the bass guitar he's carrying. The boy's name is David Palmer, and he has no idea of the chain of events he's about to trigger. Hyper at the best of times, Julian hums like a hot valve when talking music, so of course within ten minutes he's completely rewired this suburban kid's brain with his infectious talk of the Velvets and the Stooges and how he needs to buy these incredible psychedelic records by The Red Crayola and The Thirteenth Floor Elevators, Syd Barrett and Soft Machine—and as soon as possible. There's more: right here, right now, in Liverpool, there's us, Eric's, Roger Eagle, Big In Japan, Jayne Casey, Pete Burns, Probe Records, Déjà Vu, the Atticus bookshop. The list of wonders is endless. Narnia awaits! All young Dave has to do is simply choose to enter the wardrobe.

Dave walks home with his brain leaking out of his ears. That'll teach him to talk to strangers. Swallowing all this magic like a whale swallows krill, he rewards his new music tutor with the latest records Julian wants but can't afford right now. Showing me the fantastic singles Dave has bought for him from Probe and Penny Lane Records, Julian grins. I'm jealous until I too start receiving similar presents of vinyl. Living with his mum and helping out on his dad's market stall twice a week, Dave has more disposable income than we do, so, from his perspective, a few singles now and then is a small price to pay to get to hang out with such intrepid weirdos.

Rechristened 'Yorkie' by our mate Pete Wylie, Dave offers us the cellar of his mother Gladys's large and rambling house as a rehearsal room. When we see it, we are ecstatic. Give it a sweep with a stiff broom and it could be Television's rehearsal space on the inner sleeve of *Marquee Moon*. When Mac unexpectedly hooks up with my pals Will Sergeant and Les Pattinson, intending to start a band, they also rehearse down there, and we pool our minimal equipment. Yorkie, spurred on by Copey's bleached semi-dreadlocks and my *Love On The Dole* clothes, begins a slow but thorough metamorphosis. With his dyed-black Henry V haircut, incrementally followed by black jodhpurs, calf-high leather gaiters, and a Victorian cloak, he's a terrifying sight to meet on a foggy night. When he adds a genuine cavalry officer's sword to his ensemble, Ju and I suggest to him that he might, just might, be overdoing things.

—

Hanging out in Rodney Street one afternoon, Julian, Mick, Dave Pickett, and I are discussing possible names for the new band line-up. Between mugs of tea, we chew over a few surreal-sounding nonstarters. After an hour or two of no one agreeing, I start flicking through a 1971 *Daredevil* comic that I presume was left by my bedsit's previous tenant, Ozzie Yue, bass player in local boogie band Supercharge—a group I'd watched many times in the Sportsman bar in the mid-70s. I'd found the comic among a box of lost property that included pornography, mouth mirrors, sickle tooth probes, and a full bottle of dental ether that I take the occasional risky hit from.

Woah! What's this?

Drawing everyone's attention to a panel in the comic that appears to bear no relation whatsoever to the rest of the story, I hold it up while reading it to them.

AND THEN . . . IT HAPPENS—FILLING THE WINTERED GLADE OVER CENTRAL PARK WITH AN UNEARTHLY WHINE—PAINTING THE LEAF-BARE BRANCHES WITH GOLDEN FIRE—THE TEARDROP EXPLODES!

Snatching it from me, Julian is on his feet. He thinks it's psychedelic genius. Mick, Dave, and I aren't convinced at first. Isn't it a little insubstantial, a little lacking in gravity? Mick and I consider ourselves to be the conscience of the group, the front and rear brakes for Julian's occasional hyper-enthusiastic over-steering. But while we aren't bowled over by it, Julian's excitement is, as ever, so total, so infectious, that we agree that, until something better comes along, we are The Teardrop Explodes.

—

Bill Drummond, man-giant and rhythm guitarist with local art-rockers Big In Japan, asks to see us and blows our minds with the news that he wants to release a single by us on his Zoo Records label. Being a *glass is completely empty* kind of person, I'm initially dubious. A few months earlier, I'd been an accidental witness to Bill's trial-by-jury late one afternoon in the Open Eye café in the Merseyside Visual Communications Unit when he was called to account for some untoward dealings by his fellow band members in Big In Japan. I was stuck out of sight in the far room of the café, nursing my cold cuppa, but once Jayne Casey had started proceedings for the prosecution, I couldn't leave without them seeing me and embarrassing us all. It seems Bill had re-pressed Zoo's first release, the *From Y To Z And Never Again* EP, without bothering to tell his bandmates.

Bill's new business partner in Zoo Records is Jayne Casey's current squeeze, David Balfe, or 'Smurf', as he's unflatteringly known. 'Balfie', as Bill prefers to call him, is an annoyingly upbeat bloke from the Wirral. As if his bleached-white Andy Warhol haircut weren't reason enough for us all to distrust him, he also wears expensive leather trousers with baseball boots. Nothing wrong with baseball boots—the Ramones wear them after all—but Balfie's are made from white leather. To our charity shop sensibilities and Paddy's Market budgets, he looks like one of Cheap Trick—or, worse, a daytime Radio 1 DJ.

Dave Balfe is so bullish and opinionated, he argues over every point. None of us can stick him at first, but as the weeks go by, we warm to him and his high-concept, five-minute-ahead-of-his-time thinking. What we really can't forgive him for, though, just twelve months after The Clash's proclamation of 'No Elvis, Beatles, or The Rolling Stones', is his unabashed love of the Fab Four. As a kid, I adored The Beatles, but this is 1978, and I'm hardly going to admit that to anyone now, am I?

—

Still in search of his muse, Julian hasn't yet tapped into his subconscious, so for now he writes prosaic lyrics about wandering aimlessly around town.

Dave Pickett suggests 'Sleeping Gas' as a song title, which we like a lot, and I suggest 'Camera, Camera' as another. To my ear, the latter has some European art-house flavour, but I'm such a pretentious twat that last year I considered changing my name to Paul Strangeways. When Julian 'Speed Novak' Cope chanced upon my page of trial signatures, he took the piss out of me for a week.

Around this time, Dave Pickett is ousted from his drum stool. He's not a bad drummer; it's more of a chemical mismatch. We like him a lot—he's funny—but unlike Mick Finkler's positive negativity, Dave's constant sarcasm and background radiation gloom is collectively wearing on us. At Spitfire Boys drummer Pete 'Budgie' Clarke's suggestion, Deaf school roadie and young Ed Gwynne lookalike Gary 'Rocky' Dwyer, becomes our new drummer. Gary can't play too well at first, but that's okay—none of us can either. After I dye my hair for David Bowie's concert at Stafford's Bingley Hall, Gary Christens me 'Joe Bowie', and late in the evening, often just as I'm falling asleep, I hear his drunken voice shouting '*Joe Bowieeeeeeeeee*' at the top of his lungs as he crosses the intersection of Hardman and Rodney Street.

One evening, Julian calls in, fresh off the Tamworth train, to see me at my bedsit. Oh my God! He's had his bleached blonde dreadlocks chopped off into a short, rough approximation of my wartime haircut. Cool! If he didn't look about twelve years old, he could be blowing a whistle and telling his men to charge into no man's land.

—

AUTUMN 1978. Our first gig arrives: a private party at Eric's in front of our friends, peers, and friendly enemies. We've still only got five songs, so, to fulfil our thirty-minute slot, we decide to top and tail our set with the fastest one, 'Seeing Through You'.

As we climb onstage, I'm wracked with nerves.

Be cool, Paul. Just be cool.

To our astonishment, the moment we begin to play, Julian transforms into the frontman we doubted he could be. He pulls it out of the bag big time. Jabbering in schoolboy Russian down the microphone, why . . . we *almost* sound like a cool band, but apologising to the audience after every number? Not quite so cool. I get it, though: I'm so frozen with fear I've got cramps in my fingers from pressing down so hard on the keys. Gary, counting the bars in his head, fucks up on the outro of the penultimate song and everything nearly collapses, but no one in the audience seems to care. We finish to huge, supportive cheers and applause from Will, Les, Mac, Pete Wylie, and assorted girlfriends.

It's done. We are a band.

VI

MONKEY OPIUM BLUES HORSE

OCTOBER 21, 1978. LIVERPOOL. The Teardrop Explodes have just come offstage after playing what was only our second ever gig—a matinee at Liverpool's Eric's Club—when my girlfriend, Karen K, appears. Odd. She didn't attend the show, so I can't understand why she's here now, or why her eyes look so red. Between sobs, she tells me that Merseyside Drug Squad just raided my city-centre bedsit. While she was putting on her make-up to attend our evening show, a Transit van full of police officers with sniffer dogs forcibly entered and ransacked the place. While she was body-searched and questioned by a WPC, the male officers upturned draws, pulled suitcases from under the bed, and scoured my frugally stocked kitchen cupboards.

As if I am not already nervous enough about playing tonight's sold-out show supporting Wire in front of our friends, enemies, and peers, I now have to deal with the added pressure of knowing that the police consider me a suspect in some yet-to-be-ascertained crime. With just two hours before showtime to get to the bottom of this, I sprint across town to find my bedsit in disarray: clothes drawers open, books and records strewn on the floor. Upsettingly, a dozen small photo-booth photographs of my friends and me that were tucked into the frame of the mirror over the fireplace are missing. Mistaking her for a suspect, they've also taken a small 1960s promo pic of German actress Hildegard Knef peering out of a broken window.

When I call in at my local police station on Hope Street to complain, a porcine desk sergeant smelling of chips denies all knowledge of the event. Without even looking up from his well-thumbed copy of *The Sun*, he tells me that no such raid has taken place. I politely ask if he can please check with his superiors. Sneering, he raises both eyes and voice to inform me that he doesn't need to check anything with anyone, because NO SUCH RAID HAS TAKEN PLACE.

A week later, I'm sitting eating dinner while watching *Who Pays The Ferryman?* on television when there's a firm knocking on the door of the bedsit. This will be my elderly postman neighbour, Tommy, come to ask me, yet again, if he can have a few more of the vintage pornographic magazines that were left here by a previous tenant. But it isn't Tommy: it's two middle-aged men with crumpled suits, kipper ties, and matching Graeme Souness moustaches. Inviting themselves in, they introduce themselves as Detectives Merter and Thompson. I'm on the first floor; the ground floor is a medical herbalist's day surgery, and there's no tenant down there, so where did they get the house key?

I can't help but notice that Detective Thompson closely resembles fictional detective Dermot McEvoy from the BBC television series *Gangsters*. Thompson's the sort you might see in an old episode of *Z-Cars*. He'll be the one stamping his feet under a lamppost, saying, 'It's bloomin' taters out 'ere, Sarge,' while Merter is the image of *Hazell* actor Nicholas Ball—more of a 'Gotcha! Thought you could outfox an old pro like me? You're nicked!' Sitting together on my too-small sofa, they look like a couple on an awkward first date. Poshing-up the diction of their scouse accents a little, they begin to question me in a ludicrous prewar *PC 49* fashion.

'So, Mr Simpson,' they begin. 'You're in *the game.*'

The game? Am I? What game? What's it called? Did I win? I wish someone had told me.

'The *music* game. The *rock'n'roll business.*'

'Er . . . well. No. Yes. Not really. I am in a band,' I reply nervously, 'but it's early days. We've only played three gigs so far, and two of those were last Saturday night when your men rai—'

'We'll level with you, Mr Simpson. We didn't find any illegal substances on the property this time, but we must inform you that you are a *person of interest* in our investigations.'

Fucking hell! Great. Twenty-one years old and I'm already a marked man. My dad was right: he said I'd never amount to anything. Look out, McVicar! Move over, Papillon! Alert Interpol, I'm on Europe's most-wanted list. Maybe I should cut my losses now and hurl myself out of the window shouting, 'You'll never take me alive, copper!'

'Even if you can convince us you are not a supplier of narcotics to your contacts in the music business, you must come across people who do use illicit compounds.'

'Illicit compounds'? What? Are we Edwardians now?

'My colleague is referring to recreational drugs, Mr Simpson. You know, like—'

Oh, God. No! Please. They're not going to start listing drugs, are they? I'm cringing. Pausing for effect, the pair lean forward in unison scrutinising my face for the slightest hint of guilt, as if I'll give an involuntary nervous tick when they reach my drug of choice.

'Cocaine? Smack? Marijuana? Lysergic acid? Brown?'

Lysergic acid? Brown? If I wasn't so nervous, I'd burst out laughing. If I were running an underworld drugs ring, do these two seriously think I'd be living in an eight-quid-a-week bedsit? Hardly a villa in Marbella, is it? Hardly Operation Julie. Jesus! It's no wonder the crime rate is soaring on Merseyside when our detectives are so clueless.

Ignoring my offer of cups of tea—probably scared I'll put lysergic acid in it—Detectives Thompson and Merter continue with their ludicrous list of forbidden substances.

'Uppers? Downers? Mescaline? Grass? Monkey? Opium? Blues? Horse?'

Horse! He just said horse! And monkey. Fuck me! What's next? Orangutan?

'Mandies, Quaaludes—'

Wow. Now I'm imagining Mandy Quaalude. She'd be one of Warhol's burned-out Factory stars, very CBGB's, all smoky eyeshadow and no bra. She'd be Johnny Thunders' girlfr—no! She'd be David Johansen's girlfriend. Come to think of it, Opium Blues Horse is a great name for a Sunday afternoon pub band from Skipton. They'd have a song called—

'China White.'

Oh, God. Will this ever stop? What's next in their list of antique drug slang? Reefer? Tea? Laudanum? The Milk Of Paradise and The Mauve-Skirted Woman?

Unable to take much more of their comedy double act, I raise my hand as if I'm still at school.

'Sorry to interrupt you, but could I just ask you something? Erm . . . why me?' Desperately wanting rid of these two, I'm bursting veins trying to be as polite and semi-honest as I can. 'Why would you suspect me of being a drug dealer? I mean, look at this place; I don't even have a fridge. I was eating baked beans out of a can when you arrived. I'm wearing second-hand clothes. If I was an underworld kingpin, why would I dress like this? Surely I'd be trying *not* to attract attention.'

'Is that a prison shirt you are wearing?'

Oh, bollocks.

'No,' I say. 'Well, yes, but I didn't get it in jail; I bought it on Paddy's market.'

Oh, God. Now Thompson's eyeing my toe-capped boots. Seeing myself through the eyes of these detectives, I must look like I'm already doing jail time.

Exchanging glances with Thompson, Merter gives an assenting nod.

'All we can tell you,' says Thompson, 'is that on multiple occasions, a person of interest to us was observed communicating with you.'

Seeing the look of confusion on my face, Merter continues, 'That person was seen ascending the lamppost beneath your window and engaging in conversation with you, and subsequently, items were passed.'

Items? I'm confused now, and fidgeting because I desperately need to pee, but because the bathroom I share with the house's two other tenants is on the landing above, I'm frightened to leave these dodgy coppers alone in here in case they plant some of their Victorian drugs down the back of my sofa. I'm also genuinely wracking my brains. *Climbing the lamppost?* Who out of my bohemian circle do I know that does that? All of my close friends toss coins up at my bedsit window to get my attention, but there's only one person I can think of who actually climbs up the lamppost to do it, and that is my bandmate Speed Novak, aka Copey, aka Julian H. Fucking Cope! But what are these 'items' we are supposed to have passed?

'You're talking about my house keys!' I exclaim. The detectives tilt their heads and narrow their eyes like baddies in a Clint Eastwood Western. 'When friends visit, to get my attention, they throw a coin at my window. In return, to save me the effort of getting up and down two flights of stairs, I throw my house keys down, wrapped in a ball of newspaper. The paper is so I don't give anyone a black eye, and it stops the keys going down the drain in the road if my aim is off.'

Wow! That made absolute sense. Brilliant. Right! Time to drive this mother home.

'Until recently, all my friends were punk rockers,' I continue. I'm trying to use a *Daily Mail*-like jargon these jaded coppers might understand. 'The thing is, we punk rockers hated hippies because hippies take drugs. You see? They are our enemies—a bit like the rivalry between the mods and rockers in the early 60s? Drugs are unfashionable to my generation; you know, like tie-dye and flares.'

Oh, shit. I've just noticed that the algae green and silage brown suits these detectives are wearing have flared trousers. Involuntarily drawing their feet and legs together, they nod. I think they just might be starting to understand me.

'What are you now, then?' asks Merter.

'Sorry? What am I now?'

'You said, *Until recently we were all punk rockers.* So, what are you now?'

Fucking hell. Is he memorizing everything I say to use against me in court?

'Erm . . . I don't know. I suppose I'm *post-punk.*'

'And are all your friends and acquaintances *post-punk rockers?*'

God, that sounds so shit.

'Yes. Yes, they are.'

Surely now Merseyside's finest must see that I'm just some hapless new wave Frank Spencer character and this has all been a costly waste of the constabulary's time and recourses?

Standing up, the detectives prepare to leave. *Thank goodness.* I'm knackered. Maintaining one's innocence is surprisingly tiring.

I move to extend my hand for them to shake, but Cannon and Ball aren't leaving, they're just stretching their legs. Thompson asks for an ashtray before fishing out his John Player Specials, while Merter removes his jacket before sitting down again. Idly picking up a book from the top of a stack on my coffee table, he reads its title aloud:

'*Confessions Of An English Opium Eater.*'

Damn! Please, God, stop there, because beneath it is Huxley's *The Doors Of Perception*, Burroughs's *Junky*, and Baudelaire's *On Wine And Hashish.*

'Hmm. Well, post-punk rocker or not, that's as well as maybe, Mr Simpson, but you are in the entertainment industry, you must come across people who do use—'

Oh, God! Here we go again.

'Smack? Hash? Blotter? Bennies? Tar? Scag? Trips? Pane? Shrooms? Junk? Blotter? Dexies? Leaf?'

If I didn't know better, I'd swear these two detectives are stoned.

Meeting my fellow Teardrops Julian and Mick Finkler for a cup of tea in Sayer's café the next day, I regale them with the whole story. Mishearing my pronunciation of Detective Merter's name, Ju substitutes it for Mercer when including him in the lyrics to our new song, 'Camera, Camera'.

—

DECEMBER 1, 1978. OPEN EYE RECORDING STUDIO, WHITECHAPEL, LIVERPOOL. According to Dave Balfe, Bill Drummond's co-producer in The Chameleons, my organ part keeps going out of time with the bass and drums, so I have to argue hard to retain my position behind the keyboard. We've blasted through 'Camera, Camera' in one take, but 'Sleeping Gas' is taking forever. I start at a brisk tempo, but when Gary's drums come in, the song slows to a crawl, and my ludicrous two-finger, one-note-an-octave-apart rhythm starts to slide until it's on the offbeat.

In his manic desire to play it himself, Dave is bullish in trying to convince the entire room why he should: 'It's the end product that matters, not how it's achieved.' Yeah, right, you non-magical gargoyle! Hitler would have agreed with you. Upsettingly, Julian is not defending me but saying that he'll play it instead. I'm seething. They can both fuck off. Bill and Mick Finkler are both on my side, but I'm hurt, and Dave's created a horrible atmosphere in here now. There's a definite vibe of, *if I don't get it right, or show any crack in my resolve, I'll be forced to step aside.*

I'm thinking back to eighteen months ago and the first time Julian, Mick, and I saw Subway Sect support The Clash at Eric's. Their unwillingness to play the game, even the punk-rock game, was half of the band's shambolic appeal. Would our hero, Mark E. Smith, have told Una Baines to stand down to let a technically 'better' keyboard player infect the band's sacred chemistry so some godawful pre-punk muso notion of perfection could be achieved? Fuck no. Who are we, 10cc? Fuming inside, I stand my ground, insisting on playing the actual fucking organ parts I wrote for these songs. 'Camera, Camera' is both my riff and my song title, after all.

Red *RECORDING* light on, we play 'Sleeping Gas' one last time, with me going out of time yet again but absolutely on-the-money 'right'. It's not only me being criticised today: Julian and Balfie are driving us all demented with their constant bickering over every little detail of the EP's recording. Mick and I can't understand why Julian is even listening to Dave's opinion—he's not in the band, after all. I can't even imagine what a nightmare that would be.

After overdubbing a ship's bell onto the instrumental 'Kirby Worker's Dream Fades', we call it a day. The song's title I stole from a *Liverpool Echo* newspaper seller's advertising sandwich board. Beyond its politics, there is, to my ears, some descending-a-staircase six-syllable poetry and magic in it. When the song is dismissed as 'Simmo's dirge', I sigh. The tune is comprised of only four descending notes, each of them mine. To my mind, my 'dirge' adds some much-needed shade to our otherwise breezy debut EP.

Leaving the studio after the session that evening, I boost a family-sized banana cake from the café downstairs. I hate doing it, but I have not eaten since yesterday, and I am so poor right now I'm having to steal to get by. Divine punishment comes the following morning when I realise that I've left my dad's brass ship's bell behind, and I can't go back in case I get collared for the theft of the cake.

Although we recorded four tracks at Open Eye, amiable house engineer Mike 'Noddy' Knowler erased 'Seeing Through You' from the quarter-inch tape shortly afterwards so he could use it to record a session by the next paying band in the studio. When I find out, I'm livid. My improvised played-with-my-fists organ solo in the middle eight was my favourite thing we'd recorded that day.

Recording in the bag, Bill informs us we urgently need cover artwork for our three-track *Sleeping Gas* EP. With a paucity of solid ideas that's typical of the band, we decide to make do with simply lifting the logo of a grand piano from the sign that hangs outside Liverpool's stuffy classical instrument shop, Rushworth & Draper. Entirely by accident, it looks zeitgeisty and DIY—warm, industrial cool.

VII
TANZMUSIK

FEBRUARY 2, 1979. ERIC'S, LIVERPOOL. I ask Andy McClusky, the singer in our support band, Orchestral Manoeuvres In The Dark—formerly The ID, formerly progressive-rock outfit Pegasus—if we can borrow one of their two amplifiers, just so my organ and Mick's guitar don't have to share inputs on the same amp.

'Oh, no!' comes Andy's outraged but civil reply. 'They are brand new, you see.'

Hmmm. That's hardly the spirit of punk, especially coming from a band who had the gall to finish their set with a version of 'Anarchy In The UK'. I've been listening to Kraftwerk since 1974, so if they really are the massive influence this band claim them to be, why is it they are still dressing like Leo Sayer and Rick Wakeman? I've got them sussed. They probably think *Autobahn* or *Radioactivity* are their best albums, whereas anyone with real taste knows that it's *Ralf und Florian*.

—

FEBRUARY 24, 1979. GRANADA STUDIOS, QUAY STREET. Along with drummer Joe McKechnie, Dick Witts is one half of Liverpool/Manchester band The Passage. And along with Mike Riddoch and Margi Clarke, aka Margox, Dick co-hosts Granada television's regional culture and listings show *What's On*. When he contacts the Zoo Records office to offer us a TV appearance, we can't believe our luck.

Julian, dressed in a faded blue French chore shirt and pleated 1940s trousers, checks himself in the TV monitors. He looks brilliant, very *Emil & The Detectives*. Mick, wearing my battered brown leather jacket, looks suitably moody and cool. Gary, in a double-breasted brown suit and tie, his hair in a Brilliantine'd quiff, is looking very 1956 while I, still trying to grow out the faded carrot colour from a black hair-dye disaster last month, am the Little Prince in a muted plaid shirt buttoned to the neck.

Poor Gary is terrified. In a post-punk power move, we've reversed the usual setup and placed his drum kit in front. It looks fantastic, but playing live with nothing but a massive camera lens in his face, where will he get his chorus cues from?

Before we go live, a very cool and polite young man introduces himself as Jon 'without the *h*' Savage and tells me it's his first time in the building, and how much he likes our song 'Camera, Camera'. It's great to have someone, apart from the hosts, who honestly get what we are trying to do.

At the end of the programme, Dick introduces the band but forgets to namecheck me, and likewise the cameraman manages to almost entirely leave me out of frame, but what the hell—it's the end result that matters.

The following day, while exiting a second-hand sub-basement record shop on Victoria Street, I'm approached by a young teenager.

'Was that you playing on TV last night?'

'Yes,' I say, surprised. I can't have been that invisible, then. 'Was it okay? What did you think?'

He tells me he thought it was brilliant and asks me a gazillion questions about our instruments and where we buy our clothes. He says he wants to be in a group but doesn't know how to go about it.

'Do you play any instruments?' I ask.

'Nah.'

'Me neither, really,' I say. 'I'm not being modest—I only play the keyboard with two fingers, and I was petrified the whole time.'

The kid looks encouraged.

'But you should sing,' I say. 'You look like a frontman.' I go on to tell him I know a boy his age called David Palmer who plays a bit of bass and is looking to form a band.

The kid is thrilled, and he writes down his contact details for me to pass on. Before he goes, I ask him his name.

'Mick. Mick Head.'

'Okay, Mick, I'll pass your number on to Yorkie, and hopefully something will work out. See you again.'

See him again I do. Within a couple of months, Mick and Dave have formed a band together called Egypt For Now, and they are rehearsing in Yorkie's basement, along with us and Echo & The Bunnymen.

—

When 'Sleeping Gas' is finally released, Julian wakes me by throwing pennies up at my bedsit window. He's carrying the music papers.

'Simmo! Quick! Throw the keys down!'

Bursting in like an excitable Labrador pup, he proceeds to blow my mind. 'We're Single Of The Week in *Sounds* and the *NME*!'

'No way!'

'Yes way!' he says. 'They compare it to "96 Tears" and "Louie Louie"!'

'Holy shit!'

We are stupidly happy. *Look!* There we are in print, next to Gang Of Four, Scritti Politti, and Wire. Oh my God. We exist! Mac's going to be so pissed off. Wylie's going to freak.

—

At Lancaster University, drunken skinheads invade the stage. We're terrified but, to our bemusement, they love us, and we have to finish our set with bare-chested sweaty hooligans draped around our shoulders. After the show, Julian is livid to find drummer Gary receiving a blow job backstage. 'Surely that's the singer's department!'

When The Teardrop Explodes play at the Band On The Wall in Manchester, we are thrilled that our mates—Mick from The Frantic Elevators, Mark E. Smith and Kay Carrol, and the rest of The Fall—keep their Eric's club promise to come and see us. When their new keyboard player, Yvonne Pawlett, compliments my playing afterwards, I nearly die of pleasure. I've copped my whole approach from her and her predecessor, the mighty Una Baines, who is also here. After we come offstage, Yvonne, Martin Bramah, Andy Zero, and John The Postman play a ramshackle but incredible ten-minute-long version of 'Louie Louie'. It's brilliant.

Smoking ciggies outside after the gig as we wait to load the gear into the back of our rental van, Mick Finkler and I get chatted up by two local girls who watched the gig. When Julian comes out, he visibly flinches. Once we're on the motorway travelling home to Liverpool, he asks, in all sincerity why, if he's the singer, isn't he getting the attention?

Several weeks later, returning home from twenty-four hours in Hulme, I'm horrified to find a note propped upon on my mantelpiece.

Paul, you are one bastard! And when you get back you are going to sample my anger. Karen.

My girlfriend, suspicious about my lack of contact, has let herself into my bedsit and has been rooting through my belongings, looking for evidence of foul play. Going through my jacket pockets, she's discovered the letter of invitation from one of the sweet girls from the Band On The Wall gig, inviting me to spend the weekend with her and her flatmate in Manchester. Yes, I stayed over, and we even shared a bed, but beyond a bit of snogging, nothing happened. But I can't prove that, of course, so, not for the first time, I am hung for a sheep as a lamb.

The Masonic Arms on Renshaw Street is a bad hangover of a pub with flock-velvet wallpaper and hand-painted half-tone portraits of blues and rock legends surrounding the stage. As we traipse into the bar at 6pm, carrying our ridiculously minimal gear, a table of flared-trouser-wearing long-hairs burst out laughing. It's our aggressively unsupportive 'support' band, Zero One Five. They openly guffaw as if five Aubrey Beardsleys have just walked in. Meanwhile, we are all wondering why auditions for a Budgie covers band are being held in Liverpool. I swear to God, they are wearing leather wristbands, and the (admittedly pretty great) drummer keeps preening his hair as if he's already famous. They completely undermine and humiliate us by openly laughing throughout our soundcheck, and we hate them unreservedly for being so mean-spirited.

UK punk is well over two years old now, so we can't work out how these guys only a little older than us have managed to completely miss it. We're as disgusted with their cliché-filled macho rock posturing as they are with Julian's accent, my army conscription haircut, and our guitar-solo-free, Lego-brick-simple post-punk songs. When they finish their set with 'Jumping Jack Flash', we Teardrops roll our eyes incredulously. *Really?*

Snickering into their lager, Zero One Five think our toy-town Fall-influenced racket is hilarious kiddie-pool shite until they hear the loud and prolonged reception given to us by our audience, which is swelled with Eric's regulars. They also seem genuinely confused to see that we all have girlfriends.

—

APRIL 6, 1979. After a few more local gigs, my £40 electric organ starts breaking up and I have to play with a house brick resting on the top right-hand corner to keep the power connected. Borrowing money from my mum, I buy a new keyboard from an electrical shop on Leece Street. It's an Eastern European-made, wood-veneered monster with no external output; instead, it has a separate wooden loudspeaker connected by what looks like 1930s lamp flex.

When we turn up to play at the Russell club in Manchester, the sound guy can't believe I am serious about using this ludicrous instrument.

'It's Russian,' I tell him, as if that's a plus.

'It's a piece of crap,' comes the considered reply.

Meanwhile, we can't believe that the support band, the drummer-less but cool A Certain Ratio, have snaffled the Lilliputian-sized dressing room for themselves and filled it with their shrink-wrapped, dry-cleaned-for-the-occasion stage shirts. Tony Wilson gives us a warm welcome and them a loud telling off for not saying hello to us. Much to our annoyance, Orchestral Maneuvers In The Dark, now on Tony's Factory Records label, are headlining and not supporting. We wouldn't have played if we'd known.

—

'You fucking hippies!' Julian sneers, while flashing us the peace sign. 'Yeah, let's get high, man!'

Julian is the only person we know who actually pronounces the *g* in the F-word. He's being so unreasonably puritanical right now, you'd think Dave Balfe and I were negotiating a major heroin deal here in the Zoo Records office, rather than haggling over the price of a small lump of dope. Saying that, we have been wrangling for half an hour over this thumbnail of rocky as if bartering over an antique carpet.

We just laugh. It's like being told off by Prince Charles, we tell him. On my way home, I buy cigarettes and a pack of Rizzlas and retire back to my freezing bedsit. Clueless on how to skin up or how much gear to put in, my first attempt looks like a tampon applicator, and smokes like one. Extinguishing it, I try again, and five minutes later I'm holding a very loosely packed, cigar-sized paper cone. Impatiently sparking it up and inhaling a couple of massive drags, I'm instantly in the throes of my first whiteout. Waves of nausea burst over me like seasickness. I'm simultaneously hot and cold, with a side-order of paranoia. Even Eno's *Another Green World* manages to sound threatening. Turning it off, I climb fully clothed under my bedcovers and grit my teeth, as if it's a bombing raid I'm riding out.

Like one's first disgusting drag on a cigarette or the first taste of your dad's whisky as a child, you wonder why on earth you go back, but two hours later I try again, and a mellow glow spreads through me, transforming my tea and toast into angel food and making my Joe Gibbs *African Dub Chapter One* and Prince Far I *Psalms For I* albums sound like the stone God's truth they really are.

—

MAY 13, 1979. The Teardrops are on the rise. There's a definite hum in the air, locally and nationally, that we could be the next big thing, but, frustrated at how our sound is changing, I'm struggling to understand. Any trace of our core influences has evaporated of late, and any edge the music had has been eroded and replaced by a more conventional sound. There's nothing wrong with pop music, but my heart just isn't in it as it once was.

It's not like I'm in a position to steer it back, either: I'm an ideas man, not a musician, and, as I perceive it, my role in the band has shrunk of late. I may be paranoid and possibly depressed right now, but I am starting to believe that my only real value to the band is to look good and provide free wardrobe for gigs and photos. Not being a natural musician, I can't lead us, and Julian's not listening anyway. Balfie has his ear now.

Today, on the eve of recording the 'Bouncing Babies' single, I have a major wobble. The song is too light, and, career suicide or not, I don't think I want my name on it. As Julian and I are walking below the Radio City tower outside St John's shopping precinct, I take a deep breath and tell him how I'm feeling. He's hurt and defensive, and he does that snappy aggressive thing he does when his pride is damaged.

'Well, why don't you leave then?' he fires back.

Fuck it, I think, and I do, then and there. I may be paranoid, but I suspect there's a part of him that's wanted to get a conventionally accomplished keyboard player in for a while now.

When Dave Balfe and Bill Drummond hear the news that I've quit, I'm surprised to get individual visits from both of them later that evening, earnestly trying to persuade me to stay. Bill is genuinely worried—he knows that without my eye and my very defined aesthetic, the group's cool factor will be depleted, but after listening to my arguments for leaving and my just-occurred-to-me-in-the-moment idea to front my own band, he does a U-turn and agrees that it's the right move.

It's Dave's concern that surprises me the most. I honestly thought he'd be delighted at the news I'm gone, but he's not. Has Bill bent his ear, I wonder, or has he finally recognised my contribution to the band? Because I'm now exactly two hours into my fantasy of fronting a twin guitar, bass, drums, and string-synth band, so it's too late. My mission has begun; I couldn't go back if I wanted to.

VIII

THE ARMOURED DILDO

MAY 1979. Forced by some *Winter of Discontent*-fuelled directive of Herr Thatcher's government, I am forced to sign off at the Benson Street unemployment exchange for a minimum period of six months. What the hell am I supposed to do now? I have Penguin Modern Classics, records, and army surplus to buy—let alone food and the £8-per-week rent on my bedsit to find.

Having just left The Teardrop Explodes, and not wanting to leave my ex-bandmates in the lurch, I arrange a job swap with a quiet young man I vaguely know who works behind the counter in the Armadillo Tea Rooms, situated on Matthew Street, just thirty yards away from Eric's. His name is Gerrard Anthony Quinn, and I've heard that he plays the piano. Gerrard—or 'Ged' as he's known to his friends—is a civilised soul, more into Elgar and painting than rock'n'roll, but he looks good, adores John Cale, and owns a Victorian harmonium. What's not to like?

Ged and I bond over a love of haunted-looking women, the near literary porn of Henry Miller, and the writings of Norwegian author Knut Hamsun. Ged doesn't bat an eyelid at my proposal of a job swap, and after I introduce him to Julian, Gary Dwyer, and Mick Finkler, Ged proposes the idea to café proprietor Martin Cooper, who says it's fine by him.

Wow. That was surprisingly easy. Within days, I don Ged's apron and take his place serving lunch and afternoon tea to all the bands who are playing at Eric's in the evenings, and he takes over my old role of keyboard player in The Teardrop Explodes.

Living just a ten-minute walk up the hill on Rodney Street, this is a perfect arrangement for me. I can sleep in late, bathe away the excesses of the previous night, saunter down to work for 11:30am, eat for free, and make the rent each month with plenty of money left over for music and books and dead men's suits from charity shops.

Depending on my mood, I dress for work in either my 'Great

Depression' grey tweeds, my Spanish Civil War jodphurs, or my WWI army-conscript look. It's quiet when I arrive, just the core staff prepping meals for the lunchtime rush. My first job of the day is to open the vast cast-iron window shutters using a hooked pole, take down the chairs from the tabletops, then drag a jute sack of potatoes in from the huge storeroom out back before pouring them, twenty at a time, into the infernal peeling machine, an electrically operated metal drum containing rotating serrated rollers. Spuds go in the top, peeled ones fly out of the bottom. It's a dirty, noisy job, and no one in my circle who sees my hands covered in soil and potato peelings can quite believe I've willingly chosen to do this over playing in Liverpool's band-most-likely-to. The thing is, I like it here. I have time to think and plan my next move. Bill Drummond aside, I haven't told anyone that I'm thinking of fronting my own band yet.

By noon, potatoes peeled, I serve behind the counter. The first arrivals are the staff and DJs from nearby Radio Merseyside, visiting actors from the Playhouse Theatre, and a few market traders wanting bread and cheese to go, gradually building to a rush from 12:30 to 2:00, where I am joined behind the counter by more staff. From 2:15, it begins to quiet a little.

Mid-afternoons are when the local bands come in to hang out and plan their revolution. My ex-bandmates from A Shallow Madness and The Teardrop Explodes come in requesting 'tea for four' but usually only ever passing me enough coins for tea for one. There's Bill Drummond and Dave Balfe and the Zoo Records secretary, Pam Young; Pete Wylie arrives with his bandmates in Crash Course—Andy Eastwood, Rob Jones, and Mick Reid—and after them their slightly younger satellite friends, Johnno, Timmo, Bernie Conners, Kev Connolly, Tempo, and Boxhead.

In between load-in and soundcheck, bands playing at Eric's come by— The Heartbreakers, Siouxsie & The Banshees. Younger customers with spare money might buy a millionaire's shortbread or a quarter of a loaf of bread and Bel-Paise cheese to go with their tea, but most of the afternoon clientele treat this place as an annexe of Eric's—a cheap, cool place to hang out. Everything a young music fan could want is located on Button Street and Matthew Street: Eric's, Backtrax for second-hand records, and Probe Records for new ones. The Zoo Records office is nearby, in Waterloo Buildings, as is my barbers, the Victor Salon.

Though I've now left The Teardrop Explodes, one wouldn't know it. I just carry on hanging out with them and talking music as if nothing has happened. I still travel to local gigs with both the Teardrops and the Bunnymen as if nothing has changed.

The café's proprietor, Martin Cooper, is a fair and pleasant boss. Along with Paddy Byrne up at the Everyman Bistro on Hope Street, he's serving the best food in the city right now, or certainly the most affordable. Martin has a small but tasteful stack of pre-punk vinyl albums behind the counter but most of it is too square for our clientele, so I only play the only records I can stomach: Taj Mahal's debut album, *Fotheringay* by Fotheringay, and *Greetings From LA* by Tim Buckley. The latter I play to death, particularly the closing track. When Julian first hears me playing 'Sweet Surrender', he bounds over demanding to know what it is and scans the sleeve, desperate for info.

When Martin goes out to get supplies, I take the opportunity to play whatever single or album I've bought for myself this week from Probe. I'm earning decent money now, so what isn't going on books from Atticus and Progressive Books, or second-hand clothes from Déjà Vu or Ollies, goes into Probe's coffers. Records by Manicured Noise, Magazine, Durutti Column, Robert Fripp—I'll play whatever I can get away with. Most of it gets vetoed as 'off-putting' to customers, but if it's getting late and we need to put the chairs on the tables so we can mop the floors for the morning, I'll play 'We Are All Prostitutes' by The Pop Group, which never fails to clear the place of the last of the norms. Since I started working here, my circle of friends has quadrupled. The staff, mostly female and all just a little older than me, are a witty, flirty bunch:

Sue Crook, Annie and Sue Flackett, Martin Yarker, and a young Nathan McGough.

My friend Dan Brennan, Mereyside's answer to Syd Barrett, comes in wearing his signature vintage double-breasted tweed overcoat, collarless evening shirt, and WWI field officer's boots. Speaking in whispers, he passes on the titles of obscure novels and occult books he thinks I should read, shows me the majolica plates covered in ceramic eels he's bought, and describes scenes from strange films he's importing into the UK for his Mannesty's Lane film club. On a bedsheet in an abandoned warehouse near the Bluecoat Chambers in the city centre, Dan is the first person in the UK to screen David Lynch's *Eraserhead*, and it blows the minds of every one of us freaks in attendance.

—

Travelling with the still three-piece Echo & The Bunnymen to their first out-of-town dates in Chester, Sheffield, and York is exciting, and I love that my old friends want me here, just hanging out and giving them support. The Buns get better and more confident with every gig they play. The downside to accompanying them is manager Bill Drummond's idea of safe driving. Bill thinks nothing of doing U-turns at speed across the central divide or reversing back down a motorway slip road when he misses an exit. Cowering in the back of the Transit van, it feels like being on The Big Dipper rollercoaster at Blackpool Pleasure Beach—but with the added danger of an un-flight-cased guitar headstock smashing in your teeth, or the corner of an unsecured amplifier caving in your eye socket.

In York, I buy some sheepskin boots from a market stall, thinking they look like something a medieval farmer might have worn. When Mac sees them and learns they were only three quid, he wants a pair too. The difference is, mine are for indoors; Mac wears his onstage for the next two years until they look like he's trodden in his Sunday lunch.

IX

A PALE NUDE RECLINING IN A BATH
OF HER OWN BLOOD

AUGUST 1979. 3 BROMPTON AVENUE, TOXTETH, LIVERPOOL. I'm sipping tea in the dimly lit attic flat of my newly made friend Ged while he explains some of the brush techniques he's learned from studying the Victorian and Edwardian watercolours of Scottish wildlife artist Archibald Thorburn. As Tom Waits's *On The Nickel* rumbles quietly in an adjacent room, I set down my tea to investigate whatever it is that is protruding into my back from the art-deco sofa behind me. Removing a cushion to plump it up and reposition it, I find myself holding the limp corpse of a large duck. Arching an eyebrow, I cough to get Ged's attention.

Glancing up, he corrects my initial assumption.

'It's a mallard,' he says casually, as if putrescent wildfowl stuffed behind soft furnishings isn't unusual.

'Thank you for the clarification,' I reply, as if we're in a GP's consultation room. I'm soon to learn that Ged often has something with claws, beak, fur, or feathers in his rooms. A sparrow hawk or a shrew on his mantelpiece, or a half-defrosted ptarmigan draped over his painting easel, a field mouse in a fruit bowl.

'I know a gamekeeper in the Lake District,' he tells me. 'He sends me dead things to paint. My freezer is full. That one's almost had it.'

'No kidding,' I say, as I wipe the congealed blood from my fingers.

Over more tea and endless French cigarettes, we discuss how we might best manifest our idea to record an instrumental album based on Knut Hamsun's 1890 book *Sult*, or *Hunger* as it is known in its English translation. Something in Hamsun's writing chimes with our impoverished, permanently hungry bedsit existence.

Apart from our shared love of the literature of nineteenth-century counterculture, one of the many things Ged and I have in common is the frequency with which we fall in love with women who don't even know of our existence. Women with scars, women with backs the shape of cellos, Roman noses, unshaven armpits, speech impediments, flat chests, full chests, limps . . .

More tea, another cigarette apiece, and it is time for me to start walking into town to begin my shift at the Armadillo Tea Rooms. As Ged sees me out to the top floor landing, I hear a familiar voice coming from the direction of his bedroom.

'Fuckinel, Ged, are you coming back to bed or what?' I don't ask, but I'm convinced that is the heavy scouse accented voice of a well-known bottle-blonde singer and regional TV presenter. Bloody hell. My new pal Ged is a dark horse and no mistake. Knowing him, he's probably got one decomposing behind his curtains up there somewhere.

A fortnight later, when Julian Cope visits Brompton Avenue for the first time to co-write new Teardrops songs on Ged's Victorian pedal-pump harmonium, his eye is caught by a clear plastic carrier bag hung from a nail on the sitting room wall. Inside the bag, reclining like a pale nude in a bath of her own blood, lays a long, slim, white fur-covered mammal.

'Hey, man, what's that?'

'What's what?' answers Ged.

'There, in the bag!'

'Rye bread. Do you want some?'

'No, the other bag.'

'Oh. It's a stoat.'

'I see,' says Julian, going in close to examine it.

'She's just defrosting,' says Ged.

'It's beautiful,' says Julian. 'Can I have it?'

X

BEAUTY AND THE BEAST

NOVEMBER 1979. Saturday and the winter sun is up there behind the clouds like a one-bar electric fire, barely keeping Merseyside above freezing. There are five whole days until my dole cheque arrives, and I've got fourteen pence to my name. With a hot water bottle on my groin, a hat and mittens on in bed, trying to read Jean Genet's *The Thief's Journal*, I'm going to get hypothermia if I don't get a hot drink inside me soon. I've got to do something.

Sneaking downstairs and using a hairpin and a penknife blade on the Yale cylinder lock of the medical herbalist's day surgery, I tiptoe in and steal just enough milk and teabags from his fridge to see me through the night. I'm dying here. Thank fuck for the Benylin that is keeping my blood sugar up, dulling my senses and suppressing my hunger.

When Thursday finally arrives, I cash the giro at the post office on Leece Street and request that £10 of my £32-a-fortnight be given to me in fifty pence pieces. Back in my bedsit, I scatter the coins to the four corners of the room like a farmer dispersing handfuls of seed. Next time I'm starving, I'll at least be able to find enough for milk and bread on top of and behind the wardrobe, under the bed, or down the back of the sofa.

—

Ian McCulloch has just arrived at my place, and we're going out tonight to cop off with some girls. At least that's the plan. I've had girlfriends since I was sixteen, but Mac has only just started actively pursuing women in earnest.

At eight o'clock, Mac goes straight up to the communal bathroom on the landing to fix his hair with a massive can of hair spray secreted in the pockets of the old herringbone tweed coat I've gifted him. When he comes downstairs, twenty-five minutes later, he looks exactly the same as when he went up. He's obsessed about his hair and thinks nothing of dipping his fingers into his pint of lager and running them through it.

Battling raging hormones, Ian and I openly lust after an Amazonian goddess known to us only as The Body. Although she smiles at us encouragingly, we never talk to her because we know she'd eat the pair of us alive and spit out the bones. I don't know what we think can ever happen—our combined weights wouldn't make up that of a normal bloke.

This evening, as we stand in another half-empty club, staring out across the deserted dance floor, Mac turns to me and says, in hushed tones, 'Don't look now but I'm getting optics!' *Optics* is Mac's Beatnik expression for being stared at provocatively by a member of the opposite sex.

I subtly scope the room.

'Where?' I whisper.

'Over there, the tall one,' he says, gesturing to a spot on the deserted dance floor just eight feet away.

I look to where he's indicating, but there's no one there, just a thin, plaster-coated support pillar painted red. The evening is a washout; we spend most of our time slagging off the Bowie clones, not for one second realising that's exactly what we are.

One particularly dead night in the Continental—or the Conti, as it's known—just as it's closing and we're putting our coats on, I notice an attractive older blonde girl sitting with some friends, giggling and smiling in our direction. Fuelled by a long-nursed half of lager, I slink over and ask her if she wants to come back to my place for 'coffee or something'.

'I'll pass on the coffee,' she fires back, 'but I'll have the something.'

Bloody hell, I've tapped!

Mac is very quiet as the three of us walk back to Rodney Street. I feel bad, as he's meant to be sleeping on my sofa tonight, as is usual when we go out together. He must be feeling horribly awkward—but, then again, not awkward enough to fuck off and leave us to it.

Jimmying open the lock of the tiny and newly vacated bedsit next door to mine, I usher poor Ian in where has no choice but to spend the night on a damp mattress, shivering under his coat while listening to me get it on with the mysterious older woman.

In the early hours of the morning, she whispers to me that she is twenty-six.

'Shhh! That's not old,' I whisper back, but in my head, I'm screaming *Twenty-six! Twenty-fucking-six! I've just turned twenty!* She may as well be showing me her pension book.

The next morning, after a slap-up breakfast of anaemic Sunblest toast and weak tea with stale milk, I walk her to the bus stop.

'I'll call you,' I shout, while miming a telephone handset.

'No you won't,' she says.

—

It's now that I first lay eyes on my future wife. I'm at an art-college party held at Plummer's, a vast, gilt-pillared nightmare opposite Kirkland's wine bar on Liverpool's Leece Street, with Ged Quinn, newly liberated from keyboard duties with the Teardrops. We're sitting in a darkened booth, talking to Sue and Lori Larty—both ex-Eric's babes who look amazing in their homemade 60s A-line minidresses with clear vinyl belly windows—when Ged leans over and whispers in my ear.

'I know that girl who's just come in—her name's Jan, she's gorgeous, but she's got a boyfriend.'

Half-heartedly turning in the direction of the entrance, I am struck by gentle lightning. There she is. I recognise her instantly. Now all I have to do is go and tell her.

Before I can, a rival suitor enters the frame and joins her at our table, and I am forced into action. I can't risk her falling for some gonk in a rugby shirt. From her point of view, I must look like a madman as I climb over the tabletops, spilling drinks and forcing this potential rival out of the way.

A week later, Jan confesses that, as I approached her, she had a flashback to when she was a little girl, half-watching a war film on television one Saturday afternoon. She had fallen in love with the actor playing a U-boat captain, and when she saw me in Plummer's wearing a cream-coloured polo-neck jumper and black leather jacket, my dyed-blonde hair cut with wartime severity, she thought I was him, finally come to find her.

We start seeing each other but, unfortunately, we have entirely forgotten to inform our respective partners. There are royal fireworks when I take Jan back to my flat for the first time, only to find my actual girlfriend, Karen, lying in ambush in the doorway of the house. Attacked with the heel of one of Karen's stilettos, I'm concerned that Karen may turn on poor Jan, who's standing there looking very pale and diminished by this undignified scene.

Finally out of puff, Karen gives up and limps off, sobbing and broken, in the direction of Skelhorne Street bus station. I feel terrible. She's a sweet girl, and that shouldn't have happened. Jan is physically shaking. She's not used to this depravity.

'This isn't typical of me,' I plead, and I have to work hard to convince her that I'm not some serial-cheating lothario. I feel less bad when, a week later, I find out she hasn't fully broken it off with her boyfriend, either.

—

According to my esoteric friend Dan, the microdot of LSD he has placed in my palm is four times stronger than the standard blotter version. His warnings to treat it with caution make me want to try it all the more. *Yes, I'll be careful. Of course, I'll treat it with respect. No, I promise I won't take it alone. Yep, yep. Thanks. See you now! Byeeee.*

The moment he is out of the door, I swallow the tiny red planet. After twenty minutes, I become aware of a dull ache at the base of the spine—a sensation I will later recognise as the spirit loosening itself from the body, and a signal the trip is about to kick in. I must prepare myself to enter the sacred reality at the core of everything.

I can hear bells ringing. Why are bells ringing? Peeking through the net curtains down onto Rodney Street below, I become gripped by paranoia. A pretty girl is frantically waving at me. Who is she and what does she want? Oh! It's Jan. She is ringing the doorbell. I've forgotten that we arranged to go to the cinema tonight. After meeting for the first time at an art college party just a fortnight ago, we've been for coffee a few times since then, and kissed, but this is our first actual 'date'.

The Odeon is a brisk fifteen-minute walk away, but it takes her double that to get me there because the lampposts wave at me like Walt Disney animations as we pass beneath them. The German-language film we are here to see is being shown in screen 3, and due to my dawdling we have missed the trailers. The room is nearly full; the only remaining seats are on the front row, far left, uncomfortably close to the screen. As my backside hits the seat, the lights dim, the screen widens, and I let out a loud *Ooooh* for which I get a gentle dig in the ribs from Jan.

The film starts and she passes me a sweet. After several moments, I start making choking noises.

'What's wrong?' she whispers in the darkness.

'Dis schweet,' I reply, spraying her with saliva. 'Itch gwowing.'

It's just a Cadbury's chocolate éclair, but it feels like it is expanding into a giant redwood in my mouth. Jan is looking at me sideways now, wondering who the hell she has got herself involved with. Never having taken drugs of any kind, she has no frame of reference to negotiate my erratic behaviour.

Volker Schlöndorff's film version of Günter Grass's extraordinary novel *The Tin Drum* is a weird and wonderful thing, but enhanced by LSD it is a seismic event. When little Oskar Matzerath hurls himself down the cellar steps to 'explain' stunting his growth, I feel the impact of his fall. When his mother gorges herself on pickled herring, I writhe in my seat; it is the most sexually arousing thing I've ever seen. When eels slither from the mouth of a severed horse head pulled from a river, I think all hell has come.

Halfway through the feature, I become aware of a sensation located somewhere beneath my stomach. Unable to tell if it is pleasant or not, I ignore it until it dawns on me that I probably need to pee. So as not to disturb the audience, I get on all fours and begin to crawl to the foyer, until Jan hoiks me back onto my feet. Once in the foyer, I spot the sign reading *GENTLEMEN'S TOILETS*. Gentlemen? How wonderfully posh! Smartening my clothing and combing my hair, I stride into the toilet in the exaggerated fashion of an eighteenth-century duke. Once inside, I find myself alone in a vast hall of mirrors. Rooms within rooms, all of them containing clones of myself.

Having forgotten the room's purpose or why I came in here, I ruffle the fur of the four St Bernard dogs whose heads line the wall like trophies in a hunting lodge. When I put my hands near their mouths, they pant excitedly. They are my new best friends. I love them and their hot breath, and I want to live here with them forever.

It is only when I remember that I am in a cinema toilet that the dogs revert to their true form of wall-mounted hand dryers. When I finally return to my seat, Jan tells me that I've been gone for twenty minutes, and to sit down quickly so the person behind me can see the screen. The moment I do, I am gripped by fear. The 'person' she referred to is a psychopath. Angry at my blocking his view just now, he is digging the toe of his shoe into the open space at the back of my seat, twisting it into the cheeks of my bottom. Too scared to move, I sit motionless, enduring his sadism for the rest of the film.

When the credits roll and the house lights come up, we stand, and I risk a glance behind me. There is no hate-filled maniac, just a mild-mannered student eating popcorn; I've been sitting on my house keys. Probably time to go home. Only another six to eight hours for Jan to endure until the effects of the drugs wear off. As boyfriends go, I'm quite a catch.

XI
DANGER QUENTIN, THERE'S
A DOG BEHIND YOU

DECEMBER 19, 1979. GAETANO'S RESTAURANT BASEMENT, BACK PICCADILLY, MANCHESTER. The Tingle Tangle club is filling up nicely. Because this is 1979 in northern England, where magic and madness are gushing from the ground like an oil geyser blowout, Gaetano's is obliged, in order to circumnavigate some live music licensing law, to serve everyone in attendance a plate of sausage and chips. Echo & The Bunnymen's minimal gear is set up onstage, the red light on their drum machine Echo glowing red. Their manager, Bill, is deep in thought.

'We need a support band!' he says.

'Yes,' I say. 'It's a pity we didn't have time to organi—'

Cutting me off, Bill continues, 'Strap on Will's guitar.'

'What?'

'Strap on Will's guitar. C'mon, Simmo! You and me.'

No fucking way, I'm thinking. *As if I'd humiliate myself by playing an unrehear—*

Considering I haven't got a clue as to what Bill is intending to play tonight, or in what key, and ignoring the fact I play the guitar about as well as I play Mahjong, I'm feeling uncharacteristically calm as I climb onstage. Ah well. At least I look good. My barber Victor—whose catchphrase is 'I can take it off but I can't put it back on, sir'—only refreshed my Tommy Atkins haircut this morning, and I'm rocking these baggy, pleated demob trousers and prison boots. If I'm going to make a complete cunt of myself in front of The Fall and the hippest of the Manchester hip, at least I'll look good doing it.

As ever, Bill is rocking his 'Squeal, piggy, squeal' serial killer look of faded blue chore shirt, Levi's, and work boots. I just wished we'd had enough time to think of a name for our pop-up pop group. Still, it will be more mysterious if we don't introduc—

'Good evening, Manchester. We are called Danger Quentin, There's A Dog Behind You.'

Of course we fucking are. This is classic Drummond improvisational genius. Left to me, I'd have come up with something po-faced and Manchester-friendly like Industrial Giant, but Bill, hot-housed in the prankster Discordianism of Ken Campbell's Liverpool School Of Language Dream & Pun, is channelling greatness tonight.

Daft as it is, I am thinking that Bill's playfulness perfectly illustrates the difference between our great Northern post-punk power cities. Manchester elevates itself by taking itself seriously, all gravestone typefaces and greyscale, while Merseyside is so confident of its musical heritage that we just throw any surreal shit at the wall and laugh at the whole game. Glasgow is playful too, but, for reasons Manchester and Liverpool can't quite fathom, has an unhealthy attachment to cowboys and the American West. Meanwhile, all of us are waiting for London, the cradle of UK punk, to stop fannying about with eye shadow and frills.

Covering the microphone with his hand for a moment, Bill leans back and whispers to me.

'Just go mad.'

Not quite the detailed song notes I was hoping for, Bill, but as motivational speeches go, it's surprisingly effective. I don't know what I've been expecting him to play on that beautiful old Gibson 330 of his, but it isn't this deranged country and Delta blues he just opened our set with. It's so completely unexpected, and so massively out of step with the post-punk aesthetic of the event—so desperately un-Tony Wilson—that it's the coolest thing imaginable. Why? Because we are Danger Quentin, There's A Dog Behind You, and we just declared it so.

If I was being kind, I'd say that Bill's singing is Dylan-esque; if I was going for accuracy, I'd say he sounds like a low register Kenneth McKellar singing 'The Skye Boat Song' while being attacked by midges. Bill's Galloway accent has never sounded stronger, deeper, or more insane than right now. You know when you accidentally play a warped copy of a Bay City Rollers B-side single at 33rpm? No. Me neither, but it probably sounds like we do right now. *Has Bill prewritten these chord progressions and words*, I wonder, *or is he just making up this deranged shit as he goes along?*

I'm no longer *playing* this Stratocaster, I've entered into an abusive relationship with it. I've tortured it, kissed it, masturbated it, tickled it, gouged its strings, pleaded with it to tell me where the gold is hidden—and all within our first three minutes onstage. By the second song, I'm already out of ideas, so I'm reduced to ripping off Bill Nelson's fab 'Sister

Seagull' technique of sliding one's fingernails down the B and top E string from the twenty-first fret. These young Mancunians won't recognize it as a Be Bop Deluxe thing, they'll just think I'm the natural successor to Jimi Hendrix. (Jimmy Krankie, more like.)

So far, so ridiculous. There's clapping. My God! We are actually getting away with this. I've passed from abject horror into 'enjoying myself' territory. Thinking this, our third 'song', will be our last, I completely detune all the guitar strings until they resemble a giant plucking the wires of an amplified electricity pylon.

Damn. I was wrong. Bill just announced one last 'song'. Having nowhere left to go with this floppy stringed guitar wreckage, I simply drag its neck back and forth across the plastic-coated front of the amplifier for five minutes, possibly irreparably damaging both.

WEEEOOOOONNNNNGGGGGGGGNNNNNNNNNOOOOOEEEEEW!

NNNNUUUURRRRSSSSGGGGRRRREEEERRRRGGGGSSSSNNNNEEOW!

It sounds Satanic, particularly when paired with Bill's impersonation of a tubercular Muddy Waters trying to escape an iron lung. Incredibly, Danger Quentin almost go down better than the Bunnymen, and when our mates Mark E. Smith, Kay Carroll, Yvonne Pawlett, and my idol, Martin Bramah of The Fall, gather around praising the 'wild noise', I almost levitate. But, of course, Bill has some debriefing notes for me.

'Simmo. You didn't go mad enough!'

Story of my life.

PART FIVE

| NORTHERN ENGLAND
| 1980–1982

I
RIDDLE OF THE SPHINX

SUMMER 1980. FLAT 3, 14 RODNEY STREET. Once a week, the stairs and hallways of my house are cleaned by an irascible housekeeper. Because she's older, colder, and stonier than the Great Pyramid of Cheops, the residents have cruelly nicknamed her The Sphinx; and by 'the residents', I mean me.

Acting for the landlord, The Sphinx possesses Yale keys not just to the house but to the four bedsit rooms within it. These she keeps together with the individual meter keys on a jangling metal ring tied at her waist. Rude, unsmiling, and dressed entirely in black, she resembles a sadistic jailor in a Dickensian Bedlam. On the last Friday of the month, without knocking, she enters the tenants' rooms to empty the meters. We can be eating, sleeping, playing Scrabble, or performing ceremonial sex magic in the nude—it doesn't matter. In her eyes, we are beneath contempt, ex-cons and perverts all. Why else would fully grown men be living alone? She reserves the worst of her scorn for me, which is perplexing as, at just twenty-one, I am the baby of the house and am only ever polite to her.

The coin-operated electricity meter mounted next to my bed runs on ten pence pieces. Depending on how often I use my record player, three-bar heater, and Baby Belling hotplate and grill combo, one coin provides between fifteen and twenty minutes worth of power. At the end of each month, when The Sphinx unlocks and empties the coin box attached to the meter, it contains somewhere between eight to ten pounds. One afternoon, watching me feed the meter for the second time in an hour, Ged asks me why I don't just pick the padlock. Seeing the confusion on my face, he whips out his penknife and a straightened hairpin, slides them into the padlock's keyhole, and—*hey presto!*—the lock springs open. My God! This will revolutionise how I live. As long as I remember to replace the coins I take out before the meter is emptied, I now have access to a twenty-four-hour bank. This also means that even when I'm down to my very last coin, simply by passing it through the meter slot multiple times I will always have heat and light.

At first, I only 'borrow' from the meter box when I am desperate, but as the months go by I begin to raid it whenever there is a new record, book, or dead man's overcoat that I can't live without. One week, realising that my meter is five quid light, I pin a 'Sick & Contagious' note upon my door to stop The Sphinx from discovering my deception. Subsequently, I make a promise to myself that from this point on, even with my belt tightened to the point of strangulation, I will only risk raiding the meter to buy the barest essentials needed for subsistence living: French cigarettes, Benylin, Tia-Maria, *NME*, *Melody Maker*, and new David Bowie albums.

Today being the last Friday of the month, the meter in my bedsit should contain about nine pounds worth of coins. Right now, it contains my last 10p in the world. I've been intending to replace the missing coins every day for the past week. I had the money to do it, after all, but because I'm an idiot I went out last night and squandered the last of it on an elegant supper complete with fine wine. By 'supper' I mean chips and curry sauce, and by 'fine wine' I mean two cans of stout and a miniature of mescal. By 'elegant' I mean I used a wooden fork for the chips instead of my fingers.

This morning at 8:30, The Sphinx has let herself into my bedsit and unlocked the meter box located just a foot away from my sleeping face, and is now bending over me, shrieking at me at the top of her horrible voice, 'Where is it? Where's the money? You thief!' I've really messed up this time. The only thing I can think to do is to feign confusion.

'Ugh! Hello Mother. How did you get in? Is Dad with you? Are you a ghost?'

Immune to my acting skills, The Sphinx screeches, 'Just you wait! Mr Roberts will have the Bobbies on you.'

The Bobbies? She thinks it's 1922. Storming out of the room (if someone pushing ninety years old can storm anywhere), the desiccated harpy is off to find a public phone box.

Taking into account the rush-hour traffic and the Mersey Tunnel, I calculate that I have approximately forty minutes before my Birkenhead-dwelling landlord, alerted to my crime, arrives to either evict me or indeed call the Bobbies. Dressing in nanoseconds, I vault the stairs to the ground floor, three at a time. Hurtling along Rodney Street, I cross the road, turn left, race up Hardman Street, and fall, panting, into antiques and bric-a-brac shop Déjà Vu, where my friend Dan Brennan is taking off his coat, having just this moment unlocked the door.

'Dan! Thank God!'

Breathlessly, I speed-explain my predicament. Saying nothing, Dan opens his mouth in a faux-surprise *o* shape before handing me a ten-pound note—the only money in the ailing shop's petty cash box.

'I'll get it back to you within the hour,' I shout, as I charge out, setting the bell over the door ringing loudly.

Sprinting back down the hill, I pass the Atticus bookshop (nice copy of *Journey To The End Of The Night* in the window), past Kirkland's wine bar (not been in there for ages) and Chaucer's pub (met my girlfriend Jan in there), into the Midland bank on the corner of Leece Street. Oh, crap! There is a massive queue. Obsessively checking the bank's oversized wall clock, I estimate that I have a maximum of about eighteen, maybe twenty minutes left to save myself. Seconds appear to last hours in here—it's like 'The Zone' in Tarkovsky's film *Stalker*. Finally, I'm served.

'Ten pounds worth of ten pence pieces, please.'

Sighing dramatically, the bank teller meticulously counts the coins into a small transparent bag. *Come on, come on!* Darting along Rodney Steet, keeping my eyes peeled for The Sphinx, I explode through the door of number 14 and leap the stairs back to my room. Throwing off my overcoat, I dive to my knees and quickly pick the meter padlock. Replacing all the missing coins—plus an extra pound's worth—I snap the lock shut and drop both knife and hairpin behind the headboard of my single bed. Stripping to my underpants, I turn out the lights and jump back between my still-warm sheets, where I lay panting, like I've just enjoyed terrifying sex.

Moments later, the street door slams. Heavy footfalls on the stairs are followed by a hammering upon my bedsit door. Without waiting for an answer, a key is turned and the door bursts open. As the overhead light is switched on, I sit up in bed, rubbing my eyes like a bewildered Stan Laurel.

Mr Roberts glowers, all fury in a cheap suit. Although he's scowling at me, one eyebrow is raised in confusion. Having driven over from Birkenhead to turf me out of his property, he wasn't expecting to find me still abed and looking as if I am the affronted party. Behind him, out of breath from climbing the stairs, The Sphinx quickly steers him to the electricity meter at my side.

'We have him now, Mr Roberts,' she caws, fumbling with her ring of asylum keys. 'We have him now.'

The instant her key turns in the meter lock, a fountain of heptagonal silver coins clatter noisily to the floor, as though she's won the jackpot on a one-armed bandit.

'What the bloody hell is going on?' I demand in an indignant voice.

Momentarily dumbstruck, my landlord is hugely embarrassed. When he does speak, he can't apologise enough. Explaining his version of events, I shake my head as if uncomprehending.

'Is my electricity meter broken?' I ask.

Meanwhile, The Sphinx is scuttling about on her hands and knees like some witch-crab hybrid, scooping up the spilt coins in the folds of her skirt while muttering to herself. She's desperately trying to work out what sorcery I employed to achieve this horrible miracle.

Catching the landlord's eye, I twist my index finger to my temple in the universally recognised 'she's cuckoo' mime. Nodding his head back sadly—as if to say, 'Yes, you're right, the old dear has finally lost it'—he apologises to me for the rude awakening before escorting her by the arm out onto the landing for 'a little chat'.

Collapsing back into my pillow, I exhale. Fucking hell! That was close.

—

A week later, I bump into my neighbour, Tommy The Postman. At the end of a riveting conversation about his shift being changed and the eggy smell emanating from his sink, he asks, 'Did you hear that The Sphinx has retired?'

Uh-oh.

'Retired as in *she's* retired,' I ask, 'or retired as in she's *been* retired?'

Tommy doesn't know the details, or indeed what the fuck I am talking about.

While I don't exactly feel good about it, I don't feel like Raskolnikov after murdering the pawnbroker either. I'm twenty-one years old and almost starving to death in a one-room garret during Margaret Thatcher's 'managed decline' of the city. Sparring with piss-taking scallies by day and depression by night, I have more than enough monsters in my life.

In bed now, I'm taking long glugs from the Benylin bottle that I keep on top of the electricity meter. Switching off my bedside lamp, I lay in the darkness, watching the amber headlights from passing taxis bend and warp across the ceiling. As the codeine in the cough syrup begins to pull upon my eyelids, I imagine The Sphinx laying in her bed in the dark. In my head, she's drawing invisible equations in the air, still trying to work out how I did it.

II

MILK

SUMMER 1980. Friday evening in Liverpool, and The Teardrop Explodes, minus Julian, are travelling down to Rockfield Recording Studios in Monmouthshire to resume work on their debut album, *Kilimanjaro*. Unable to drive and wanting an extra night at home with his wife, Julian asks if I will drive him down tomorrow morning in a hired van. Having nothing better to do, and feeling a little twinge of jealousy at the mischief I'll miss out on if I don't, I agree.

When I pick him up outside his flat in Prospect Vale, Kensington, at 10am, Julian throws a small bag of clothes into the back and leaps into the passenger seat like a hyperactive puppy. *FFS!* Why did he specify my hiring a whole bloody van if he has no equipment? But I don't really mind as Ju is great company, and I know there's going to be a lot of music and madness talked in the next few hours.

We've only got as far as the end of Prospect Vale when Julian turns to me and says, 'Simmo, I'm starving, man. Can we pull in at that corner shop over there? I need to eat.'

Parking up, I think I'd better get a Mars bar and a can of something for the journey myself.

As we enter the shop, a bell rings over the door. It's dark inside, hardly any stock on the shelves and a neon strip-light buzzing loudly.

Julian is rocking his knee-length Moroccan striped robe worn over jeans and biker boots, and I'm wearing my classic 1940s baggy pleated trousers. At the sound of the doorbell, the woman behind the counter starts to snigger. She's not shy or being subtle, she's openly laughing at us. Not in a timid, can't-help-it way, but in a 'what *do* you two fucking clowns look like?' kind of way. I don't know what Julian is thinking, but I'm incensed. I'm used to getting grief from young scallies in Liverpool, but never from women. Still, it's the man in the dress with the blonde bowl cut that's really got her going. It can't be often that Lawrence Of Arabia walks in, shopping for snacks.

Selecting some biscuits and a family-sized bags of crisps, Julian places them on the counter and busies himself fishing coins out of his jeans. Then, as if he's Peter Falk in *Columbo*, acting out one of his fake afterthoughts, Ju very politely asks her for a pint of milk. Retrieving one from the refrigerator behind her, still smirking, she totals up the bill. We are a hilarious joke to her, and she wants us to know it.

Julian pays, and while he's pocketing his change, he whispers to me, 'Pavel, go and start the van.'

Just as I reach the door and set the bell off again, I look back to see Julian calmly opening the top of the milk carton as if he's going to take a swig, before leaning over the counter and pouring the entire contents over her head. She's so incredulous at what is happening she doesn't even attempt to move out of the stream. *Glug, glug, glug.* She just stands there, letting it pour over her, until she and her ill-mannered conformity are soaked.

Oh, shit!

Turning the van around, I indicate and pull out, and we head out past the abattoir in the direction of the motorway.

Julian opens the biscuits, with no mention of the woman or the milk. He just asks, 'Hey, man, is there a cassette player in here?'

III
CAESAR'S THUMB

AUTUMN 1980. 'Wow!' says Dave, looking me up and down. 'You have a great image.'

In offering to pay for demo time for The Wild Swans—the band I've formed with Ged, drummer Justin Stavely, bass player Jim Weston, and guitarist Jeremy Vincent Kelly—Phonogram A&R man Dave Bates is hoping to scoop up his next Teardrop Explodes. Thanking him for the compliment, I feel compelled to correct him.

'This isn't an *image*, Dave. I wear these clothes every day of the week. Some nights I have to literally fight my way home.'

Dave looks confused.

'Scallies and Neds are conformists,' I continue. 'They like labels. You know: Slazenger, Lois, Diadora. They don't understand wartime haircuts, prison shirts, and demob suits. It's a hangover from school—an ingrained fear of being laughed at by their mates.'

Dave nods his head, deep in thought. What is wrong with me? Dave meant it as a compliment, why am I so defensive all the time? Sensing that he's already thinking that The Wild Swans may be more trouble than we are worth, I compound things still further.

'I always fight back.'

—

Departing from Liverpool a little after 6am, the knackered Ford Transit van we've hired pulls up sputtering radiator steam outside Matrix Studios in Little Russell Street, London, a little after ten. Carrying our drum kit and guitar cases into the live room, we are incredulous to discover Marianne Faithfull seated at the mixing desk, louche, semi-comatose, and possibly on the nod after an all-night recording session.

'Hello boys,' she slurs, her voice all peacock feathers and burgundy-coloured velvet. 'Do forgive me. I've been attempting to conjure magic . . . didn't notice the time.'

Ged, Justin, Jim, and I exchange glances. *Oh my God. It's her! Of Hampstead, heroin, and Mars bar fame.* Clueless to her rock pedigree, young Jeremy sidles up to me, whispering, 'Who is the old hippie bint?'

Adjusting the settings on his Moog Opus 3, Ged searches for the perfect glacial keyboard tone he has in his head; some impossible mix of Elgar and Captain Oats limping to a heroic death in the blizzard. Sitting behind his drum kit, Justin sips tea with one hand while combing pomade through his hair with the other. Six months ago, when Justin and I first met, he was dressing entirely in black, as if David Sylvian had fallen on hard times and moved to Birkenhead. After we became close friends, he absorbed my CC41 wartime demob aesthetic, washed, starched, and rewound it to the late 1920s, and is now wearing spats and sock suspenders.

Smashing out 'God Forbid', 'Now You're Perfect', and 'Infidel' in record time, we sound as raw as oysters, with about the same chances of making people ill. Tim, the engineer, is bored. To him, we're northern chancers. He can smell it on us. He's not that much older than us, but he's the delusional type I fucking love: considers Barclay James Harvest underrated, knows his scales, probably used to play guitar or bass in a band called Caesar's Thumb or Odin's Fire—definitely someone's something. He thought punk rock was a horrible joke and can't believe that wankers like us are afforded studio time by major record labels when proper musicians like him and his pals in Titan's Trousers never were. He is clueless to the heavy truth that the more technically proficient a musician is, the less their chances of ever creating anything original are. Give Tim sixteen bars to play with and he'll fill them with a 'scorching' guitar solo because it wouldn't occur to him to do anything else. Ask the same thing of a post-punk 'chancer' and they'll expand the art form by miking up the studio fridge.

In the nightshade fraught with danger,
In the grey, dark wanton umbra.
We ponder the unpleasantness,
where mistral sculptures wander.

Our song 'Infidel' is clunky northern goth, and thanks to nerves it races faster than a hormonal nerd with a porno mag. Jerry's fingers are strobing, doing that weird helicopter-blade thing—he could burst into flames at any moment.

This being my first time behind a studio microphone, I have no technique whatsoever. I'm not singing, I'm bellowing like a calf that has been separated from its mother. I am clueless as to what these words I've written mean, but it's hugely atmospheric in a lost-in-fog-at-twilight,

Arnold Böcklin *Isle Of The Dead* kind of way. I suspect Phonogram will think it atmospheric in a nobody-will-ever-play-it-on-the-radio-or-ever buy-their-records kind of way.

Braced for rejection, we are astounded when Dave Bates offers us a record deal with a £10,000 advance. *Finally!* we think, until Dave explains to us that our recording budget comes out of that sum—and that he insists upon producing our album himself. Despite Julian speaking very highly of him and us liking 'Batesey' a lot, Ged and I are determined that The Wild Swans are not going to be anyone's vanity project.

IV
PAPERCLIP JIM

WINTER 1980. Just as the acid is kicking in, Jim arrives. Seen through the funhouse mirrors of a quadruple-strength microdot, he is fast becoming two-dimensional. In my rapidly deconstructing world, my elfin-faced pal has become Paperclip Jim—a fictional character like Peter Pan, or Pinocchio. Striding across the room toward me in stop-go animated strides, he is a cardboard puppet from a Victorian toy theatre, his head and limbs attached to his torso by brass, split-pin butterfly paperclips. Jim's voice is two octaves higher than I remember it, and where did he get those ting-a-ling jester's boots? Surely he didn't catch the train from Birkenhead to Liverpool Central with those ridiculous pheasant quills in his hat?

Experiencing the beginnings of a panic attack, my mind is throwing out grappling hooks, desperately trying to gain purchase on some fragment of reality. Sensing my agitation, Jim attempts to calm me down by making me a cup of tea, but in trying to impress upon me the dangers of scalding myself while the balance of my mind is disturbed, I'm too scared to drink it, so I hold it at arm's length, as if it's a radioactive isotope, until it is cold.

Hearing a coin tossed up at my window, Jim glances out before throwing down my door keys. Expecting our friend Yorkie to walk in, I freeze as I turn in my chair to say hello. A Nazi in full SS uniform is standing there, his arms full of Tequila and brightly coloured Indian confectionery.

'Don't say hello, then,' the Commandant snaps, as he goosesteps past me into my tiny kitchenette on his quest to find glasses and plates. It's Yorkie all right, but not the one I was expecting.

There's no time to worry about the gift-bearing Angel Of Death in my kitchen right now, though, as a more urgent crisis beckons. Having swallowed his microdot, Jim is putting on his army raincoat, preparing to leave. I feel compelled to warn him of the perils he will face while tripping on the streets of Liverpool, but his name suddenly sounds wrong in my mouth.

'J-i-m.'

Those three letters are far too short to contain the inner and outer space of him. How can this massively complex person be known to the world by just one syllable?

'Jiiiiiimm. Jiiiiiiiiiiiiiiim.'

'What?'

'I forbid you to go out. It's not safe. You'll be murdered.'

Ignoring me, Jim continues to comb pomade from the jar he's found on my sideboard through his ultra-short wartime haircut.

'You must listen to me. You are safe here, but out there, when the acid kicks in, your brain will become mince.'

Jim isn't having any of it. 'You're being paranoid, Paul. I'll be fine.'

Before I can respond, I spy the Capuchin monkey perched on top of the framed *Rock Of Ages* painting on my wall. Dressed in a velvet waistcoat and Moroccan fez, the tiny primate must belong to me, yet I can't remember ever buying myself such an exotic pet. The image on the painting beneath him portrays a repentant prostitute clinging to a massive granite cross in a storm while waves lap at her feet. I've had this Victorian picture on my wall for years, so why have I only just noticed how deeply disturbing it is?

'I'd love to stay and hang out with you chaps,' Jim says, while checking himself in the mirror over the fire surround, 'but I'm meeting a girl in town. It's a date.'

Rolling my eyes in disbelief, I look to Yorkie to back me up.

'Dave! Tell him he mustn't go out. He'll listen to you.'

'It's absolutely fine, Jim,' Dave shouts from the kitchenette. 'Don't listen to Paul. He's paranoid. Last time we took acid, he thought he was one of those rub-down figures from the Letraset catalogue.'

And with that, Jim leaves.

'Dave ... your boots, they're scaring me. Can you take them off?'

While I know now that he is not the embodiment of evil I thought he was when he first arrived, I still recoil at the menacing, creaking sound his leather gaiters make when he walks. Not yet under the influence of the LSD he has swallowed, Yorkie has little truck with my paranoid whimpering.

'Paul, don't be so fucking daft,' he says, while passing me a tray of sticky Gulab jamun.

The sword at Dave's waist is not a hallucination. He really does wear an antique cavalry sword attached to his belt. Incredibly, he never gets stopped or questioned by the police for carrying this fearsome weapon on the streets of Liverpool. I can only presume that when they see the sword combined the black cloak he wears, they think that he's an actor from the nearby Everyman and Playhouse theatres.

Time is meaningless on acid. We can't tell if an hour, a decade, or an ice age has passed. The acid is peaking now, and as if to prove it, Dave and I have discovered that we can toast bread by using the radiation from the TV screen—a revelation, to us, on a par with the discovery of penicillin.

Sometime after 9pm, Will Sergeant calls in for a cup of tea. Seeing us both holding floppy slices of Sunblest against the television, he susses the situation immediately and offers to stay and babysit while our minds turn to Plasticine. Will appears so friendly to us, and his voice so reassuring, that we think Johnny Morris from Animal Magic has dropped by.

'Don't sit so close to the telly,' Will warns. 'You'll knacker your eyes. Your noses are almost touching the screen. In fact, turn it off, and I'll put a record on.'

Turn the telly off? Is he mad? Dave and I are engrossed in the greatest fantasy film ever made. Having missed the opening credits, we don't know what it is called or who directed it, but we are convinced it is a lost masterpiece of abstract expressionism. When we explain the intricacies of the plot to Will, he consults the TV listings in the *Liverpool Echo* and starts to laugh.

'You are on BBC1, right? It's not a feature film, you dickheads! According to this, you've been watching *Family Fortunes*, *Knots Landing*, and a documentary about Morris dancing.'

Dave is not having it.

'Well, who was the man with no face who walked under the giant arch of lady's legs in the plastic cathedral? Was that a dream sequence?'

I am equally confused.

'And who was the priest in the red robe who said that thing about crystal tongues of liquid fire?

'What, are you on about?' Will replies. 'It's a black-and-white telly— and the sound is off.'

When Jim returns after an hour, he's visibly shaken.

'Why are you back so early?' we ask. 'And how did your date go?'

Slumping down onto the sofa next to us, Jim sighs and begins to tell us all about his all-too-brief encounter. Arriving at the club just as the acid was coming on, he had some trouble locating his date. Just as he was starting to think she'd stood him up, he found her sitting in a corner, looking miserable. Not recognising her, he had passed by her several times while ignoring her attempts to get his attention. Thanks to the acid, rather than the ethereal, pre-Raphaelite beauty he was expecting, Jim thought she resembled a Gloucester Old Spot.

'Whaaaat! But you didn't tell *her* that, though?'

'Erm . . .'

'Oh my God, you did.'

'Jim. Tell us exactly what you said.'

'Well, I was polite about it. I think I just said, It's remarkable how much you resemble a pig.'

'What! What do you mean?' she shot back at him in alarm.

'Well . . .' Jim continued. 'What is the word? You, know, for when someone's features resemble those of a pig? Is it . . . Porcine?'

Attempting to be as accurate as possible, Jim compounded the insult by repeatedly pointing at her face and hands.

'Look, you even have a snout and trotters.'

I can't stop laughing.

'But you did tell her you were on drugs, right?'

'I didn't get the chance,' he says sadly.

Oh my God. That poor girl will be in therapy for years.

Switching off the TV, Will begins flicking through my record collection.

'Right,' he says. 'I know what you *Teds* need.'

As the opening bars of 'Let There Be More Light' from Pink Floyd's *A Saucer Full Of Secrets* fill the room, the monkey leaps from the painting, onto the shade of my standard lamp, where it hangs by its tail momentarily before slinking down onto my shoulder. In a sultry tone reminiscent of Fenella Fielding, it breathes softly, '*I think, we are in for an interesting night.*'

—

Three years later, having relocated to London, Jim is killed by a speeding motorcycle while crossing the road at Marble Arch.

V

FRAZZLED

SPRING 1981. 108 PRINCES ROAD, TOXTETH.

'Can you feel anything yet?'

'Nope. Nothing yet.'

'What about now?'

'Nope.'

I'm lying. I can feel something, but waiting for drugs to come on is like waiting for a delayed train; it tends to cause anxiety. I am convinced that the psilocybin we swallowed forty minutes ago is not going to compare with its synthesized LSD equivale—

'Bloody hell!'

On turning the key in the door to my flat, my mouth hangs open. Not only has the place been entirely renovated but it appears to have been bulldozed, moved to the Southern Hemisphere, and rebuilt by Pacific Islanders. The walls of the sitting room are constructed entirely from bamboo and dried clay, the linoleum floor tiles now buried beneath a leafy forest floor, complete with creepers, vines, and tropical oogly booglies. Mounted on the wall above my bookcase, beneath a roof of layered palm leaves, is a stuffed silver marlin. I know this enormous fish is a hallucination, yet as I move closer to it, the iridescence of its skin takes my breath away. For reasons I don't understand, my bed, record player, three-bar electric fire, and six-person sofa with its original 1950s 'atomic'-patterned fabric all appear unchanged and not out of place in their new Bikini Atoll setting.

Two hours ago, I was sitting in the basement of the Everyman Bistro on Hope Street, drinking Guinness. At closing time, I moved next door to the Casablanca, where members drink until as late as its license allows. Having arranged to meet my old friend Les Pattinson there at midnight, I'd killed time smoking French cigarettes while pretending to be Alain Delon or Jean Marais—anyone but myself. When Les arrived, he came bearing gifts. Hidden beneath his jacket, disguised inside a multi-pack bag of Frazzles, were five ounces of dried psilocybin mushrooms, acquired from a country type out in the wilds of Hesketh Bank.

Sitting in a dark corner of the Casa's basement, nursing pints of lager, we shovelled great handfuls of what tasted like shredded cowpat into our mouths. We'd both taken acid before, but never together, and never psilocybin. Entering uncharted territory, we were clueless as to how many individual mushrooms to take. Worried we may be underdosing, we decided to consume the lot, sharing from the bag as if it really did contain smoky-bacon-flavour snacks.

I only moved into this flat last month, so this being his first visit, Les can't fully appreciate the radical redecoration that has occurred. Seeing the startled look on my face upon entering the flat, he tells me not to panic. There's a simple explanation.

Preparing myself for a convoluted tale involving string theory, or possibly some kind of fairy-tale talking flute, I'm all ears. In a soothing voice, Les tells me that the flat's décor hasn't changed—we have. By ingesting several hundred mushrooms each—a quantity he now realises was a colossal dose—we have overshot the quantity of psilocybin needed for a 'heroic' trip by some distance.

Hmm . . . that does make significantly more sense than my theories.

Sitting cross-legged on the floor with a blanket draped across his shoulders, Les has transformed into a Medicine Man from Central Casting. As he stares into the 'embers' of the electric fire with his back to me, I sense that Les has chosen a non-participatory role in the evening ahead.

Feeling too animated to sit quietly and in the need for 'input', I select only the most beautiful and non-threatening records to play, starting with 'Sketch For Summer' by The Durutti Column.

'Take it off!' orders the shaman.

I try again with Phillip Glass's 'Music In 12 Parts'.

'Noooo!' commands the voice.

He's right. Every record I put on changes the vibe too dramatically. We're tripping in unfamiliar surroundings, and I suspect that Les is experiencing a radically different voyage to mine. Using the psychic powers newly gifted me by the magic Frazzles, I intuit that my old pal is not leaning into the trip but actively resisting it, determined not to succumb to hallucination. Concerned that we may have inadvertently poisoned ourselves, Les has chosen to sit quietly and monitor events, should the evening necessitate calling out paramedics or the fire brigade.

As I lay down on my single bed in the corner with my hands behind my head, Les shouts, 'Don't go to sleep!'

Sleep? I couldn't if I wanted to. I'm just making myself more comfortable, to better enjoy the cosmic cinematography that has begun playing across the inside of my eyelids. Golden gyroscopes the size of Pluto spin in a complex orbital mechanism, generating sound and light across the vast firmament inside me. Intricate as watch innards, each harmonic oscillator emits its own unique vibration: a musical note, and with it, a corresponding colour. These vibrations blend together in a constantly evolving audio-visual symphony of perfection. Just half an hour into my trip and I am on a subatomic-level sightseeing tour of the sacred engine room of creation, nanoseconds away from illumination and beholding the glowing countenance of—

'Paul?'

'What?'

'Don't go to sleep.'

Rising to use the bathroom, I find myself pancake-flipped into an *alternate*, alternate reality—somewhere significantly more primal. Apparently, I now pay rent on a quarter-hectare village in a dense and humid tropical rainforest, in a country that is some hallucinatory mash-up of Central Brazil, Borneo, and Papua New Guinea. What's more, my skinny young body has morphed into that of a short, bent-backed, potbellied old man.

Barefoot, I take painful steps down a winding path strewn with vines toward the village toilet situated at the edge of a vast, impenetrable jungle, where macaws and howler-monkeys scream warnings at my approach. My bath and toilet suite are gone, replaced by a hole in the ground. Looking down, I find myself standing precariously on the lip of an enormous waterfall. A thundering torrent cascades a thousand feet down before disappearing into a billowing cloud of mist. While I know that in the physical world, I am in my bathroom unzipping the fly of my trousers, in this reality, I have porcupine quills through my lips and am wearing a Koteka—a huge and ridiculous-looking penis gourd made from some kind of dried pitcher plant.

Meanwhile, back in the sitting room, Les is acting strangely. He's got it into his head that the water in the goldfish bowl above my fire surround urgently needs changing. It doesn't. I know this because I cleaned it of algae and put fresh water and pondweed in just two days ago. What Les cannot see in the orange glow from the electric fire—the only light source the medicine man considers permissible—is that the glass walls of the bowl are thick enough to lend it a green cast. He's adamant that the water inside is dirty, but it is not. Feeling spiritually connected to all life on earth, he cares little for practicalities and reasons why not to act. The shaman by the fireside only feels empathy with the fish.

He's right, of course—it's horrible keeping any animal captive—but the goldfish was a present from my girlfriend, who is away in Canada. Mashed on drugs as I am, I know that in our drugged state, siphoning water from one container to another, washing slippery glass, and refilling it with the water of the correct temperature would not only stress the poor creature out but in our state be a task akin to rescuing Theseus from the minotaur's labyrinth. By his silence, I presume that Les concurs.

As dawn breaks over Merseyside, the long night ends, and with it the effects of the mushrooms. The village in the rainforest has faded now, along with its wild pigs, moon moths, swallowtail butterflies, and giant centipedes. I'm finally straight enough enter the kitchen and apply a match to the cooker's gas jets to make Les and me a pot of P.G. Tips without killing us both.

God only knows where Les's hallucinations took him last night. In my trip, he was the village wise man from every Joseph Campbell documentary and ludicrous safari suit adventure film I've ever seen, but in his, who knows? He may have retreated to childhood, grown fins, and sprouted gills, or been piloting a spaceship through his own neuroanatomy.

Too sleep-deprived for a post-trip debriefing, my friend and I sip tea and munch toast in exhausted silence. Eight hours have passed in material reality, but under the influence of psilocybin, countless eons have elapsed. I can't speak for Les, but I have been on a dozen adventures in as many realms and in as many realities. But what's this?! I've just spotted my goldfish, 45, floating lifeless on the surface of its bowl. The water is oddly clouded and smells of spearmint.

Like some stupefied Columbo, it takes me several moments to work out that something fishy has occurred. In the early hours of the morning, while I was coral diving in the methane oceans of Neptune, or in the angelic realms, communing with the multi-eyed Ophanim (the 'spinning ones'), Les, clearly worrying about the well-being of my goldfish, must have left his vigil by the electric fire and gone rogue on a *Heart Of Darkness*-style rescue mission to the bathroom. Now I've come down from my trip, I can sympathise with his drugged logic. If fluoride in toothpaste can clean teeth, it can also clean water.

Just after 9am, Les leaves for home and some much-needed rest, while I give 45 a burial at sea courtesy of Armitage Shanks. Exhausted, I fall asleep at 9:35am only to be woken ten minutes later by a ringing on my doorbell.

Hang on! This makes no sense. My bedside clock reads 09:16, so unless time is running backwards, that can only mean that I have slept for twenty-four hours straight!

It's Les at the door, en route to rehearse with Echo & The Bunnymen. He won't come in, he's just called by to drop off a gift. Aww, good old Les. He's gone to some significant trouble to locate the golden sliver of light staring vacantly at me through the walls of a plastic bag. There was no need. I could never hold the events of last night against him, and for one good reason. No, not because I've known this guy since we started school together at the age of five, or because, at sixteen, he saved me from near drowning at Ruskin's View in Kirkby-Lonsdale; I can't hold it against him because yesterday evening was so absolutely, hilariously, and archetypically *drugs* that I can only see the funny side. One day I must write this all down as a warning to young people. Drugs can kill.

—

When I hear that Mick Finkler has been sacked from the Teardrops, I am incredulous. What were they thinking? Mick is fucking brilliant. It's what he *doesn't* play as much as the lean elegance of what he *does* play that is one of the strengths of the group. Never needing to think about it, he just knows the coolest, most minimal thing for any given song. Mick's limitations as a guitarist, along with my naïve playing, helped define the band's post-punk sound. With Mick gone, Julian will be entirely surrounded by 'yes men', and I'm worried for the band's future.

Understandably, Mick is *destroyed* by the news, and we don't see him down at Eric's for the next three months. When he does finally appear, he's both physically and mentally changed. He's been working out in a gym; he's muscular but unsmiling, and he doesn't want to talk about it. We're all wondering if he's come back to kick Julian and Dave's heads in.

—

'That's the best haircut you've ever had,' says Bill, as I walk into the Zoo office dressed in vintage military fatigues. This ultra-severe 1940s hairstyle soon becomes so widely copied in Liverpool that it eventually becomes *the default indie look*, and I laugh to myself as, one by one, my friends, local bands, and outright enemies follow me down to the Victor Salon on Whitechapel for a 'Simmo'.

Like Beau Brummell and his three different glove-makers, I'm not satisfied with just one haircut every three weeks. I return to Victor's two or three days after a cut for crucial minor adjustments. Frustratingly, I'm increasingly forced to wait in the lengthy queue I helped to create, having unintentionally turned about the fortunes of this tiny ailing barbershop. So in-demand are Victor's poison-oil lubricated clippers these days that he develops kidney problems from not being able to leave his shop for the building's only toilet three flights up. I plead with Victor to get an assistant—he has two barber chairs in the shop, after all—but he refuses. He has no idea how long this 'short back and sides' golden age will last, so he needs to milk it while he can.

Walking into the downstairs Everyman Bistro on Hope Street these days is like finding yourself in Weimar-era Germany, and it's all my fault. At least one member of every band in here is sporting a variation on my CC41 Utility theme. The Wild Swans jodhpurs and Spanish Civil War leather jacket aside, the best of the bunch are my young friend Michael Head's new band, the elegantly named Pale Fountains, who this week are dressing like members of Baden-Powell's original Boy Scout movement. Yorkie's new band, The Balcony, look like the terrifying cast from an expressionist movie, while The Passage, Modern Eon, Black, and The Room have all discovered the less-likely-to-get-your-head-kicked-in indie uniform of black denim and Air-Wear shoes.

—

Julian has invited Yorkie, Tempo, Will Sergeant, Les Pattinson, Ged Quinn, his wife Kath, and me to appear in the Don Letts-directed promo video for the Teardrops' next single, 'Reward', which is being shot on location at one of Liverpool's abandoned North docks. That's me hanging on to the back of the hurtling jeep with Tempo and Ged; Kath, dressed like a French Resistance fighter is seated next to drummer Gary in the back seats. Bill's Bristolian friend Bill Butt, the Bunnymen's lighting engineer, is driving.

This is the first time most of us have heard the new Teardrops single and met the three newly recruited members of The Teardrop Explodes, and we are shocked. Not by the song, which sounds super-commercial, but ... well, no wonder we've been drafted in for the video! Julian and Gary aside, the new Teardrops look awful. Friendly as they are, I see their type every week on *Top Of The Pops*, in bands like The Tourists and The Korgies. Left unchecked, they'll wear aviator sunglasses and Hawaiian shirts, roll their sleeves back *Miami Vice* style, and play slap bass high up under their chins. You have to keep an eagle eye on this stuff or, before you know it, they'll be turning up to do TV shows wearing baseball caps and American football shirts like Steely Dan or Supertramp, and that's only one step away from piano-keyboard ties, treble-clef lapel badges, and T-shirts overprinted with a fake Tuxedo and dickie bow.

Meanwhile, Ged and I have turned up in our current 'Hell Drivers' look—Ged's in my late-40s belted raincoat, mountaineering socks, and prison boots, and I'm in a vintage 40s brown leather jacket, pleated tweeds tucked into mountaineering socks, and brown toe-capped boots. Yorkie, meanwhile, looks like the baddie in one of Fritz Lang's monochrome silent films. Now we understand why we've been invited. The song might be called 'Reward', but we're not getting paid or even fed for supplying our visual aesthetic to the proceedings.

'Ged, look!' I whisper. 'The trumpet player is bald with a massive moustache, and that other one has a mullet!'

Ged winces. 'Hanging offence in my book.'

By the end of the day, I've met them all. Troy, Alfie, and Jeff. They are sweet and excited to be here and part of something outside the London norm, and I feel bad for thinking badly of them, but tucking one's nasty leather pants into white tube socks and baseball boots is the devil's work. It just is.

VI

THE GLORY CHORDS

AUGUST 19, 1981. PLATO'S BALLROOM, FRAZIER STREET, LIVERPOOL. Standing in isolation on bulldozed waste ground, Mr. Pickwick's nightclub is an unlikely crucible for alchemy, but once a month my friend and occasional workmate at the Armadillo Tearooms, Nathan McGough, transforms this faux-Dickensian scampi-in-a-basket supper club into Plato's Ballroom, a magical, walk-in curiosity cabinet full of bands, performance artists, film projections, and variety acts.

Since the closure of Eric's in March last year, nothing has come close to this as a locus for the city's counterculture. Finally, Merseyside has a venue as eccentric as its bands, and thanks to artists Mick Aslin, Julia Percy, and Arthur McDonald, even the Situationist International-inspired posters for these monthly Wednesday night events are works of art.

Tonight's headline act are Glasgow darlings Orange Juice, with support from The Wild Swans and Mick Head's Pale Fountains. Introducing myself to Orange Juice frontman Edwyn Collins, I politely ask him if it would be okay for us to move just one of their guitar amplifiers a foot to the right, just for the half-hour that his support acts are on. With three bands playing tonight, space onstage is severely limited.

'No,' Edwyn replies frostily. 'You can't.' Hmmm, not quite the playful kitten portrayed on his record labels then.

Taken aback by this icy wind from the north, I relay the news to my friends and bandmates. Jake 'Fifth Bunnyman' Brockman is convinced that Edwyn has guitar envy from spotting the sex-shop pink, semi-acoustic Fender Telecaster with pearl scratch-plate I'm playing tonight. On a stage full of vintage guitars, 'Pinky' is by far the most beautiful—and, more importantly, the most kitsch. She isn't mine, of course: she belongs to my pal Ian, but Edwyn doesn't know that.

Speaking of guitars, it's almost time for our soundcheck and there's no sign of Jerry. Panicking, I run to the nearest phone box and dial his parents' number. Exasperated to hear him pick up, I jam in a handful of coins.

'Jerry! Why aren't you here?'

Through mouthfuls of his mother's home cooking, he dumbfounds me with, 'But, I haven't had my pudding yet.'

For fuck's sake! How old is he, six?

Infuriating as his immaturity can be at times, we tolerate nineteen-year-old Jerry because of his exceptional musical talent. Having only caught the tail end of punk rock, he has little interest in the guitar gods of the 60s and 70s, no love for psychedelia, and he doesn't even aspire to be Tom Verlaine, Keith Levene, or John McGeoch. With barely any vinyl at home to inspire him, he has created a sound and a style entirely his own. Intricate classical arpeggios, ornamented as gothic cathedrals, morph into wild Gitano strumming, Neapolitan subdominants, and Coltrane changes I don't understand—all of it unfashionably free of effect pedals.

Luckily for us, his bandmates, this trainee electrician at Wavertree bus depot is clueless as to just how remarkable a guitar player he is. One day, Jerry's hot-headed impetuousness may cause him to jump ship to another band—or worse—but right now he's my teenage electric Segovia and the brightest gem in a band of musical jewels.

My fellow Wild Swans and I can hardly bear to look at Nathan tonight. Acting in his role as temporary manager of The Pale Fountains, he has reneged on the deal we agreed upon last month by allowing the beautiful posters for tonight's event to be printed with their name above ours, making it appear as if we are bottom of the bill. Whether it's typographic problem-solving at the layout stage or wilful games-playing, we are hugely pissed off. I love young Mick, his brother John, bass player Chris, and drummer Jock, and I only wish them well with their new band, but surely Ged Quinn and I, having both helped in the creation of the two-hit-singles-and-counting Teardrop Explodes, have some proven form? Nathan elevating his group at the cost of ours by fly-posting this enforced demotion across the entire city feels like a shitty power move.

Humiliated in front of our friends and peers, we feel betrayed, and I am regretting leaving my box of records stickered *P* for Paul in Nathan's DJ booth earlier tonight. These are the tracks that I believe should be soundtracking this incredible scene: 'Faith' and 'Metronome' by Manicured Noise, 'You're No Good' by ESG, 'Beyond Good And Evil' by The Pop Group, 'Aya Mood' by Lizzy Mercier Descloux, 'The Flood' by The Blue Orchids, and a few ye-olde curveballs like 'Some Velvet Morning' by Lee Hazelwood & Nancy Sinatra, Noel Harrison's 'Windmills Of Your Mind', and the incendiary Tom Jones B-side 'Promise Her Anything'. My last record of the night is 'The Electrician' from The Walker Brothers' *Shutout* EP, the first Scott Engel-penned song that I turned Julian Cope on to in 1978, and the catalyst for his about-to-be-released complication, *Fire Escape In The Sky: The Godlike Genius Of Scott Walker*.

If I jerk the handle
You'll die in your dreams.

It's taken what feels like an eternity to reach this moment. Since walking away from The Teardrop Explodes on May 13, 1979, I have willed The Wild Swans into existence. From the first exploratory letters I exchanged with Ged while he was studying art in Edinburgh that autumn, I scoured the city in search of unknown musicians prepared to crucify their minds and follow us into a future unscripted. It took some time, but we got there, and now, on the very night of our live debut, we are being denied our promised launchpad.

I envisaged tonight's bill as a three-stage rocket: The Pale Fountains up first, warming the room with their gentle, L7 postcode take on Bacharach; us, the neo-romantic Wild Swans, as propellant, raising the temperature a little; and headliners Orange Juice delivering the joyous, jangling payload. Disappointingly, the collaborative movement I'd envisaged doesn't exist. There is no revolutionary spirit. 'Pop Jerusalem' will not be built here.

Incapacitated by nerves and devitalised by the absence of bonhomie on display this evening, I swig down two-thirds of the bottle of Benylin I have secreted inside my jacket pocket. The codeine takes me in its sticky, slow-motion embrace, and I no longer care who opens tonight's show—Sooty and Sweep, Ken Dodd's Diddymen, or the fucking Krankies.

Rise up, O Lord, and may thy enemies be dispersed and those that hate thee flee from thy face.

By 8:30, the venue is packed. Every head from every credible band in the city has turned out, most of them, in my drugged imagination, here to witness us fail. The girlfriend of one of Dead Or Alive tells me that Pete Burns has forbidden any of his group from even watching us tonight, let alone clapping.

With nothing left to lose, my bandmates and I stand our ground with Nathan over the billing, and The Pale Fountains go over the top and into no man's land first after all. Psychic equilibrium has been at least partially restored. Ten minutes ago, no one in the audience knew what to expect from the young Michael Head and his brother, but it certainly wasn't the breezy bossa-nova now entering the darkened venue like a shaft of Brazilian sunlight. Across the country, the tight circle of barriers that punk erected around itself in 1977 is being extended incrementally, band by eclectic band.

Androgynous performance artists Mick Aslin and Julia Percy are up next, with their shaved heads, white shirts, and identical black suits covered in a layer of white ash. There's no music—no 'act', per se—just the two of them attempting to break out of a man-sized black box onstage. Their railing against conformity is entirely lost on the crowd, who stand, mouths agape, failing to understand or applaud.

We are on at 9pm, after the variety club act. It's a different guest artiste each month—knife throwers, stage magicians, Wild West lasso tricks. God knows when these living fossils were last hired to perform, but Nathan adding them as between-course palette-cleansers is a stroke of the kind of pretension-bursting genius that prevents Plato's being perceived as just another music venue and helps to propel it into the city's most anticipated monthly event.

While Jerry and the boys tune guitars and copy setlists, I chain-smoke French cigarettes to hide my nerves. This poster business has all but destroyed my self-confidence. I'd pull out if I could—I'm excellent at running away, after all—but if we are to follow our former Zoo Records stablemates from penury to pop glory, we have to plant our revolutionary flag tonight.

Desperate not to trip on the steps, I take my place centre stage, Justin at my back, Jerry to my right, with Ged and Richard 'Rolo' McGinty— newly installed on bass after Jim's lackadaisical attitude to rehearsals forced us to seek a replacement—to my left. Forgetting to mute Pinky's volume control, I plug her into my amp. *Bzzzzzzz!* Mortified, I turn my back to the audience as my inexperience echoes through a delay effect set up on the mixing desk.

KER-CHUNK, KER-CHUNK, KER-CHUNK . . . CHUNK . . . CHUNK.

Justin counts us in, and the twin-guitar interplay of 'God Forbid' explodes into the room. The nerves are working for us—we sound remarkably tight. Jerry, head down, is giving his all, bobbing about like a Thunderbirds puppet while Rolo brings some much-needed, rock-solid 'pro' to the stage. Ged's beautiful minor chords add some class to the racket, and behind me, Justin, skinny arms at ten-to-two, is looking cool and keeping it all grounded. Thank God for these guys, the actual musicians in the band, because, let's face it, all I am really bringing to the table is this radical haircut.

Twenty-five minutes pass in what feels like five, and we end our set with our newly written song, 'Revolutionary Spirit'.

Lost in the delta of Venus, lost in a welter of shame.
Deep in the forest of evil, we embark on the new crusade.

It builds, it falls. It builds and it falls. Christ! I can hear my voice coming back through the monitors. I sound like Derek Nimmo, the bishop's chaplain in the late-60s TV show *All Gas And Gaiters.*

All is quiet where angels fear,
Oh my heir-apparent the revolutionary spirit is here.

Finally, rising leviathan-like from the depths, the potential of this group breaks the surface just momentarily before concluding with a colossal seven-step stagger—bam, bam, bam, bam, bam, bam, bam-baaam!

It is done.

Climbing offstage to the cheers and applause of our friends and girlfriends is gratifying, but it's the approval of our peers that we seek. Will Sergeant and Les Pattinson, watching from nearby, give me the thumbs up; Jake, all smiles, seconds it; and enigmatic Syd Barrett lookalike Dan Brennan takes me to one side as if he's about to break some terrible news.

'That line in "Flowers Of England"? *Asleep and awake, something is here, beyond belief . . .* is that a Tarkovsky reference?'

If Dan, one of the brightest minds I know, is working that hard to understand us, there is hope.

As Orange Juice take to the stage, Jerry beckons me over to join him and the rest of the band.

'Paul! You stole my thunder!'

'Eh? What, are you talking about?' I ask.

'You!' he laughs. 'At the end of every song!'

'What did I do?'

'You hang that guitar around your neck, but you only play it for the last few bars of every song. I'm doing all the heavy lifting, fingers a blur. Then you come in playing the glory chords and take all the applause!'

Note to self: play the glory chords at every gig.

Tonight's sets by The Pale Fountains and The Wild Swans were not stellar genius, but neither were they a fiasco. What is important is that our Mersey budget euphoria was heard, and registered, by the local scene. We're not just talking about it anymore, we're having a go. This is Merseyside under heavy manners; Thatcher's horrible eye is everywhere. Like wildflowers shooting through cracks in concrete, it's a miracle we exist at all.

Walking home by starlight, I glance back at Mr Pickwick's. Plato's Ballroom won't last. The best clubs never do.

VII
ALL IS QUIET

AUTUMN 1981. Not only does Echo & The Bunnymen's remarkable young drummer Pete de Freitas resemble Guido Reni's painting of the archangel Michael, but he's also about to embody him by lifting us out of our dole-queue purgatory and into the light. Home from touring with his first substantial royalty cheque banked and accrued per-diems in his pocket, Pete calls into our weekly practice session unannounced. He's been following our progress for a while now and listening to cassette recordings of our rehearsals. Why he didn't mention this to me before, I don't know, as in an instantly regretted, lets-shake-things-up-a-bit moment, I've recently moved out of my ideally located and stupidly cheap Rodney Street bedsit and into a damp two-room basement flat on Princes Road in Toxteth, in the same frequently burgled house where Pete and Zoo Records' brilliant but beleaguered secretary, Pam Young, reside.

Pete tells us that he'd like to fund the recording of a Wild Swans single, and of course we are ecstatic. But our luck doesn't hold. Just a few days before the recording session, despite our repeated knocking, our drummer refuses to answer the door to his bedsit.

Up until yesterday, Justin and I have been nearly inseparable. Preferring the crackle of Liverpool's city centre to his old life in Birkenhead, for six months of last year he slept on my sofa, even spending Christmas day with my parents when he couldn't get home to Bahrain. So, what has happened? Sleuthing around within our shared circle of friends, we discover that an acquaintance of the band has been causing trouble, and for reasons as yet unknown has dripped poison into Justin's ear, leading him to believe that he is about to be sacked.

This isn't shit-stirring, this is blitzing it in a Moulinex. If Justin ever missed a rehearsal without letting us know in advance, we might have been a bit pissed off, but we'd rather lose an eye than lose him. Posting a note under his door that contains the studio address, phone number, and start time, we live in hope, but it's too late—the poison has done its work.

With Justin extricating himself from both the recording session and the band, Pete offers to play on the two tracks we've chosen to record. It is not what any of us wanted, but my God, it could be worse. With Rolo on bass, Jerry at his youthful fevered peak on guitars, Ged on the studio's almost but-not-quite-in-tune upright piano, and Pete occupying the drum stool, this is an incredible band.

Clapping his hands to test the acoustics, Pete decides to set up his kit in the wood-panelled former billiard room adjacent to but not a part of the

Pink Studio he has hired. After tuning his drum skins, he begins a tom-tom-heavy warm-up routine. The volume is *titanic*.

After a perfect first take of 'God Forbid', Pete removes his headphones and looks up to find himself surrounded by a semi-circle of heavily pregnant women. They are members of the Ananda Marga socio-spiritual movement who live in the upper levels of the house. Having been violently ejected from their group meditation, they are understandably furious.

Apologising profusely, Pete implores them to be patient for just ten more minutes. Because he's handsome and charming and speaks like he's from RADA, they agree and leave the room for a herbal tea break. True to his word, Pete finishes the drum tracks in record time, but not before the sisterhood of perpetual calm have returned, screaming at him, three more times.

With seasoned engineer John Brierly on loan from Stockport's Cargo Studios, technically we are in very safe hands today—or at least that's what we believe until he surprises us all by fucking off at 5:30pm to drive home. Whether it's a fault on the desk or the smidgeon of cocaine in Pete's system affecting his judgment, there is hardly any low end audible on the finished mixes of the tracks. Worse still, when it's too late to do anything about it, we discover that 'Revolutionary Spirit' has accidentally been recorded in mono. Looking for clues as to the cause, we ask our old pal, studio manager Hambi Haralambous, if he knows what could have occurred. Closing his eyes and placing an index finger to his temple, he pretends to think for a moment before offering a suggestion.

'Drugs?'

Mono or stereo, we honestly don't care—something has been trapped in amber today, and, anyway, it's not like either of our songs is ever going to get played on the radio. Taking a cassette copy of the tracks to Bill and Dave at the Zoo Records office in the Chicago Buildings on Whitechapel, Pete is told there is nothing to play it on. Reduced to utilising the office answer machine, Bill and Dave lean in closely to the tinny, low-volume playback and decide then and there to release 'Revolutionary Spirit' and 'God Forbid' as a twelve-inch-only single. Its catalogue number will be ZOO CAGE 009.

Bill immediately contacts Dutch photographer Anton Corbijn, asking him to shoot our band's promo photographs, but—ignorant of our close connection to Mac & co—Anton refuses the job, accusing us of being mere Bunnymen copyists unworthy of his massive ego. My old friend Les Pattinson, an actual member of Echo & The Bunnymen, offers to do the photoshoot himself.

VIII
DESTROYER OF WORLDS

DECEMBER 1981. THE PYRAMID CLUB, TEMPLE STREET, LIVERPOOL. Julian is seriously compelling onstage tonight. During the extended dropdown section of 'Sleeping Gas', he is extemporising in the style of his current obsession, Jim Morrison. By voicing imaginary altimeter readings, he is piloting the song, bringing it in to land as if it were a 747. In a city infamous for deadheading its tall poppies, this takes some serious balls.

The mk3.1 incarnation of The Teardrop Explodes that Ged and I are watching no longer looks or sounds like the same band that we were ever a part of. They're more post-funk than post-punk, and our eyebrows raise when we hear a few of the early songs that we co-wrote with the group writ large, with added keyboard trumpet we thought banned under the Hague Convention. We've seen them on *Top Of The Pops*, but drummer Gary and keyboard player Dave aside, the new guys in the line-up are strangers to us. The current Teardrops sound is tighter and slicker than anything local musicians could ever have provided, but from their over-shortened guitar straps to their over-studied stage moves, it feels a little homogenised. I suspect these new session players were grown in a lab using test tubes and a centrifuge.

Employing guns-for-hire probably made sense on paper, in the same way that Yes asking their producer, Trevor Horn, to become their singer made sense at the time. But bypassing traditional band chemistry is a dangerous strategy.

Dave Balfe's attempts to co-pilot the Teardrops are not sitting well with Ged and me. We may be minor characters in the band's history, but we still feel protective of Julian and the Teardrop Explodes brand name. Dave isn't stupid. Far from it—he is one of the few people I know who can smell the future coming. He's been conceptualising the fuck out of everything that moves for a while now. I love the two Lori & The Chameleons singles, and the Turquoise Swimming Pools tracks he played me recently, but they are fabrications in the same way that 'The Laughing Policeman' and 'Gimme Dat Banana' are fabrications.

There's nothing wrong with conceptual pop music—I adore 'Telstar' and 'Everyone's Gone To The Moon', after all—but it's a dangerous mindset for a musician to bring with them into a pre-existent, organically formed rock band. If Dave was to engage hyperdrive on his two Prophet 5 synthesizers, it might just propel the Teardrops into a credibility-swallowing black hole. Just because you can, doesn't mean that you should. I just hope this 'fuck authenticity, I'm going for it' rejection of punk attitude is not a pre-shadowing of the decade ahead.

Of course, Ged and I can't broach any of this with Julian. He'd just feel insulted and think we're ungrateful, jealous cunts. Right now, Ged and I feel more kinship with tonight's opening act, The Ravishing Beauties. Bewitched by their melancholic songs about love, grief, and dead children, we watched like lovestruck schoolboys as English roses Kate St John, Nicky Holland, and Virginia Astley giggled nervously through their set. Burn your synthesizers! Chintz is the new black, and pressed flowers are the new rock'n'roll.

It was Bill's former landlord, original Beatles manager Allan Williams, who suggested the Pyramid Club as the location for Bill's latest four-dimensional chess move. In the early 60s, this club was called the Iron

Door and hosted gigs by The Silver Beetles, Cilla Black, and The Searchers. After two decades, this hard-to-locate three-floor labyrinth in the arse end of the city's business district is back in the music press. As is often the case with Bill's more outlandish ideas, the concept is proving better than the slightly damp reality.

With further Club Zoo events booked ahead in Dublin and London, the expectation in the music weeklies is that it will be an 80s version of The Rolling Stones' Rock & Roll Circus. In reality, it is a six-week-long 'residency' by the Teardrops; two sets per night, with a different support band each week. The Ravishing Beauties are up first, then The Wild Swans, with Cheshire's The Colours Out Of Time in week two, and Leeds band The Expelaires in week three. Because fans are having difficulty locating the venue, audience numbers are significantly lower than anticipated. More conventional management would have had the Teardrops playing at the thousand-capacity Royal Court tonight, but where would the reckless magic be in that?

In a fortnight, The Wild Swans will be supporting the Bunnymen on their UK tour, so Club Zoo is a low-pressure opportunity for the band to get tight—and, for me, a chance to learn to be less shit. In week two, after our first soundcheck, Ged and I are instructed by security that we are not allowed access to the top floor of the club without Julian's permission. Apparently, he has taken to ensconcing himself in a tent up there between sets, holding audiences with his former Liverpool circle. One can no longer visit Julian on spec—one must be invited into his sanctum. Young Caligula is losing the plot.

Once I'm finally admitted inside the canvas-sided holy of holies, Julian introduces me to his soft-spoken publicity officer, Mick Houghton. Mick is polite and charming, and I like him immediately. Spotting my pre-gig nerves, he suggests I partake of 'a little toot'.

Clueless as to his meaning, I look to my old bandmate for enlightenment. Ju just widens his eyes in an expression I take to mean *Simmo, you'd be fookin' mad not to.*

Under instruction, I inhale a three-inch-long line of whatever pulverised madness this is. Immediately told not to 'fly on one wing', I go 360-degree stereo and vacuum up another line.

Ten minutes later, I am onstage, biting chunks out of the air like a scrapyard dog. I am just one microgram short of grabbing my crotch and shouting, 'Good evening, motherfuckers! We are called Gargantua, and this song is Destroyer Of Worlds.'

At Bill's suggestion, Mick becomes The Wild Swans' first manager.

—

JANUARY 1982. LONDON. Julian and I are hanging out in his room at the Columbia Hotel in Lancaster Gate. Having not seen each other since Club Zoo, we are catching up on some radical changes in our private lives. While he's been enjoying hit records and filming promo videos, I've been twiddling my thumbs, waiting for our debut single to be released and for a record label to commit to us in the way Phonogram have to the Teardrops. Having both recently dynamited our long-term personal relationships, Ju and I have a lot to discuss, so I am surprised when he pulls a handbrake turn during our co-confessional in order to tell me how, just yesterday, Bill had played him our upcoming single, 'Revolutionary Spirit'.

'Oh yes?' I say, eager to hear his thoughts.

Julian leaves a pregnant silence while staring out of the window.

'It's a bit . . . *Robin Hood*.'

What? What did he say? Has he just equated our Blakean epic about transforming human carbon into spiritual gold with the theme tune of that crappy 1950s children's television show? His words land as a bruise upon a bruise. Flushing red, I turn away so he can't read my face.

I had a similar casually dismissive reaction last week from Bunnyman Mac, whose only comment upon being played the acetate of our single was, 'I prefer the B-side.' I shouldn't care what either of them think, yet I do, these friends and ex-bandmates of mine still exert significant gravity in my world.

IX
ACID DROPS

The further north we drive on the motorway, the more appalling the weather becomes. Abandoned cars and lorries are everywhere. With visibility down to just a few yards, we could smash into the back of a stationary vehicle at any moment. The radio reports that with temperatures in double-minus figures and the country nearly immobilised by deep snow, the Met Office has declared this the coldest winter for a hundred years.

Finally forced to surrender, we abandon the hire van in a snowdrift and walk miles across farmland in a whiteout to find a pay phone. Eventually safe and warm on the back seat of the Bunnymens' coach, The Wild Swans arrive at Glasgow's Apollo Theatre just in time to soundcheck. Warned by the venue's security team to be careful while exploring their 'lively' city, we reply, 'Pffft! We're Scousers! We aren't afraid of anyone.'

Before heading off to Radio Clyde to be interviewed by Billy Sloan, assorted Swans and Bunnymen are milling around outside the theatre, blowing on our fingers and deciding where we can go to get warm. As I count the shrapnel in my pockets and Ged attempts to roll a cigarette without removing his gloves, something large and heavy explodes through the window of the takeaway adjacent to the theatre. The noise is biblical. At our feet lays an upended chair of chrome and leather.

What the hell? This is 5pm on respectable Renfield Street, not half-past midnight on Sauchiehall Street. Picking splinters of glass from our hair, we can't get over how this Scandi design classic has been lifted above head height and hurled through the plate glass window of Mr Chips from the inside.

—

Rolo is acting strangely onstage tonight. Staring up into the lighting rig, he appears mesmerised. This is Scotland, home to The Scars, Josef K, Aztec Camera, and the mighty Associates, and we are desperately trying to look choc-ice cool up here, but right now, Rolo resembles a French schoolgirl experiencing a visitation of the Virgin Mary.

The Bunnymen are aflame at the moment—possibly at their artistic peak—so supporting them on their *Heaven Up Here* tour is huge for us. I'm fuming with Rolo. For me and my ex-Eric's circle, smiling at the audience is a crime up there with introducing the band. I can't berate him after the show, though, as he's already upset and is being ministered to by Bill Drummond. Between sobs, he recounts how, after our set, while he was watching Mac, Will, Les, and Pete completely relandscape the current music scene, someone snuck backstage and stole his bass from the dressing room. What? Am I tripping here? How could anyone sneak backstage without a pass?

After some light interrogation, Rolo admits that it's not me who's tripping but him. Before walking out onstage tonight, he thought it might be fun to drop a tab of LSD. Bill is shocked to hear that Rolo has risked jeopardising our show like that, but I am incredulous. It may be early days for us, but I take what we are doing extremely seriously. No stranger to hallucinogens myself, I've learned that drugs are a sacrament not to be abused. To prove my point, just look at what has happened. To my mind, it is no coincidence that Rolo's bass was stolen tonight, rather than at any previous gig on the tour. In being so cavalier about it, he has invited the shapeless chaos in. Being heckled offstage mid-song at Liverpool's Royal Court last night was damaging enough to my psyche.

A band's rhythm section can't take acid while performing any more than an orchestra conductor can. Drummers *rat a tat* and bass players *dum de dum* while looking arrogant, sexy, or bored—that's the deal. Only Hendrix-level frontmen sorcerers are qualified to risk the void and invoke the sacred fire during a show. This unwritten rule ensures that no matter how fucked up, dribbling, and abstract the singer's performance is, at the bare minimum some semblance of the band's music, as promised on the gig posters, is delivered.

Because tomorrow is the final gig of the tour and we don't want Rolo's already bad trip to turn into a full-blown lysergic nightmare for him, we keep quiet. Bill covers the cost of the stolen guitar and Les offers him the use of his spare Fender for tomorrow night's, gig, but as far as Ged, Jerry, and I are concerned, Rolo has made a fatal mistake tonight. He's a brilliant musician—scalpel-sharp—and we like him as a friend, but The Wild Swans are messengers, not entertainers. This isn't just two bands on the road, it is an artistic seed dispersal. I cannot allow the revolutionary spirit to be diluted, or the credibility of our group compromised, by a band member grinning at the audience. I mean, that could be misconstrued as us actually 'enjoying' ourselves onstage.

By placing that LSD-impregnated blotter on his tongue tonight, Rolo has sealed his fate. To make us all feel less hypocritical and cunty, we remind ourselves that it was never his intention to join The Wild Swans. Travelling up from London to audition for The Teardrop Explodes, Rolo only lost out because they had an East Coast US tour booked and his criminal record would deny him entry. To soften the blow, Bill and Dave suggested that, as he was in Liverpool anyway, Rolo might as well audition for The Wild Swans, a group without a major record deal. No wages, no per diems, not even a bed for him to sleep in while in town. Hardly the offer of a lifetime. He's got the chops, he should front a band of his own.

—

Catching an evening train to Liverpool Lime Street, The Wild Swans have an entire carriage to ourselves. Having bought a music paper at the station, tour drummer Joe spots that we've been mentioned in a review of the Bunnymen's opening night in Oxford. It reports how the singer in support band The Wild Swans *walked onstage looking like Marlene Dietrich.* Imagining their singer in fox fur and high heels, the rest of the band are taking the piss out of me, but I'm taking it as a compliment. I know the writer was referring to her looking androgynous in her tailored suit.

Forty minutes outside of the city, I cup my hands to my eyes like a periscope to block my reflection in the carriage window and stare out across the moonlit fields. A lone grey mare is sheltering under the snow-laden boughs of a nearby oak tree. Belly deep in the drift, the horse is nearly invisible in her surroundings, but on hearing the train she raises her head to watch us as we speed by. As the amber carriage lights flash across her from muzzle to rump, I feel her loneliness as my own. It brings to mind my favourite painting in Liverpool's Walker Art Gallery, *The Falling Star* by James Hamilton Hay. There is a sadness at my core, some cellular-level Sehnsucht that has been there since I was nine. Wherever I am, whoever I am with, I feel at best lonely, and at worst at war with myself. I worry that I have inherited this hypersensitivity couched in coldness from my dad and that I may pass it on to my kids one day.

Hours later, approaching Liverpool Lime Street Station, we crane our necks to see multiple thirty-foot icicles suspended from the Victorian railway arches. The last winter I can recall being as severe and as beautiful as this was the Great Frost of 1962–63, when I was four. Woken early one morning by my mother, I sat up blinking as she opened the curtains and told me to look outside.

'Quick, get dressed,' she said. 'It's been snowing.'

Snowing? What is snowing? Swaddled for the cold in multiple jumpers, tartan trousers, wellington boots, and mittens, I took my first exploratory steps out onto the spotless lunar surface.

Oh! I wondered. *What magic stuff is this, that makes the dirty clean?* I sank to my chin into the frozen mystery.

X
BY STARLIGHT

JANUARY 1982. After the Christmas break, Jerry starts to panic. Worrying about money, he voices the opinion that we've made a mistake in turning down the offer from Phonogram. Ged and I tell him he's wrong, and, as if to prove it, right on cue, the producers of the David 'Kid' Jensen show offer us a BBC Radio 1 session.

At thirty-three years old, Jensen is rebranding, dropping the 'Kid' from his name and commissioning sessions by some credible indie bands. We can't believe our luck. Recording 'Now You're Perfect', 'Opium', 'The Iron Bed', and 'Flowers Of England' in just six hours at their studios in Maida Vale, we think the recording has gone well until I ask the house engineer to remove the flange effect that he's added to our temporary bassist Phil Lucking's parts.

'It's too late,' he says. 'I've recorded it to tape.'

I am outraged. That bass effect is synonymous with groups like The Cure and Magazine—nothing wrong with those bands, but our clean amps and minimal use of effects *is* the Wild Swans sound. How dare a house engineer make creative decisions on our behalf? When I suggest to him that we quickly re-record the worst-offending song, he looks at me like I've lost my mind.

'Er . . . no! You guys should try being more grateful,' he scoffs, with all the jaded arrogance of a man still wearing flared trousers and Hush Puppies in 1982.

Come February, 'Revolutionary Spirit' single is released on Zoo Records, and just like the Teardrops' 'Sleeping Gas' two years ago, I am thrilled to see it achieve Single Of The Week in the British music press. Spending nine glorious weeks in the UK independent chart, we peak at the portentous number 13.

In March, shortly after the Jensen session is broadcast, we get the telephone call that we secretly hoped for but thought we'd never receive. It is John Walters at Radio 1, offering us a session for legendary tastemaker and fellow scouser John Peel. For young indie bands like us, John's approval is akin to a provincial butcher getting the Royal Warrant.

Spotting a crumpled paper bag on the stairs of the Ministry rehearsal rooms where we have been preparing for the session, I feel oddly compelled to pick it up. Peeking inside, my mind starts spinning like a turbine. Hurriedly stuffing the bag down inside my baggy tweeds, I speed-walk outside to our waiting Transit van, grinning like a chimp. Ged, Jerry, and our brilliant, hyperactive new drummer, Alan Wills, look horrified to see their glorious leader rummaging around inside his trousers like this, but once the bag is retrieved, their eyes go wide like pirates inspecting a chest of Doubloons.

Alan is virtually inside the bag and sniffing like a police dog. According to him, it contains good quality black, rocky, red Leb, and something new called 'sputnik'—a particularly incapacitating variant of dope laced with animal tranquilliser. It's a drug dealer's taster menu.

Before we reach the Mersey Tunnel just a few hundred yards away, the inside of the van is thick with smoke and hysterical laughter. No one, including our driver for the day, is in a fit state to navigate a conversation, let alone the route to and from the BBC's legendary recording studios in north Paddington.

With the recording session falling on a Sunday, the famously subsidised canteen at Maida Vale is closed. Ravenously hungry after our long drive and feeling cheated out of lunch, Jerry and I break into the carousel of the vending machine of the near-deserted studio complex, entirely emptying it of chocolate bars and crisps. A fiver's worth, at least. That'll hit the millionaire director general of the BBC where it hurts.

Dale 'Buff' Griffin, former drummer with Mott The Hoople and producer of the session, turns to me, wincing, as if he's just found a condom in his korma.

'*Did a ghost kiss your eyes or rot the leather on your boots?*'

He's quoting from the lyrics to 'Enchanted', the first of the three songs we are recording in today's session.

'What does that even fuckin' mean?' he asks, with all the sensitivity of plankton. 'Very sixth-form poetry class.'

Owning four of Mott's brilliant run of seventies albums as I do, his sarcasm hurts. Upper sixth? I left my secondary modern just a fortnight after turning sixteen, and the only poetry I ever read there was 'Kevin Keegan Is God', 'Gladys Street Mob Rules', and 'Mr O'Neil Is A Bender' scratched with a penknife on the changing room walls.

Attempting to shift Dale's acidic focus from me, I tell him that, in the 1940s, TV actor Leonard Rossiter attended my school. Dale just shrugs his shoulders.

'You know,' I say. 'Rigsby from *Rising Damp*?'

Taking a swig from his mug of tea, Dale sighs. 'Well, that fucking figures.'

I'd rather die than share this with anyone, but decoding my influences regarding lyric writing is hardly cracking the Unified Field Theory: drop some Berlin-era Bowie into a blender with some *Foxtrot*-era Peter Gabriel, add a pinch of Bill Nelson's Be-Bop retro-futurism, a soupçon of Peter Hammill's faux Shakespearean gravitas, fold in some Dante and Blake, liquidise to a paste, and serve cool with sacramental bread. Voila.

Because Peel is regularly playing both sides of our debut single on air, and discounting the four songs from our Jensen session, we only have two new songs to record today. Bound by the terms of our BBC contract, we have no choice but to pad out the session by improvising a third track, ideally something of five minutes or more. We decide on 'Bomber Command', a one-chord dirge that we have been consistently failing to get off the runway at rehearsals. Partially inspired by the instrumental 'India' on Roxy Music's *Avalon*, our piece is so linear and turgid that I can't find anything solid to anchor a vocal melody on. Once the backing track is down, I am clueless as to how to proceed, so our intrepid drummer, Alan, overdubs protracted trumpet squalls across it. What we can't understand is why Baz Hughes, our stand-in bass player for today's session, who actually is a trumpet player, doesn't do it.

Re-christened 'Thirst', the track sounds nothing like Roxy Music—or The Wild Swans for that matter—but is sufficiently weird for Peel to let it pass without sarcasm. Thankfully, Jerry's superb Hispanic-influenced guitar picking, Ged's gorgeous five-note keyboard melody, and Alan's cross sticks on the snare rim have elevated 'Enchanted' into a thing of crackle-glazed beauty. And, in terms of sheer ambition, our newest song, 'No Bleeding', has surpassed everything we have recorded to date.

As Dale fine-tunes the mix, Simon Potts, the A&R director at Arista Records, enters the studio. How he's blagged his way past security we don't know. Casually nodding hello as if he were expected, Simon sits down, folds his forefingers into the shape of a church steeple, and closes his eyes.

Black clouds approaching,
once my mettle held fast,
Now my courage is melting,
with the ice in my glass.
Head under covers
so awesome a goal
Poor boy you suffer,
faint heart thirsty soul.

When you've lost the will to carry on,
when your wretched spirit's broken,
and all hope of it is gone.
Do you tell your troubles to a bottle?
Scrape each barrel that you find.
Curse the woman that conceived you,
can the world be so unkind?
To a boy with ambition,
lost and drinking heavily
braving jeers of sad derision
on a harsh and foaming sea
Do you tell your troubles to a bottle?
Scrape each barrel that you find.
Curse the woman that conceived you,
can the world be so unkind, to a boy?

'This is … brilliant,' says Simon. 'Really! It's incredible. But why is it called "No Bleeding"? It's not mentioned anywhere in the lyric.'

I am stumped. *Why* did I call this epic new song of ours 'No Bleeding'? For someone who has grown up with depression, these lyrics about keeping going when everything appears to conspire against you just came to me as a dam burst upon first hearing Ged and Jerry's first attempts at cycling the verse pattern at rehearsals. Put on the spot like this, it suddenly becomes obvious to me that the song's title concerns self-harm and the willpower needed when suffering in silence.

Despite its unusual one-verse, six-chorus arrangement, 'No Bleeding' is a quantum leap in songwriting for Ged, Jerry, and me. Even grumpy Dale Griffin grudgingly admits, 'Okay, this one is not total shit.'

Rolling himself a joint, Simon turns to Dale. 'This is the best song I've ever heard from an unsigned band. Don't suppose you can run me off a cassette of it?'

The boys and I are desperately trying not to smile. Simon is going to offer us a deal—we can almost touch it.

Broadcast on May 1, 1982, our Peel Session establishes us as indie contenders, and hearing John enthuse about us live on air is about as good as it gets. With The Thompson Twins, Huang Chung, and Fashion on their roster, Arista may not be the coolest major label on the planet right now, but with Patti Smith and Lou Reed also there acting as ballast, it's more than good enough for The Wild Swans. Our future home with Simon Potts—the only 'suit' who sees our potential—is assured.

Before we've even finished loading the van for the drive north to Liverpool, we're clearing imaginary space in our homes for the Ivor Novello awards and anticipating sprinkling cocaine and Veuve Clicquot on our cod and chips. By the time we stop for a pee break at Keele Services, I'm already walking my wolfhound pups, Neptune and Merlin, around the moat of the in-need-of-renovation chateau I've purchased in the south of France. By the time our clapped-out rental van is limping over the Runcorn bridge, I've married Tina Weymouth and we're laying among the lavender fields of Roussillon, eating chocolate-covered figs by starlight.

XI

THERE'S A GHOST
IN MY HOUSE

SPRING 1982. 20 DEVONSHIRE ROAD, LIVERPOOL. With hoarfrost on the windows, two-bar fire radiating orange light but no heat, coats worn indoors, and last year's tinsel still hanging, this could be Eastern Europe. Nothing works properly here, and even the kitchen taps give electric shocks. The top-floor flat I'm sharing with Pete de Freitas has terminal lung disease and a deeply troubled psychic history. Previous tenants of the house include Julian Cope (pre-acid) and Pete Burns (pre-cosmetic surgery). Before these beautiful freaks, it was home to a coven of black magicians who raised something they couldn't put down; a malevolent entity that won't let me sleep.

Being the largest room in the flat, the lounge also doubles as Pete's bedroom, and with his mattress in one corner and his motorbike dripping oil into a turkey-roasting dish in another, it's not the most convenient arrangement for me. On the nights when one of his girlfriends sleep over, I hole up in my room, shivering under layers of army surplus blankets reading nineteenth-century accounts of delirious young men in cold rooms.

There's no TV or radio to ease our days here, but we do have two record players and more vinyl than an indie record shop. Right now, I'm lost in the malarial haze of Dr. John's *Night Tripper* album, and thanks to the Sputnik we've been smoking night-blooming cacti blossom from the walls. Weak from a diet of packet soup and Benylin, I'm hallucinating, and although I know that the noise from the street below is just a bin lid blown off by the wind, it's still the machete-wielding Tonton Macoute I see when I close my eyes.

Pete emerges from the bathroom, damp-haired and smiling, wearing just a bath towel tied at the waist. Taking up a yoga position on his mattress, he recites a passage from his favourite book, *Cat's Cradle* by Kurt

Vonnegut. It's beautiful, like Ginsberg reading *Howl* or Christ preaching on the Mount of Olives. Pete's giving it Bokononism and ultimate truth, but I can't concentrate; I'm too fucked up on this tranquilliser-laced pot to know what's Stork and what's butter any more. Like every other job-fearing poet in town, I'm using this cheap street anaesthetic not for kicks but as a survival tool; a temporary means of escape from Margaret Thatcher's reign of terror, DHSS fraud-squad investigators, and the southern menace of Spandau Ballet and the New Romantics.

Down at carpet level, our teenage drug-buddy neighbours, Mike Mooney and Paul Green, share a bong with Ged Quinn and Jeremy Kelly. Sporting Tommy Atkins haircuts and baggy tweeds tucked into thick socks and mountaineering boots, my bandmates look like drunk extras from *The Heroes Of Telemark*.

The bong is a homemade affair—all sinuous pipes, rubber bungs, tin foil, and sticky tape. When Pete suggests exchanging the dirty water in the glass demijohn for the Courvoisier that he lifted from last night's Bunnymen gig rider, we don't understand. When he explains to us that we'll drink the cognac after it's been fortified with half an ounce of pot smoke passing through it, our faces light up like pre-schoolers. I told you he was a genius. Now, I'm a sucker for a ritual of any kind, but we are already so cabbaged that the idea of us getting any higher than this is preposterous. If I wanted to see magnesium suns exploding on the head of a pin, I'd start dropping acid again.

—

I'm bored with Dr John now, and I want to browse through my record collection for something to elevate the mood—Eno's *Evening Star* or The Blue Orchids' *The Greatest Hit*—but the door to my bedroom is proving a lot harder to open than it should. When I do manage to force it, there's a noise like a spaceship's vacuum seals being blown as the air is sucked from my lungs. Through heavy white smoke, I can just make out the outline of my bed. I call it a bed, but it's just a three-quarter-size mattress on bare floorboards. Whatever it's called, it's on fire, so, running to the kitchen, I wet a tea towel, cover my mouth with it, and re-enter the smoke-filled room. Feeling my way to the sash window, I hurl it wide and then retreat.

Five minutes and several trips ferrying jugs of water back and forth later, the mattress finally stops smoking. Just as I'm wondering where I'm going to sleep tonight, a violent knocking on the door of our flat jolts me back into the moment.

Shit! This will be the Griffiths from flat 2 downstairs, come to complain about the volume of the music.

I answer the door with a prize-winning apology ready on my lips, but it isn't our downstairs neighbours, it's a fireman wearing a face mask, oxygen tanks, and what looks like a deep-sea diver's suit. Behind him, in a descending spiral down the stairwell, are three more firemen, similarly kitted out with axes, fire extinguishers, and enough machismo for a gay calendar shoot.

Now I'm worried. You see, Pete and I are already living here on borrowed time. Not only has the owner discovered that we are illegally sub-renting his flat from his newly separated tenants, Julian and Kath Cope, but he's also fielding weekly complaints from the house's other tenants concerning the twenty-four-hour traffic of freaks to and from flat 3 and the Old Testament levels of noise we generate. But how else is Pete going to get his motorbike up and down the three flights of stairs except by riding it? I just know that whatever happens next will almost certainly result in the landlord throwing us out.

The fire chief tries to get past me but I block his way.

'It's all right,' I yell as if he's concussed, 'my bed was on fire, but I've dealt with it.'

'Have you, now?' he replies as he pushes me aside. Once inside my bedroom, the first thing he does is hurl a chunk of my record collection to one side so he can unplug the tangle of electrical cables dangling from the wall socket.

Shit! Doesn't he realise that's an import copy of the first Modern Lovers album on Beserkely and the acetate of 'Rev Spirit' that he's just Frisbeed into the wall?

Throwing back the blankets, he stands smartly back as the mattress reignites in an impressive *whoomph!* of spectral blue flame. After zapping it for sixty seconds with CO2, he looks across at me, shaking his head in that world-weary *I pity you* way before leaving, followed by the rest of The Village People.

Moments later, I'm sitting on the top step outside our flat's doorway, staring down the empty stairwell and wondering if any of that that really happened. Sadly, the stench of smoke and the wet footprints on the stairs tell me it did.

Re-entering the darkened living room, I find my friends and bandmates leaning out of the great sash windows, *oohing* and *ahhing* at the retreating lights of the fire truck like simpletons. Firing up the bong, I inhale, taking a long, slow drag, only to burst out laughing as Pete replaces Dr John with 'She Is Beyond Good And Evil' by The Pop Group.

—

Spending a shitty, dream-filled night in the damp spare room at the back of the house, I awake, shivering, to weak sunshine and the migraine-inducing sounds of Gene Krupa and Buddy Rich's *Drum Battle*. Before leaving to rehearse with the Bunnymen, Pete has put the birthday present I left for him on repeat play on the stereo and propped our mail—which I'm heartened to see includes his driving licence and my unemployment benefit cheque—up on the sideboard, next to the remains of his breakfast cereal. Welcome as it is, today's Giro brings a dilemma; Rye bread, sausage, washing-up liquid, and toilet roll versus second-hand copies of Patti Smith's *Babel* and Nerval's *Journey To The Orient* from the Tom Atticus bookshop and that chalk-stripe demob suit I've had put away in Déjà Vu on Hardman Street.

Before getting dressed, I perform a post-mortem on last night's fire damage. Lifting the still-soaking mattress, I find myself staring through a hole large enough for a circus gymnast to jump through, and there on the scorched floorboards a plug attached to a length of blackened flex. Until a moment ago, I'd been attributing last night's fire to the entity that's been targeting me since I moved into the flat five months ago: the pissed-off discarnate that the magicians who once practised from the house summoned but failed to banish. But now, un-drugged in the clear light of morning, I think it just might have something to do with me leaving my PIFCO electric blanket switched on for five days solid.

I'm perilously close to a breakdown, but I can't tell anyone because if I try to speak of the ghost I'm made nauseous, and if I try to write it down my hand is stilled and I get the urge to vomit. I'm so terrified when I fall into bed each night that sometimes I don't even get undressed or switch off the light.

While the careers of my old friends and stablemates Julian Cope and Ian McCulloch are skyrocketing, mine is sub-basement. In eighteen months, these two have gone from borrowing my clothes for gigs and promo photos to having clothing allowances, accountants, and hit records. One minute they're laughing at my army-surplus clothes, calling me 'The Gay General', the next they're arguing about which of their bands came up with the idea.

I think I now know why Bill Drummond and Dave Balfe passed up on managing The Wild Swans' righteous, holy futurism. They knew what I've only just found out: that I'm haunted, and just not malleable enough to bank on. I may be five years ahead of my time, but it's no comfort to me. I'm tired of living like a degenerate, and I'm going to get my act together, starting right now. Well, starting tomorrow, because I've just found the note Pete has left pinned to his door:

Paul,
Jake riding up from Bristol tonight, get skins. I'll knock for Mike and
Paul on my way home. Ring Ged, Jerry, and Hot Knives.
Love Pete.

XII

UGLINESS MADE BEAUTIFUL

SPRING 1982. It is a beautiful morning in Liverpool 8. Pete sits at the breakfast table, sipping black coffee while studying a motorcycle catalogue. Sitting opposite, I sip tea, lost in *Crazy Cock*, an early piece of literary pornography by Henry Miller. We caned it again last night, and as such we breakfast in silence, like a pair of hungover Oxford dons. Exposed by sunlight, dust particles fall in slow-motion to the floor, while through the open window, a startled mistle-thrush trills a warning before taking flight.

Hearing a black cab pull up outside, we glance down in time to see two teenage goths explode out of its nearside door. We know they are Americans from their Chi-Chi panda eye shadow and back-combed Gun Club hair. These are not the cool, European, nihilistic goths seen in *i-D* magazine but the quirky lace gloves and rah-rah skirt hot-weather variant. Whatever branch of the undead these two are allied with, it would appear that aliens have landed in Toxteth.

Spellbound, we watch as they study a scrap of paper, take in the ivy-covered house frontage, then look up at Pete and me.

'Hey!' one of them shouts. 'Are you guys Peter and Simmo?'

Pete looks at me, wincing. He knows that I detest being called Simmo, especially by strangers.

'Hi, I'm Courtney, and this is Robin. Julian said we could stay with you.'

Pete nearly chokes on his coffee.

Julian said what?!

Already scribbled on the first joint of the day, we look at each other open-mouthed. Every time we eat at this table by the window, extraordinary things happen, like something from a German fairy tale. Perhaps the felled oak it was crafted from once housed the trapped soul of a witch.

Hiding our drugs in a fish-shaped jug upon the fire surround, Pete clears the breakfast plates while I descend the three flights to open the front door and lead these teen Brides of Dracula upstairs. Robin is near mute with shyness, but Courtney immediately questions me on why I have sewn the logo from *The Face* magazine onto my jacket. What in the name of all that is unholy is she talking about? I'm horrified. It is the red and blue logo of FFI—the emblem of the French Resistance!

While Pete keeps the girls distracted, I slip into the hall to telephone Julian in Tamworth. Getting no answer, I try Dave Balfe at the Zoo Records office in London. We desperately need to verify the girls' story. If they are friends of Julian's, of course we'll help them out, but until that is confirmed we need to be careful. These two could just be starstruck Teardrop Explodes fans out to harvest the DNA from Copey's pre-fame underpants. They could also be Manson Family types, come to carve pentagrams on our sex bits while we sleep. They are Americans, after all.

Echo & The Bunnymen's star is in the ascendant right now, and The Wild Swans are on our way. Apart from the abject poverty, the lethal house electrics, the uptight downstairs neighbours, and the demonic incubus trying to bugger me while I sleep, I am having the time of my young life. Weeknights we spend reading, smoking dope, and listening to extraordinary, weird albums while Pete tinkers with the motorbike on its stand in the centre of the room. On Friday and Saturday nights, our friends come over and we get shitfaced on booze and drugs. Ours is a rich and rewarding life and one we are not in a hurry to see change.

With no word from Julian or Dave, we have no choice but to give the girls the benefit of the doubt. We offer them the small empty back bedroom for a few nights, and they appear relieved and thankful. Within hours, makeup bags and hairspray appear in the bathroom. Pete looks anxious. *For fuck's sake! It wasn't an invitation to move in!*

—

The girls have been here for a fortnight now, and there has been no response to the increasingly frantic, whispered answer-machine messages we leave for Julian. Something is amiss. We are beginning to suspect that he wasn't being entirely altruistic in suggesting the girls visit us at his place in Liverpool so much as attaching a geographical flea collar to himself. If this were a film, this would be the inertia-inducing zoom shot.

Oh my God! Of course! He is ridding himself of them.

In their defence, the girls have caused us no trouble so far. Robin is sweet and near limbo dancing in an effort to keep a low profile. And although she's loud and opinionated, I really like extroverted Courtney's sense of humour—she's sarcastic enough to be a scouser. She asks us about Pete Burns, Probe Records, Backtrax, Pete Burns again, and how to locate Curley Music and Frank Hessy's guitar shop. We talk about bands and albums, and they tell us how they want to form a group and how they might go about it, before asking us about Mr Burns again.

Pete leaves to rehearse with the Bunnymen, and the girls have just left to walk down Princes Avenue into town. As I'm clearing the teacups away, I see Courtney has left her diary open at today's date on the table. There is a single entry.

Paul is a perfect example of ugliness made beautiful.

I feel winded. Did she write this while we were chatting, just now?

—

A month has now passed since the girls arrived, and Pete has taken to closing the door to the sitting room. How odd. Apart from when his French girlfriend, Clothilde, comes to stay, his spacious room serves multiple purposes: gentlemen's lounge, party room, and, after midnight, his bedroom. Domestic flexibility is the price he agreed to pay for bagging the largest room in the flat for himself.

I understand that with four people now living here, Pete needs some privacy, but the knock-on effect is there is no longer a sitting room for my use during the day. As such, I now live full-time in my claustrophobic bedroom at the front of the house, with only Casper the unfriendly sex ghost for company. I could go mad in here.

In the early Teardrops Explodes days, this was Julian's music room. It still has the floorboards he painted in broad stripes to resemble the ones on the cover of Syd Barret's *Madcap Laughs*. It makes me sad to look at them now. Not so very long ago, we sat in here drinking tea and planning the revolution to a soundtrack by The Soft Machine, This Heat, and Art Bears.

Chatting with Pete one afternoon in the Victorian warehouse rehearsal room our two bands share, he tells me he keeps the door to the sitting room shut because he no longer feels comfortable leaving his personal items on display. Things have moved.

We hate doing it, but if Pete or I bump into one of the girls while en route to the kitchen or toilet, we nervously ask them how the flat hunting is going. Embarrassed, they list the letting agencies they have enrolled with and tell of all the unsuitable rooms they have turned down. By 'unsuitable', we suspect they mean that these flats require the payment of rent and utility bills. Perhaps they are waiting on money from Courtney's dad—an amount substantial enough to allow them to become independent of us.

Pete and I have been a little naive. A room in a safe Victorian house on a leafy road within walking distance of town? Why would two teenagers without jobs pay rent when they can live with us here for free?

—

Spring turns to summer, and the girls, low on funds, only leave their room to hang out with our young friend Mike Mooney and his best pal Paul Green at Mike's mum's flat just across the street. Pete and I have no idea what goes on over there, but one day, when stoned, 'Greenie' tells us that the last time the girls were over there, the four of them took it in turns to play horsey rides with each other, and how once, at Courtney's insistence, Paul became her human coffee table. We honestly can't tell if he's joking or not.

Returning from rehearsals one evening, I find Pete pacing up and down the echoing Victorian-tiled hallway of the house. He looks worried. He tells me that on arriving home, he found the door to the box room open. This, the smallest room in the flat, contains all of Julian and his estranged wife's clothes and personal possessions. Peeking in to check, Pete has noticed that things have been disturbed: draws opened, clothes pulled out, letters removed and opened. Pete and I are live-in caretakers here. Our one job is to safeguard Kath and Julian's belongings until one of them feels settled enough to retrieve them.

A further week passes, and with things left unspoken, tensions are building. After much discussion about the moral implications of our proposed actions, Pete and I let ourselves into the girl's bedroom—or, more accurately, into Julian's bedroom. Despite the girls not being at home today, we whisper like burglars.

'What if we are wrong?'

It feels creepy to be snooping around like this, but intuition tells us that something is off. Looking around, we discover that we were right to be suspicious.

Angrily gathering up the girls' belongings, we pile them into their cases before carrying them down the three flights of stairs to the vestibule. When they do return, mortified to find their bags awaiting collection, the girls leave silently, and without knocking for an explanation. Out of options, they throw themselves upon the mercy of our next-door neighbours, Sally and Camilla.

We feel genuinely sad that it has come to this. Perhaps the young Americans were starstruck by Julian and wanted to connect to him through his belongings, hoping some of his celebrity fairy dust would rub off on them via psychometry. Pete and I bear no ill feelings. If anything, we feel guilty about ejecting them so brutally. They are still adolescents, after all. But, as Pete reminds me, youth is no excuse for bad behaviour. After all, he and I are still only in our early twenties.

A month later, when Julian returns on a brief visit to Liverpool, he confesses that he knew it was us ringing him all along. Listening to our panicked messages with his fist in his mouth, he avoided our calls on purpose. Apologising now, he tells us he was amazed we even let them stay for a night.

With the girls now gone, the flat is quiet. Pete and I have resumed leaving the internal doors open, taking drugs, and partying with Mike Mooney, Greenie, and my fellow Wild Swans at weekends. But Echo & The Bunnymen are becoming a significant band, and Pete's not at home as much as he was, so breakfasts at the witch table are infrequent.

The last meal Pete and I share by the open window there is punctured by the roar of motorcycles. Looking down onto Devonshire Road, we see a motorcade approaching. Each car is flanked by outriders, with plain-clothed security men on foot scoping the surrounding buildings for snipers. Having taken hallucinogens, when we see Pope John Paul II waving up at us through the bulletproof dome of his plexiglass bubble car, we assume we've broken our brains. We've been partying for days, with no TV in the flat, so we're unaware that the roads around Princes Park are part of His Holiness's *Highway to Hell* tour of Catholic Merseyside. How are we to know that what we are seeing is reality?

If I'd known the pope was real, I'd never have flicked him the Vs.

—

It's cold tonight. Autumn has come. Laying atop my mattress upon the Syd Barrett floorboards, surrounded by my albums and towers of books, I'm thinking about the summer just gone and remembering Paul Green recounting to Pete and me that one day, while he, Mike, and the girls were scouring the music papers, Courtney had made them all shriek with laughter by declaring that her face would one day adorn the front covers of not just the *NME* but also *Vogue* magazine.

'Yeah, right,' they chorused. 'As if!'

XIII
A STAB IN THE DARK

AUTUMN 1982. At the start of summer, having heard nothing further from Simon Potts, Jerry began to somehow suspect that I may be purposely sabotaging the deal. While it is true that I have not been communicating with my bandmates as regularly as I was, the reality is I want that contract so badly it burns. But, for reasons unknown, the gates of that particular Eden are still barred to us.

After the giddy highs of the band's last winter and early spring—and having had no communication with Arista since they got us stoned to the point of hallucinating on Hawaiian grass sometime in May—I have been struggling to remain positive. Not just about the band but about everything. When the darkness falls upon me, it falls hard. With The Wild Swans' calendar seemingly clear, Ged and his girlfriend Louise take off interrailing around Europe. And now that Bill and Dave have relocated Zoo Records to London—with no plans going forward that appear to include The Wild Swans—I have become increasingly introverted.

Jan—my girlfriend of nearly three years, and the purest soul I know—tries her best to pull me out of it, but I am unresponsive. I can't be reached by her kindness. With every day I am sucked ever closer to the eye of the whirlpool.

Upon his return from Berlin, Amsterdam, and Paris, Ged is fooled into thinking that Jerry and I have spoken. He is misinformed that I no longer wish to continue with the band. Surprised and upset that his best friend has not shared this bombshell with him, Ged is frustrated. All those letters we exchanged, all that hard work, has come to nought.

Jerry disagrees. With Alan and Phil still on board, it will be easy to carry on—and, in fact, he already has my replacement singer on speed dial. It is Peter Coyle, the stage-crawling frontman from The Jass Babies, a man I had once declared my only competition in Liverpool. Unconvinced that this new guy can hack it, Ged wavers, but Jerry is persuasive. Together, they empty the contents of the Wild Swans bank account and split it between the two of them. Why not? It may be immoral, but it is not illegal. Any two of our three signatures can release the funds, after all.

With one eye already on the exit, Ged wonders if the group can maintain credibility without me. They should at least change their name. Jerry thinks otherwise—it worked for Genesis, after all.

By October, they have had a rethink. Rechristened The Lotus Eaters, they record their own Radio 1 session for John Peel three weeks after 'forming'. On hearing 'The First Picture Of You' for the first time, I feel sick. They have repurposed my chorus chords from our earliest song, 'Opium', aka 'Blessed Thing', written in Yorkie's basement in Prospect Vale in late 1980.

Shortly after their Peel Session airs, Jerry and Peter co-sign the Arista deal with Simon Potts. As their promotional postcards—bastardised from Fred Astaire—declare, 'Make it big, make it classy, give it style.'

PART SIX

THE WORST YEAR OF MY LIFE
1983–1991

I
SPEX AND KEKS

'If one does not know to which port one is sailing, no wind is favourable'.

SENECA THE YOUNGER

SPRING 1983. LONDON. Standing in the foyer of George Martin's legendary AIR recording studios on Oxford Street, Ian Broudie and I are agog to find the hallways loaded with dozens of enormous flight cases stenciled with the legends PAUL McCARTNEY and MICHAEL JACKSON. A receptionist tells us Paul is upstairs in Studio A, finishing an album she thinks is called either *Crack Pipe*, *Pipe Bomb*, or *Stick That In Your Pipe*. She can't remember—something with pipes in the title, anyway. She goes on to tell us that it includes duets with Michael Jackson and Stevie Wonder.

As Ian and I enter the immense studio complex to record our debut single, we are feeling half punk-rock and half really-fucking-stupid, because one of The Beatles is inside, and possibly Jacko and Stevie too, plus a bazillion quid's worth of instruments and equipment. We are wearing charity-shop clothes and carrying an acoustic guitar and a pair of entry-level bongos.

Stepping into the lift, we exchange nervous *what the fuck are we doing?*

Looks, and I press the 'UP' button. Not long ago, I was signing on, so this is an upward move for me in more than one way.

Unusually for a just-formed pop group, Ian and I have not discussed our sound, how we should look, or how we might market ourselves as a band. It's like we've just thrown coffee and cheese into a blender in the hope of creating something new and delicious.

On Merseyside, 'keks' are the slang term for trousers, and hilariously our old friend Ian McCulloch has christened our new group Spex & Keks after our dominant signifiers—Ian's spectacles and my voluminous, Cor-Blimey trousers. Duos are near impossible to photograph, and we are perplexed as how to portray ourselves. We don't want to do that Pet Shop Boys *I'm in a suit, he's in daft hat* thing for fear of being thought a synth-pop act.

The one strong sartorial idea I do run past Ian gets short-shrift.

'Fuck off, Paul! I'm not putting loads of pink Elastoplast around the bridge of my glasses!' he says. 'I'll look like a paedophile!'

'Trust me, Ian. It will look cool. Just a few sticking plasters where the arm meets the frame, then. It's not quite as good, but it will work.'

'Why have I got to do it?' he shouts. 'Why don't you have your leg in plaster? Will that be *cool*? No. I thought not.'

Damn! I honestly thought *orphan boy in National Health spectacles* was a winner. It would tie in with my current Dutch bargeman look brilliantly, but Ian's not having it.

A year later, when The Smiths appear on *Top Of The Pops* with Morrissey wearing a massive vintage hearing aid, I jump up, shouting at the TV. 'Ian, look! I told you! I told you! NHS chic! We could have been huge!' But Ian isn't listening; he's not even there, as by then we have split up.

—

JUNE 1983. Offered a record deal just a month after us first being introduced to each other by Will Sergeant, Ian and I have gone from naught to a hundred in sixty seconds. One of the biggest surprises I've had while getting to know Ian is that he's funny, as in stand-up comedy club funny. On our frequent drives to London for meetings with the record company, he has me doubled over and begging him to stop. On a recent trip he told me a story about an after-surgery-hours dental emergency he had recently experienced. While he was sitting in the chair, delirious with both pain and painkillers, convinced the orange juice his dentist had given him to get his blood sugar up was some secret and delicious elixir only endodontists know about, his dental surgeon made his excuses and left the room for a moment to let the cocaine injection do its work before he started attending to the cause of Ian's tooth infection. Immobilised in the surgery chair, Ian watched in horror as a little dog, finding the surgery door accidentally left open a crack, ran in from the street, jumped up onto his chest, and sat there like some canine tooth fairy, staring into Ian's wedged-open-with-swabs mouth.

Orchestrated to within an inch of its life, our debut single, 'My Boyish Days,' fails to capture the public imagination. It's not the fault of brilliant producers Clive Langer and Alan Winstanley, it's just got a bit too much going on. Because our inner circle of friends tells us our sixteen-track Amazon Studios Kirby demo with Pete de Freitas on drums was cooler, Ian decides he'll produce our next single himself, under his nom-de-plume Kingbird.

A few weeks later, we have rented an office space at 57 Roscoe Street at the back of St Luke's, or 'The Bombed Church' as it's known, smack bang in Liverpool's city centre. Inside this small white painted room with kitchenette and toilet, we've set up a demo studio comprised of an eight-track Fostex reel-to-reel tape recorder, a mixing desk, a Roland Space Echo, and a brand-new-on-the-market TR-808 drum machine.

Because I am a morning person and Ian is a night bird, I usually walk down from the three-storey Victorian haunted house we share with our girlfriends on Hope Street and begin work about 11am, leaving for home about 5pm, just in time for Jan and I to go to meet my art-school lecturer pal Colin Fallows in the nearby Ye Cracke pub. Ian usually rocks up to work in his Honda Civic anytime between 2pm and 4pm and works into the evening.

It's a beautiful spring morning today, the bells of the nearby Anglican cathedral are ringing, and I'm feeling good for the first time in a long time. I wouldn't normally come down to the studio on a Sunday, but I woke early and am feeling creative. While still bruised from the Wild Swans debacle, I'm determined not to let it kill me.

Unlocking the studio door, I find the *Alice In Wonderland*-style note Ian has left for me propped on the mixing desk.

Press play.

Having recorded a rough backing track, he is requesting my input. I like it. I really like it. Setting up the microphone through the Space Echo, I press the record button and sing along, improvising melodies using whatever words come into my head. A verse and chorus melody comes quickly, but frustratingly not the lyrics to fit. Nothing in my notebook is scanning with the tune I've created, and I'm just about to run off a cassette of the track to work on it at home when I became aware of a timid knocking on the front door. I open it and find myself face to face with a young oriental girl dressed in what looks like a confirmation dress.

Bowing her head formally, she speaks in a barely audible whisper.

'Will you buy my flaming sword?'

I beg your pardon?

'Will you buy my flaming sword?'

Upon hearing the girl's mystical sounding words, I am immediately picturing Heaven's bouncer, the archangel Uriel, seeing off demons at the gates of paradise with his undulating sword. Believing that I have misheard, I ask the girl at the door to explain herself, but she simply repeats the question.

'Will you buy my flaming sword?'

This time, I notice the lidless cardboard box at her feet. Inside is a six-inch high, blade-shaped plant, scaled like a pangolin and a peculiar shade of red. My mind is whirring. Who sells a single houseplant door to door, on a Sunday morning, on a non-residential street?

'How much is it?' I ask.

'Three pounds?' she suggests.

Hurriedly fishing out shrapnel from my pocket, I give her everything I have upon me. It looks like about five quid and includes a lint-covered Polo mint and an enamel Lenin badge. Thanking her, I close the door and hurry to get back on the microphone to record her perfectly scanning words. But wait. Did that really happen? Everything has been so strange for me since The Wild Swans ended, I genuinely cannot trust my own mind.

Hurriedly reopening the door, I walk outside and scan the length of Roscoe Street in both directions, but there is no sign of the girl. Back inside the studio, I'm fully expecting to discover that the plant has also vanished, but no, it's there upon the window ledge, where it will stand for the next month or so before it dies of under watering.

—

In May, 'Flaming Sword' is released, housed in a striking sleeve designed by our ex-Eric's friend Gary Jones, and enters the UK Top 50 singles chart. The British public are actually buying this bassoon-laden song with lyrics about trying to flog angelic weaponry. I'm starting to believe that we could, on a good day, become the 80s equivalent of Gary Usher and Curt Boettcher, masterminds behind late-60s classic albums by Sagittarius and The Millennium. As if to encourage that thought, someone reviews our music as 'intellipop'. I'm not sure how much intelligence I am packing right now, but I'll take that.

'Flaming Sword' becomes 'record of the week' on Radio 1, and for me, hearing hyper-cheesy mainstream morning DJs gushing about it is simultaneously exhilarating and excruciating. Along with a feeling of validation, I am experiencing a slight sense of embarrassment. Unlike 'My

Boyish Days', I really like this recording and its blood-slow instrumental B-side, 'Misericord', a piano reworking of the A-side by indie English rose Virginia Astley.

To make the project look better and to enable us to play live, we recruit bass player Paul Sangster, a fellow scouser. Paul is younger than us and looks ridiculously cute in his Noddy hat. Our drummer, Tony Wheelan, drove his kit down from Glasgow on spec; asking around, he eventually found out where Ian and I lived and simply rang our Hope Street doorbell to ask us for an audition.

Promo videos, TV appearances, live Radio 1 interviews, and six weeks on full board in Micky Most's RAK studios in St John's Wood can't stop the ache inside me. The old black dog depression is back, and in a horribly selfish moment of cowardice, I abandon ship midway through the recording session for our debut album, *Love Crowns & Crucifies*, leaving my brilliant friend Ian completely stranded. It's The Wild Swans. I can't get past the pain and injustice of our end, and until I can, I can't fully commit to anything else.

II
THE AUTUMN STAR

MARCH 1984. Vaulting a 'no entry' sign, I sneak up onto the deserted crew-only deck of the ferry, where, under cover of darkness, I fall asleep shivering under *Fomalhaut*, the Autumn Star. It rains in the night, and I wake at first light in agony. The ship's funnel has become so hot during the crossing from the Hoek of Holland to Harwich that it has scorched through my jacket and burned the skin on my back. Ravenously hungry, I eat the last crumbs of Pumpernickel in my pocket. After paying for my Transalpino continental train ticket and a week's food and lodging in Amsterdam, I have less than a guilder left in change, and I can't afford a drink to wash it down.

Sleeping on the train into London, I walk the two hours back from Liverpool Street station to my tiny rented room in Kensington, where I collapse exhausted and hungry. Not only can I not meet my rent this month, I can't even afford the tube ride to the Warner Bros offices to ask my music publishers, Bill Drummond and Dave Balfe, for a small sub on my advance. I'll have to walk.

Dave is in a meeting, so I explain my situation to Bill. In leaving Care before our album was delivered, I have broken the contract, kissing goodbye to £10,000—the last instalment of my share of the Arista Records advance. I'm broke. If I am going to launch myself as a solo artist, I'll need a sub on the publishing agreement I signed with Zoo Records way back in 1978.

Leaning back in his swivel chair, Bill asks, 'Is £3,000 enough?'

With my stomach cramping from hunger, I'd settle for £200. Christ, I'd settle for £20.

Bill tells me that he will need to run it past Dave first, so to telephone back at four. Fantastic. Now I just have to kill four and a half hours.

Using the last of my penny-sized Dutch cents in a pay phone, I eventually speak to Dave.

'Hi Dave, how are things?'

'Listen, Paul, I've given this matter some thought. I have concluded that a period of poverty would do you good right now. You'll write better songs.'

I'm standing in a piss-stinking telephone kiosk in Notting Hill Gate, being lectured to by the man that killed The Teardrop Explodes. I should have known that 'phone back at four' was just a ruse to get rid of me. In Bill and Dave's eyes, I am not a perfectionist, I am a quitter. My whole adult life has been one long 'period of poverty'. What the fuck do they think I have been doing of late? Dining on hummingbird soup? I am picturing Dave dunking biscuits in his coffee in his office at Warners while Bill listens in, cringing, their guilt only lasting for the duration of the phone call. What happened to the madcap pair who created the situationist-inspired Zoo

Records? When did they swap adventure for gold discs, smoked glass, and chrome? I don't know about Bill, but what could bourgeois Dave possibly know about poverty?

Floating somewhere above the public telephone kiosk, I watch myself smashing the handset into shards of Bakelite.

It's 11pm and I'm creeping past my landlady's door, doing a runner. I can't decide which weighs more, my luggage or my guilt. With a two-mile walk to Euston station ahead of me, I am the very definition of exhaustion. All I have in the world right now is the return portion of a train ticket from Liverpool. Near hallucinating with hunger, I am remembering how, earlier this year, there had been a poster of Ian Broudie and me in *Smash Hits*. Looking relaxed and healthy, we'd just returned from an A&R expense-account lunch of sushi and chilled Mosel.

Back in Merseyside for the first time in six months, I have no option but to stay out in the sticks with my parents. Pleased as they are to see me, I could go mad here. How have I messed my life up so badly?

Christmas morning and I could die of loneliness and shame. Going through some old trouser pockets, I find a paper wrap, presumed lost, of what I presume to be cocaine or sulphate, given to me at a party. The first bump tells me this isn't coke or speed but heroin. Ah well, any port in a psychic shitstorm. Floating through Christmas, I wake a few days into the new year, ready for business.

1985. Phoning from Nicosia, my sister Val tells me she's getting married and is moving to Canada after the wedding. Dad asks me to accompany Mum in flying out to Cyprus as an advance party, to give my sister some support. One evening in a restaurant on Ledra Street, my mum, a little drunk, confesses that when I was young, she had a brief affair with her driving instructor in retaliation for my father's infidelity overseas.

Whaaat? Isn't that same guy who taught me to drive in 1975? So that's why he wouldn't accept payment for my lessons!

It is 104 degrees on the rooftop terrace of my sister's apartment. In a rejection of my past, I have grown my hair to my shoulders, and it bleaches white in the sun. I look like a film negative.

While listening to the morning call to prayer from the minaret on the Turkish side of the border, I formulate a plan to revive my career. Haunted by the events of late 1982, I decide that the only way forward for my career is to go backwards. I will revive The Wild Swans. Recruiting three or four new musicians, I will secure us a Radio 1 Session and claw myself back to the righteous position I was in before 'Lotusgate' turned my world to shit.

Strolling down Liverpool's Bold Street a week later, I bump into my old friend Ged Quinn. No longer in that band, he is back pursuing his art career. Despite everything that has gone down between us, I still love him as a brother. One look at that face of his and I'm hugging him and telling him my plans.

After we part, Ged passes my plans on to Jerry Kelly, and they work together to get me in a pincer movement. Reuniting the original members of The Wild Swans is not my intention. I'm too damaged for that, but as the weeks pass, I realise that reuniting with those two could save me six months to a year of auditioning and recruiting.

When I tell Jan my intentions, she is incredulous.

'What! Are you mad? Jerry betrayed you!'

'Yes, I know,' I say, 'but it would be so easy.'

'But what about The Lotus Eaters?' she asks.

'They have split up,' I reply.

'Are you sure?'

Ignoring my gut—and Jan's infallible wisdom—I do a Jesus and turn the other cheek. We were just young hotheads in '82. We are older and wiser now. While I can't erase the damage wrought upon my psyche by the betrayal, I can slap some emotional Tip-Ex on it. After all, what could possibly go wrong?

III
RAZOR BLADE SUMMER

1987. LONDON. Holding the surgical steel razor blade just microns away from the surface of the two-inch magnetic tape as it speeds across the record and playback heads, my hand begins to shake.

Do it, Paul! Do it, you coward!

After five weeks in London, staying in a Balcombe Street apartment owned by Justin Hayward of The Moody Blues, followed by a fortnight in a cockroach-infested toilet for three in Bishop's Court, Bayswater, Jeremy Kelly, bassist Joe Fearon, and I are in the closing stages of recording The Wild Swans' debut album. We've spent three weeks on drums, bass, and keyboards, and an unbelievable five weeks on recording guitars, leaving just five days for my vocals and a week for mixing at Pete Townsend's Eel Pie Studios near Richmond.

Jerry and Joe have gone out to get some takeaway lunch from M&S, and album producer Paul Hardiman has left the two linked multi-track machines running off a safety copy of the backing tracks while he checks on his swishy Jaguar, parked a few streets away. I feel sick. I hate this album we have recorded with all my being. It's big and its shiny, full of sound and fury, and signifying nothing. To my ears, it's perfectly serviceable mid-80s guitar rock, but nothing more. My hand is shaking hard.

Do it! Do it, you wuss! Cut its bloated throat.

But how will I explain it? How can I stop myself from being sued by Sire Records?

I was in the toilet . . . I heard a noise and walked into the studio to find the tape on both multi-track machines shredding.

I'll never get away with it. One multi-track reel, maybe, but not the safety copy too. Fuck! It's too late now anyway, as Paul just walked into the control room.

Maybe I'm wrong; maybe I'm just being a perfectionist and this album isn't the overproduced, corporate-sounding, inconsequential, bombastic shite with cod messianic lyrics and Derek Nimmo guide vocals I believe it to be. Jeremy loves it, Joe is noncommittal, but deep in my being, I know it's been a horrible and costly mistake. Lacking gravity, this album will never be taken seriously by credible reviewers, and musically it's so feeble it would need a Stannah Stairlift to climb the charts.

What's the point? Where are the sweeping epics; the careering, reverb-drenched, arpeggio- and piano-driven wonders that the original band were known for? Where are the swooping dynamics heard on our Kid Jensen and John Peel Radio 1 sessions?

If this album doesn't kill the band stone dead upon its release, it will only be because every other promising UK indie band taken up by a major label of late is delivering something similar or worse. It's 1987, and in the four years since The Wild Swans were last in a recording studio, the musical landscape has changed beyond all recognition. The producer is king; colossal, gated snare drums are everywhere, along with Thatcherite plastic optimism and singer as dancing Christ. Authenticity is dead. The new, self-titled Echo & The Bunnymen album and Copey's recent *Saint Julian* solo albums are both over-produced and undercooked imitations of their former glories. Christ! Even Lou Reed is playing a headless Steinberger guitar, and Mark E. Smith is wearing mascara.

The album title *Bringing Home The Ashes* came to me in a lucid dream I'd had in which I was carrying the cremated remains of my parents (then still living) in two beaten copper urns resting upon a velvet tray. To my horror, as I walked, I tripped and spilt the urn's contents over my shoes.

Paul Hardiman genuinely thought the title track of this album was a song about beating the Australians at cricket. He's a nice enough chap, but he doesn't know enough about us or our roots to notice that we're veering so far off the righteous path we started upon that we may never find home. After attending one short band rehearsal in Liverpool, he binned off the brilliant Alan Wills as 'not good enough' and instead hired Van Morrison's drummer, Peter Van Hoek, for the session. And we let it happen; I let it happen.

I am honestly relieved when, upon its release, the album is almost totally ignored by the UK press, but Ian McNabb—newly returned from a US promo tour with The Icicle Works—blows my mind by informing me that there is an enormous photographic image of me plastered across the windows of Tower Records on Sunset Boulevard. American college radio has fallen in love with The Wild Swans. Not that it does us much good. We'll never sell enough copies to recover the enormous sum Sire has spent on recording and promotion.

Over lunch, our A&R man, John Hollingsworth—a friend and ally of the band, and Seymour Stein's long-suffering right hand in London—is looking stressed.

'Don't worry,' I tell him. 'We'll get it right, on the next one. Loads of bands have come good on their second album. Okay, I can't think of any right now but... oh, wait! Led Zeppelin!'

John, frowns, laughing.

'Paul, you are not Led Zeppelin. You are not even Fuzzy Duck.'

IV

THE URBAN FOX

JUNE 14, 1989. Late afternoon, mid-summer, and Ian 'Mac' McCulloch and I are hanging out at his lovely house in Fullwood Park, drinking wine and listening to Frank Sinatra's *In The Wee Small Hours*. Ian's obsessed with Frank right now and has almost his entire back catalogue to hand. Because my dad owned this very album, I can't listen to it objectively; it's inextricably tied up with childhood and father/son dominance issues. I'm telling Ian about how Frank would never wear a pair of socks twice and would throw the worn pair away every evening, and we take opposing sides on the *obscene versus cool* debate.

When the album ends, Ian picks up his beloved Fender acoustic and plays me one of the most beautiful songs I've ever heard. It's simply called

'Garden'. It's got that Leonard Cohen naïve-on-purpose quality that I love. Ian's melody and lyric, '*I wish I was a garden when the rain is falling down*', are both gorgeous and timeless—better than anything I've ever heard him write or sing before. Not quite knowing whether to be flattered or insulted by my reaction, he puts the guitar away.

We're midway through side one of Lou Reed's recent *New York* album when the landline rings in the kitchen. Moments later, Ian's wife Lorraine and my fiancée Jan walk in from the kitchen, ashen-faced.

'Pete's dead.'

'What?!' says Ian. 'Our Pete?' Ian has an older brother of the same name. 'Or Pete de Freitas?'

'A motorbike accident in Staffordshire. It hasn't been confirmed.'

What the fuck?

We can't take it in. Turning off the music, we all sit in silence, waiting for a promised telephone update that doesn't come. After twenty unbearable minutes without news, Ian phones his ex-bandmates Will and Les at the huge, top-floor flat they share with Pete on Aigburth Drive. They've just this minute had the definitive news. It's true. Pete is dead.

I feel sick. We all do. Everyone is in shock and crying. Lorraine is going to run Ian over to the Bunnymen house on Aigburth Drive.

'Are you coming?' he asks. But I've tipped into somewhere horrible where I can't communicate. I just want to go home and curl in a ball, and Jan is too upset to go anywhere. Pete had had a crush on her since they were both working down at Rockfield studios in Monmouth in the March of 1981, him with the Bunnymen and her singing on demos for Dave Balfe's Turquoise Swimming Pools project. Loving them both, it was a gentle attachment I never examined too deeply.

Back home now, I'm remembering gratefully how, after the best part of a year, I'd seen and talked with Pete only recently. Less than a fortnight ago, I'd been sitting outside a city-centre café, reading, when he and his buddy Andy Eastwood had walked past in their bike leathers, shopping for supplies before riding south together. It was a beautiful afternoon, and as he stood there on Liverpool's Bold Street, the sun made a corona around his head like gold leaf on a Russian ikon. Arranging to meet for a catch-up when he got back, we hugged goodbye, and I returned to my coffee and book, pleased at how 'back in the game' he looked after his New Orleans blowout of '85 and his bumpy return to the Bunnymen the following year.

Twenty-seven is no age to die.

—

I write a letter to Pete's mum and dad, Denis and Madge, trying to explain to them what Pete had meant to me and my bandmates; how he had spent his first ever royalty cheque from the Bunnymen on putting The Wild Swans into the studio when Zoo Records hadn't yet committed. I wrote about how, when we had shared homes, first on Princes Road and later in Julian Cope's old place on Devonshire Road, Pete had educated me not only in good cuisine but in all matters cultural; he was certainly the only twenty-year-old I knew who bought the Sunday papers and laid a place for himself at a table for breakfast.

A week later, I receive a gorgeous message back from Madge, thanking me for the letter and informing me that despite how devastated the family are feeling right now, these stories from me, and from many of Pete's Liverpool friends, had been a huge comfort to them.

Two days later, it's my thirty-first birthday. We'd normally have friends over—Jean and Mitch Walker, Ian and Lorraine, Henry and Jacquie Priestman, Hambi and Leslie Haralambous—but we don't because there's absolutely nothing any of us want to celebrate right now.

Lorraine drives Ian, Jan, and me down to the funeral in Goring-on-Thames and we meet up with Pete's brother Frank and sisters Rose and Rachel and everyone in the extended Bunnymen/Teardrops camp in the garden of Pete's parent's lovely home. Madge shocks me by asking if I'd like to see 'the body'. It hadn't occurred to me that Pete would be here at the house and not at the undertakers. I can't face it. I can't face him. If anyone is going to leave a beautiful corpse, it's Pete, but I want to remember him as I last saw him, not made up for open-casket viewing.

The funeral itself is bittersweet. Before we go in, I hang out chatting with Julian, who I've not seen in an unbelievable four years, and I meet his lovely wife Dorian for the first time. She's looking shy and vulnerable among so many of the old Liverpool crowd.

Former Ravishing Beauties member Virginia Astley is also here, and we exchange sad, embarrassed smiles across the church. Virginia and I had had a fling in 1984, when I was a hot mess, but hadn't seen or heard from each other since. We're not the only ones feeling awkward—every musician passing through the lychgate is staring intently at their feet today. Bandmates, ex-bandmates, wives, girlfriends, ex-girlfriends; we all have some emotional untangling to do today. Or not. Mac and Julian, weirdly both now solo artists, have not spoken to each other in years and make the largest Gordian knot. Bill Drummond, Dave Balfe, Pam Young, Bill Butt, Martyn Atkins, all the old Zoo Records gang are here, even some senior Warner Bros staff. Only Pete's devastated partner, Jonson D'Angelo; his family; and his broken-hearted best friend, Jake 'Fifth Bunnyman' Brockman, move between the factions and islands-of-one with total ease.

It's only in the early evening, when we retire to the beer garden at the back of the local pub, that barriers begin to fall. Someone passes me a joint, but it doesn't help—it only serves to amplify the sense of upset I'm feeling. Pretending to go to the toilets, I take myself for a walk around the village. This is when I see my first ever urban fox, zigzagging its way across the village green, nose to the ground, following a scent. Stopping just a yard or two away, this elegant dog-fox is not remotely scared of me, just curious.

My God. I'm looking into its wild, living-for-the-moment—there are no accidents—death-is-not-the-end eyes. *Woah!* What was that? Did I just think that, or did I say it aloud? I must be stoned.

A car's headlights bisect us, and the fox darts through a gap in a hedge and out of sight. I'm probably just high, but I feel better somehow. That brief exchange with nature has lifted something from me and liberated me from the full weight of the day's sadness. I decide to decide that whatever and wherever Pete is tonight, he's not gone; his matter has just been transmuted. I decide to decide that everything is okay and it's going to be okay forever.

Six weeks later, Mac and Lorraine are round at our place in Grassendale Park, and I ask him if he's recorded 'Garden' yet. I'm incredulous to discover that he can't remember it. I don't mean he's forgotten the chords, or the melody has escaped him; he has no memory whatsoever of writing the song. Even when I sing what I can recall of it back to him, he just shrugs in a *nope, not one of mine . . . you must have imagined it* way.

Pressing a finger to the corner of his eye to get me in focus, he squints at me. 'You'll look like Peter Cushing when you are old.' He's been saying this to me since we first met at Eric's in 1977.

Annoyed because I know he's right, I parry with the elegant Wildean retort, 'Shut up, Flobhead.'

V
THREE-SPEED CRUCIFIX POWERTOOL

SUMMER 1991. MICRO MUSIC. WAVERTREE, LIVERPOOL.

'Hello. Is that Dave? I am ringing about your *Musicians Wanted* advert, *Heavy metal band seeks vocalist.*'

Okay. I know this is by far the most ridiculous idea I've ever had, but with the promise of my third major record deal on the table but no actual band right now, I have nothing to lose. I've just turned thirty-three, the age that Jesus made his career-defining exit into ten-dimensional space. My earthly mission fronting The Wild Swans has prematurely ended, so what else can I do right now but actively pursue the ridiculous?

Because I want to make this spectacular power move in complete secrecy, I've purposely avoided the *Musicians Wanted* ads in the guitar shops in the town centre. I know I won't find the spiritual warriors I need there. For the most part, local musicians tend to follow predictable blueprints, and I'm not looking for stuck-in-the-60s scouse troubadours, trippy beat-dance remixers, pocket Springsteens, or psychedelic Byrds wannabes. I'm looking for four non-visionary wankers to blindly follow me in a high-risk, high-reward venture into the unknown. Four head-banging unknowns with no greater aspirations than getting to the dizzy heights of playing gigs with an actual rider, to help me to refocus the revolutionary spirit and beam it through the currently unfashionable prism of heavy metal.

Because recruiting individual band members is going to take too long, I'm looking for an existent group with good chemistry, low expectations, and zero vision. Throw a stone in any direction and I'll hit one of those. I'm seeking a pre-owned metal band, a 'host' that I can inhabit, steer, and subvert from within. Once secure at the head of this powerful unit, I'll lead them like Hannibal over the Alps of, err . . . heavy rock to glory and riches using nothing more than my delusional arrogance and my vintage 70s patchwork leather and velvet kick flares.

Just to be clear, I'm not talking about pastiche. I want to be taken seriously. Not hair metal, goth, grunge, or the heavy 80s indie sound of the albeit brilliant Killing Joke and The Cult. Actual heavy metal. I'm going to succeed where the years-ahead-of-their-time Zodiac Mindwarp and The Love Reaction failed because, unlike them, I have a recipe. I'm going to weld heaven and hell together. The upper world I have always aspired to and the nine circles of Hell underworld I've been travelling through since I lost my mind in late 1982.

Imagine linear 'downer' Sabbath verses married to joyous, uplifting, T. Rex 'Children Of The Revolution'-style choruses. Throw in some Wagnerian-scale abysmal drop-downs and some gorgeous Blue Öyster Cult middle-eight arpeggios. Top it all off with uplifting, mystical, Blakean,

Mirbeau, J.K. Huysmans gutter-and-the-stars lyrics and foxy-chick Mott The Hoople backing vocals. Boom!

Oh, and for once in the entire history of the genre, our albums are not going to sport crappy artwork. No werewolves, skeletons, tattoos, motorcycles, naked women, and definitely no images of Satan or cartoon depictions of hell. I want something with the simple visual impact of the first two Led Zeppelin albums and the wonder of Gustav Dore's illustrations for *Paradise Lost*. Instead of Zepp's Hindenburg in flames, I want the image of a rust-covered submarine. A seaweed- and barnacle-encrusted wartime *Unterseeboot*. Where the U-boat's serial number would normally be painted on the sides of the conning tower, we'll have our band name abbreviated to TSCP. My dad will freak. But fuck it! There's loads of sexy suggestive metal mileage to be had out of submarines and torpedoes.

So, *shhh*! Here's the plan. We go dark. We tell no one. Not even our girlfriends, as they'll only use their witchy magic of common sense and reason to try and talk us out of it. We'll disappear into a rehearsal room for a month, get tight, hone our sound until it's irresistible even to priests, then straight into the studio with Roy Thomas Baker or Bob Ezrin to record our debut album, *Sturm Und Drang*, and its killer lead single, 'Seduce, Bewitch, Destroy'.

In my head, I'm already creating an image for the band based on that historical tipping point late-60s/early 70s style where Status Quo 'Trog' meets 'Song Remains The Same' satin and stars. I'll also be ripping off the fur stole Freddie Mercury wore to perform 'Killer Queen' on *Top Of The Pops*. Around the time of the second album launch, maybe I'll start rocking a Chris Squire cape. I'm getting an erection just thinking about it.

Of course, *Metal Hammer* and *Kerrang!* magazines won't touch us with a bargepole, my indie rock and pop years put paid to that, but what will we care? Our sights will be set on America. America, where all sins are not only forgiven, they're rewarded. With the vibration of the planet raised, my life's mission will be completed and Satan will die screaming. Okay, I've got a little ahead of myself, but as a starting point, I've already written and home-demoed a handful of heavy riff-based songs: 'Demonised', '(You're) Dead To Me', 'It's Your Funeral', 'Particle Accelerator'. I've also dreamt up a band name so meta-metal, I honestly can't tell if it's shit, complete and utter shit, or stellar genius. Okay, okay! First, you have to picture it in a retro, Bolt Thrower-style typeface:

THREE-SPEED CRUCIFIX POWERTOOL

Taste doesn't enter into it with band name logos. Anything too innovative will miss the target. The template is metal, and, as such, our band logo must conform to the rules of riveted steel, flames, or lightning bolts. Okay, it may sound absurd now, but over time, when the gold discs are becoming a storage problem for me, our band name will be considered a classic; up there with the likes of Motörhead. Five years into our fame, when the original guitarist has OD'd and I'm shagging the bass player's girlfriend and he's shagging mine, on no account must we shorten the band's name to POWERTOOL, because that is just bollocks.

I have no idea what my band name means. Like all my worst ideas, it came to me in a dream. I just like the shape it makes in my mouth and the weird religio-sexual aftertaste it leaves of nuns fingering dildos in Ann Summers. Anyway, here I am in Micro Music, in darkest Wavytree, removing a handwritten advertisement from the *Musicians Wanted* noticeboard.

Heavy metal band seeks vocalist, it reads. Wow! It doesn't get simpler than that. In smaller writing beneath, *Into Zeppelin, Sabs, Deep Purple*, followed by the obligatory *No timewasters*. This is perfect! I can almost smell the hybrid Birmingham/Yorkshire accent it was written in. Exactly what I'd imagined I'd find in this *here be dragons* territory of South Liverpool.

Metal and I are not quite the chalk/cheese interface one might think. Between 1970 and 1975, somewhere between my transition from The Jackson 5, the 50p-in-Woolworths *Tighten Up* and *Fire Corner* ska compilations into Alice Cooper, Bowie, and prog rock, I went through an if not an exclusively metal phase then a metallic one. I'd owned and loved *In Rock, Fireball,* and *Machine Head* by Deep Purple; *Master Of Reality* and *Sabbath 4*; and some hard rock acts like The Edgar Broughton Band, The Sensational Alex Harvey Band, Thin Lizzy's *Vagabonds Of The Western World,* a cheap Hendrix sampler, and Hawkwind's *Doremi Fasol Latido.*

It didn't last. The more sophisticated sounds of Bowie, Be-Bop Deluxe, and Lou Reed eclipsed it, and come late 1975, a chance encounter with an arresting bus-stop poster outside Bootle technical college for Patti Smith's *Horses* and the US punk scene she spearheaded killed that shit stone dead for me. Or so I thought. When, in 1989, I asked my pal Bill Drummond to remix 'Melting Blue Delicious' off my *Space Flower* album for potential release as a single, he asked me if I wanted him to include any samples on it.

'Yes,' I replied. 'Immigrant Song' by Led Zeppelin.

As if to prove my belief that magic is real, as Bill was entering the recording studio, who should be coming out but Robert Plant. Seeing his own work tucked under Bill's arm, he asked what was afoot. Bill came clean and gingerly told Robert the plan to sample it for a Liverpool band called The Wild Swans.

'Cool,' said Robert. 'I'm just glad I'm still considered relevant.'

Anyway, right now, I've got it into my head that the coolest thing I can do—the coolest thing *anyone* can do in this, the last decade of the millennium—is to front an incredible (if not entirely credible) heavy metal band. I mean, my post-*Space Flower* long hair is now down to my shoulders. I'm at the point where people are shouting 'Catweasel' at me in the street.

I'm not stupid. I know Iron Maiden fans will never accept us, but they are not my target audience. I'm going to scoop up every lost, disenchanted, and bored indie kid, cut off the top of his head, and remove his brain before washing it in a bucket of clean, ice-cold, water before plopping it back, ENLIGHTENED. Fuck The Smiths. Kids don't want Charles Hawtrey and Ena Sharples as their role models anymore! They want Kabbalistic symbolist poetry fused to a riff machine. If Wild Swans fans stuck with me after the overproduced and bombastic letdown of *Bringing Home The Ashes*, and the bat-shit curveball I threw them with the bubblegum-pop of *Space Flower*, surely they can handle my latest nonsense.

—

Briiing briiing.

'Yep?'

'Hello. Is that Dave? My name is Paul. I am ringing about your advert in Micro Music for a singer for your band.'

I've braced myself for the forensic grilling on who my favourite bands are, so, bypassing the actual good stuff he won't have heard of, like Garmr, Fissure Of Sylvius, or German Oak, and avoiding the thorny subject of subgenres entirely, I'll play safe and answer truthfully with the holy trinity of first-generation British metal bands he's already listed. It is, after all, the metalhead's equivalent of The Velvet Underground, The Stooges, and—

'Have you got your own PA?'

'Er, no,' I reply. 'But I do have a record deal.'

'So, no PA then?'

'No Dave,' I reply. 'We won't need one. The venues we play will supply the PA. But I have got a record deal waiting.'

Incredibly, this isn't a lie. I really do have a carte-blanche offer of a major record deal from a friend who is about to head up the A&R department of a new major label.

'We're looking for someone with their own PA,' says Dave.

'Right. But I've already had two major label record contracts. I could get us up and running very quickly.'

'You'll need your own PA.'

'For rehearsals, you mean?' I ask.

'For everything. Rehearsals and gigs.'

'The rehearsal rooms I use in town already supply their own PA systems.'

'Yeah, right.'

'Really! A rehearsal PA would be far too small to use for gigs anyway,' I say. What is he? Nuts? 'We'd be playing sizable venues, Dave, not pubs. Certainly big enough that we wouldn't nee—'

'You can't play gigs without your own fuckin' PA, mate.' Only forty seconds in and Dave is already sounding pissed off with me.

'Er, well, we really can bypass all that hard work. I have a record deal in place. We can rehearse in the professional practice rooms I use in town. Every room in there has its own—'

'Have you got your own microphone?'

'Mics are supplied along with the PA, Dave. It's all set up and waiting when you arrive.' I go on. 'I was thinking we'd rehearse for a month, go straight into the studio. Get a single out this autumn, and then tour the album.' I wait for his response. 'Hello . . . hello?'

Stressing all three syllables hard, he butts in, 'Stu-di-oh? Where's *Studio*?'

Ah. He must think Studio is the name of a venue or a club.

'Err . . . the recording studio? I was thinking we'd bash out some rough demos for this label I mentioned. If we moved fast, we could have a single out in the autumn and an album out in the new year. I have a bit of a following in America and Japan already, so once the album is released, we could get out to the metal-head heartlands of LA and New Yor—'

'Mate, you gotta have your own PA.'

'Dave, I don't think you quite understand. I'm not talking about playing pub gigs. I'm talking about breaking America.' He's gone quiet. 'Hello? Dave? Hello?'

'Did you even read the fuckin' advert, mate?'

'Yes. Yes, I did. I'm holding it now.'

'*Must have own PA*,' he mimics.

Just before the phone line goes dead, I hear Dave snarl-whispering.

'Un-be-fuckin-lievable! No fuckin' PA! Fuckin' timewaster!'

Oh well. I wanted visionless wankers, and I got one.

PART SEVEN

| MIND LAGOONS
| 1998–2009

I
TINKYFUCKINGWINKY

MARCH 1998. GLASGOW BARROWLANDS. Echo & The Bunnymen are on the UK leg of their *Evergreen* comeback album tour. Mac's two solo albums and the Bunnymen's album without him, *Reverberation*, have long passed, the short-lived Electrafixion is over, and Les Pattinson is back in the band. Their new single, 'Nothing Lasts Forever', is getting airplay, and Glasgow is excited.

Dressed in a brilliant white zipper jacket and white jeans, I am standing here in the semi-darkness, playing live bass guitar to a DAT tape of pre-recorded backing tracks of the two eighteen-minute-long kraut/prog-rock instrumental singles I have released through Dave Battersby's Cheltenham-based indie label, Ochre Records.

At the lip of the stage, a pair of slide projectors face inward, shining an assortment of graphic horror sci-fi images I've hastily prepared across me and onto the projection screen behind me. Because my debut single as Skyray, 'Invisible', was released a transparent ten-inch record, the idea is that I become invisible within the projections.

After the Wild Swans mk2 debacle ended in tears eight years ago, I metaphorically lost my voice, yet after a break of five years and a twelve-month fellowship at John Moores University, I wanted an outlet for my creativity that allowed me some anonymity. Tonight, I'm trying to give this 1980s Bunnyfan pop/rock audience a *Wire* magazine-style 'art' performance. You know, a *so NOT rock'n'roll that it IS rock'n'roll* thing. Or at least I would be pushing that if the projection screen hadn't just fallen over and landed on my back.

The Bunnymen's road crew and guitar tech are nowhere to be seen—they must be off having sex and cocaine sandwiches, or whatever road crew do—so I'm up here trying to hold the screen up with my shoulders while trying to stay in the pocket of this eighteen-minute long 'Taxman'-on-Mogadon bass line.

Oh, Christ! I am dying up here. *Stan! Peasey! Where are you?*

Just to compound matters, because there is so much of the Bunnymen's gear on such a shallow stage, and because the screen has fallen on top of me, I have been forced into moving even further downstage than I already was. I am now playing just a few feet away from the lip of the stage where my two slide projectors are flickering away. There is now too little distance between me and the projectors for the images to expand to anything like their intended size, so instead of my being lost in a twelve-foot cube of sci-fi horror imagery, I'm standing here in semi-darkness with a foot-wide square of light shining onto my chest.

The die-hard Bunnyfans who are clinging to their hard-fought-for places at the forestage are looking puzzled. They can't get an angle on this support act at all. Desperately trying to maintain some dignity, I'm attempting to project some cool *Tony Conrad playing at the Kitchen in New York in the early 1970s* dealio, but nothing is getting projected tonight because I look and feel like a fucking Teletubby.

Inching slowly myself backwards until the projection screen rights itself, I unplug my bass and walk sheepishly offstage to the dressing room, where I drown the last remaining atom of my dignity in a tumbler full of vodka.

II
ZOOM THE AMPLITUDE

SPRING 1998. Tiring of the repetitive dream-kraut blueprint I have employed these past two years with my instrumental Skyray project, a pleasing Les Baxter-on-ketamine feel has found its way into my latest home-produced demos. Coincidentally, I have been engrossed in a 1953 book by Jacques Cousteau on his pioneering work developing the aqualung for the French Navy. Informed by this, a nautical concept album is born: sultry sirens, sunken ships, haunted islands. When Jon Savage drops in on the recording session at Henry Priestman's Gossamer Dome Studios on Anglesey and hears my proposed album title, *Mind Lagoons*, he jokingly reprimands me, 'Paul, now you're going too far.' Just wait until Henry zooms the amplitude on the computer monitor next door and Jon sees how the waveforms of my work in progress resemble an endless line of syringes injecting themselves . . .

While recording the album's title track with my new band, The Undersea Research Group (Henry, Alan Holmes, John Lawrence, Mike Ward, and Mike Cross), I am overtaken by the desire to break my vow of vocal chastity and narrate something on top. Out of my subconscious swims a diver who hallucinates that he is making love somewhere among the turquoise breakers of the south seas. In reality, he is trapped beneath an oil rig in the freezing North Sea, slowly dying from nitrogen poisoning.

The narration works but for one thing: my voice. To my mind, I still sound like a middle-class vicar trying to 'get down' with the kids. The psychological value of my voice is entirely wrong for both the project and for these late-period Britpop/*Spice World*/Robbie Williams dumbed-down times. I love Art Garfunkel's perfect diction, but I bet he wishes he mumbled like Lou Reed sometimes.

Midway through the ten-day recording session, I drive back to Liverpool for the weekend and play a rough mix of the title track to my wife, Jan.

'You know who would be perfect for this?' she suggests. 'Bill Drummond.'

She's right, he would, but as he has publicly declared that he has turned his back on music, he would never agree.

—

Picking Bill up from Runcorn railway station, he utters a spectacularly understated, 'Morning, Paul,' as he slings his backpack into the rear of my car. In the five years since we last saw each other—a chance meeting outside London's National Gallery—he's posted me some of his Penkiln Burn pamphlets and we've exchanged catch-up emails but nothing more. I'm pleased to see him and grateful he's taken time out to do this for me. As ever, Bill is dressed in his signature jeans and plaid shirt—the same classic beatnik look he was wearing when I first saw him climb onstage with Big In Japan twenty-one years ago.

In travelling light, Bill travels far. He's the inverse of me in every way. Bill knows that the ultimate cool is to keep it Neal Cassidy simple, while I change my clothes just to greet the postman.

While Bill had been to the National Gallery that day in 1993 to catch *The Great Age Of British Watercolours 1750–1880*, I was there to observe four exiled Tibetan Monks create, then, after forty hours of work, ritually destroy, intricate Buddhist sand mandalas. This beautiful variance in us is reason enough for Bill and me to become collaborators.

'*Could it be a devil in me, or is this the way love is supposed to be?*'

'Paul. Can we turn the music off?'

'*It's like a heatw—*'

This recent 'no music' declaration of Bill's is hard to swallow. I cannot conceive of the hour-and-a-half car journey from Runcorn to Anglesey ahead of us without listening to something of the divine art. Be it Vaughan Williams, Burzum, Funkadelic, or the Vienna Wankers Choir, tarmac loves a soundtrack. The word 'music' may be a translation of the Latin *art of the muses*, but I prefer the story of how, after the concept of rhythm and tone was revealed to the prophet Musa (or Moses) on Mount Sinai, he later tried to describe the miracle he had been gifted to his followers by simply repeating the holy command he'd heard: 'Musa ke!' or 'Moses hear!'

I used to think Bill's slight emotional detachment when communicating hid either a childhood trauma similar to my own or some terrible secret. Maybe I still do. As co-architect of the gazillion-selling, post-rave subversives The KLF, Bill certainly had the perfect cover for arson, bombings, or serial murder. Mark 'Zodiac Mindwarp' Manning's brilliantly extreme fantasy-fiction version of 'Meester Beel' in the duo's book collaborations *Bad Wisdom* and *The Wild Highway* is so convincing that it is all too easy to picture Bill hunched behind the wheel of his battered Ford Fuck-Truck thundering up and down the M25 each night like Neken, the evil spirit of the north, *Twenty Line-Dancing Greats* blasting out as he scopes the hard shoulder, looking for lone breakdowns and teen runaways.

Apart from the tongue-tripping opening line, 'Green phosphorescence swam through her fingers', once Bill is behind the microphone, he reads my story exactly how I'd imagined he would. He's laying on the Scottish accent thicker than Harris tweed, but it's perfect. I love it. Twenty-five minutes later, it is done.

After lunch at the Kinmel Arms in Moelfre, I drop Bill at Bangor railway station, and he's gone. Texting me from the train, Bill requests that I credit him on the album sleeve under his 'porno' name of Tenzing Scott-Brown. To find your porno name, you take the name of your first pet and combine it with your mother's maiden name. Mine is Snowy Atkinson.

Understandable as his decision is, it's frustrating to have Bill Drummond of The KLF on your album and not be allowed to say so, but Bill is adamant—he doesn't want to be seen to be reneging on his current 'no music' stance. Fair enough, but I can't help but be suspicious. Bill is too well-informed on all the latest musical subgenres, bands, and their releases. Maybe he gets it all second-hand from his son, but I bet if we poked about in his office down in Aylesbury, we'd find the latest copies of *Q* and *Mojo* sandwiched between back issues of *Guns & Ammo*, *Anal Witchcraft*, and *Menstruating Fuck Bunny*. Damn! Manning's dark fantasy version of Bill is bleeding over into my reality.

III

SATAN DIES SCREAMING

APRIL 2000. JULIAN COPE'S CORNUCOPEA, LONDON. I'm in my room at the Feathers Hotel on the South Bank, watching *Forbidden Planet* on TV, when my mobile phone rings. It's Liz McCudden at the Royal Festival Hall. She tells me she has been trying to reach me all day, and would I like to play 'Sleeping Gas' onstage with Julian tonight?

My silence stretches from here to the moon.

'You don't sound too keen,' she says.

Having only met me for the first time yesterday, Cornucopea festival organiser Liz hasn't quite got the measure of me yet. She's yet to discover that no matter how positively I present, I'm as negative as an electron. I kid myself that my auto-response of '*nein, danke*' to just about everything I'm offered is discernment, but the truth is, it's fear; a still-active phobia from childhood about being caught up in events beyond my control.

Backed on pianos by Welsh wizard David Wrench and Henry Priestman, I performed as a three-piece Skyray to an almost full house at the festival last night and no one died, so what am I scared of? Well, it's been twenty-one years since Ju and I last played onstage together, and a lot of dirty water has flowed in and out of the mouth of the Mersey since then. And, as such, this invitation is a big deal for both of us. But because I've been drinking Malbec since 11am, and because I love Copey to bits for asking me, I'm horrified to hear myself say, 'I'll be right over.'

—

Julian beams as I arrive. We hug, and I scan the vast stage, wondering where the keyboard is. I'd kill to play his M400 Mellotron, but I'm anticipating some sort of high-end Yamaha portable, duct-taped to a stand. His grin widens, Loki-style, as he gestures to the Leviathan that occupies the entire rear wall of the venue.

Holy mother of Odin. Does he mean to tell me that I, Paul Simpson,

Two-finger Joe, am expected to play a song I haven't heard in ten years and haven't played in over twenty, to an audience of over two-thousand people, in a venue renowned for having the best acoustics in the world, on one of the largest and most spectacular pipe organs in the country?

Stretching the entire width of the hall, this Satanic torture device could block out the sun. It has four five-octave keyboards, one hundred and three drawer stops, dozens upon dozens of thankfully disabled bass pedals, and an unbelievable seven thousand, eight hundred, and sixty-six individual pipes. The organ I played with The Teardrop Explodes had vibrato and an on/off button.

With the house doors about to open and no time for a soundcheck, Julian quickly cycles the riff on his twelve-string while I find my bearings. At Ju's insistence, his lovely sidekick, Thighpaulsandra, puts black tape on the notes that make up a D chord. Julian's saying it's so I can see them in the gloom at the back of the auditorium, but I suspect it's really so he has something to joke about with the audience when he next plays in Liverpool. Northern audiences are frequently regaled with his story of how, in the early Teardrop Explodes, I couldn't play the keyboards properly. He's right. I couldn't. I wasn't trying to. Anyway, right now my old bandmate doesn't trust me not to fuck up, and he's absolutely right. There is no monitoring back here, the organ console is lit by what looks like children's torch bulbs, and, let's face it, I can barely remember my way back to the hotel, let alone the upbeat and opiated kinder-drone of 'Sleeping Gas'.

Because tonight has been sprung on me, I've nothing remotely suitable to wear. Julian is channelling some kind of Viking berserker meets outer-space yoga instructor look, so I can't possibly wear the tweed suit and brogues I came in or we'll look like George Jetson jamming with Sherlock Holmes. All I have in my overnight bag is a dark brown leather jacket cut in the style of a Levi's and some slim, stone-coloured trousers. Brilliant. I finally get a chance of performing to an audience of thousands, and I have to do it dressed like I'm in Tight-Fit's 'The Lion Sleeps Tonight' video.

Finally, it's showtime. Incredibly, I've not seen Copey perform for over two decades, and only once as a member of the audience, when The Wild Swans supported the third incarnation of the Teardrops as part of Bill Drummond's Club Zoo shenanigans back in December 1981. Apart from a couple of his 80s hits and a handful of songs from his *Fried* and *Interpreter* albums, I don't know many of the songs from tonight's repertoire, but they sound uniformly brilliant. He's going down a storm, and his between-song anecdotes, delivered in his understated *Kevin Ayers circa 1971* speak, are hilarious.

A terrible thought steals into my mind. What if I really screw this up? Not only could I ruin our rendering of our much-loved classic Zoo Records debut, but I could neutralise the magic of this entire event.

Eyeing the exit doors, I consider doing a Stephen Fry: 10:05 from Liverpool Street to Harwich—night boat to the Hoek of Holland—first train to Amsterdam Centraal. I could be canal-side, drinking coffee with a selection of delicious pastries, by 6am. I'm on after the next song. In a last-moment attempt to appear more Red Army Faction than Mike Nolan from Buck's Fizz, I button my jacket up to the neck and prepare to enter Planet Cope.

'*Now, I'd like to introduce a very special guest. Co-founder of The Teardrop Explodes, Paul Simpson!*'

Climbing the steps to the stage, I pause momentarily to draw down some protection before walking out of the darkness and into a pool of brilliant white light. Greeted by genuine whoops of surprise and wild applause from the hall, I smile and wave as if this Dalinian situation were in any way normal for me. A quick *let's do this* nod to Copey and I stride upstage in the direction of the steps that lead up to the mighty organ. But something's wrong. Very wrong.

Where are the steps? The steps up to the organ? The beautiful solid mahogany steps that were there at the soundcheck? The massive steps that enable the organist to reach his seat at the keyboard of this King-Kong of instruments? There is an acute absence of steps.

Built into the very fabric of the building, this monstrous organ can only be played from an elevated position with one's back to the audience. Clearly not briefed on the last-minute changes to Julian's stage requirements, a member of staff, unaware the instrument was being used tonight, has, I presume, wheeled them off into the wings.

Faced with a Christ-knows-how-high wall of polished wood to scale and no discernible hand or footholds, I am clueless about how to proceed. I mean, even the Spinal Tap guys would consider this too moronic a situation to create for their seminal mockumentary. Mercifully, because of a towering wall of amplification, only people seated in the higher tiers or the boxes at the sides of the venue are witness to my humiliation. My heart is in my brogues. I'm Frodo standing quaking at the foot of Mount Doom.

Fuelled by terror alone, I leap, and somehow, miraculously, I manage to get my fingers into a recessed lip halfway up the wooden panelling of the back wall. Channelling my inner Chris Bonnington, I haul myself up and up and over the edge, where I clamber awkwardly into the instrument's cockpit. Eager to begin, I'm flexing my fingers like a brain surgeon in a horror film, but Julian hasn't finished with me. Laughing down the microphone, I hear him say, 'He's so reluctant! Paul, come down here.'

Oh, God! I'm so bad at this. I should have given him a showbiz hug when I walked on or something. In his defence, from his vantage point upstage facing his adoring audience, my old friend has no idea about the missing steps or the Herculean task I just pulled off getting up there. Reversing the process, hanging by my fingertips, I drop back down to the stage below, nearly twisting my ankle as I do so. With counterfeit bravado, I stroll back into the blazing arena of the pop damned.

Enveloping me in a huge embrace, Copey grins. He knows I'm not good at this rock'n'roll stuff. Judging from the appreciative reaction of the crowd, I suspect many in the audience honestly believe that this is the first time Julian and I have seen each other since I left The Teardrop Explodes in 1979. Trying not to let my uptight reserve spoil things, I hug him back. Am I doing this right? Am I acting appropriately? I genuinely have no idea. I know more about witchcraft than I do about stagecraft. I am, after all, the man Sire Records boss Seymour Stein reprimanded for playing most of a Wild Swans gig in London with my back to the audience.

For the second time in three minutes, I scale the polished walls of the pale wooden K2. Back on the padded organ bench, my heart is beating paradiddles no drummer could replicate. The Harwich ferry has sailed. There's no escape. Here it comes.

'One-two-three-four.'

NEE-NAW, NEE-NAW, NEE-NAW, NEE-NAW.

NEE-NAW, NEE-NAW, NEE-NAW, NEE-NAW.

'Sometimes I wonder if you're really living.'

Pumping away on these ludicrous disco octaves, I can barely hear Julian at all, so I'm counting the bars to know when to go into the big chorus chords. I catch the first chorus but, typical of me, I become preoccupied with trying to decode the symbols and abbreviations on the organ drawers. Back here all alone, my mind has wandered, and I miss the second. I can't hear anything but me. I feel like a passenger who, informed the pilot is ill—and only because he once assembled a balsa-wood model glider—has to help land a 747 full of schoolkids. Am I even vaguely keeping time?

Oh, fuck it! Paul, just keep going.

Before I know it, it's the final round of choruses and I play the sacred power chords right on cue.

Woah! That sounds incredible—like Titan rising from the depths.

I wonder what will happen if I add a lower octave again? Even with the music issuing from the pipes literally going over my head, the sound is MASSIVE. If I can just reach that last, lowest D note with my little finger, we might really have something.

BWAAAAAAAAAAAAAAAAAAH!

Huge, jagged fissures appear in the walls of the Festival Hall and masonry rains down from the ceiling. Unable to absorb the low-end vibrations, the entire roof tears off and is sucked, spinning away across the River Thames, revealing the twinkling, diamond-encrusted starry grandeur of the universe. Gabriel has blown his horn. Jericho's walls have collapsed and Satan dies screaming.

A quick bow and I'm heading for the stage door, letting Julian take his well-earned curtain call. He must be exhausted. Not just from the gig but from organising this entire weekend. The logistics of getting Coil and Klaus Schulze and Manuel Göttsching to agree to perform as Ash Ra Tempel alone!

Backstage, in the gent's toilet, strange eyes are boring a hole into the back of my skull. They belong to a striking, salt-and-pepper-haired gentleman in a polka-dot shirt.

'Was that you playing the organ just now?'

'I'm afraid so,' I say.

'Awesome,' he replies.

It's Julian's sonic reflection, King of the Brit-psych Old Gods, Robyn Hitchcock. Bloody hell. I need a drink.

—

The Green Room is, as expected, orchestra-sized, and, in order to subdue any possibility of rock'n'roll behaviour, horribly over-lit. Important-looking strangers queue to vigorously shake my hand. Apparently 'that' was amazing. Head honcho and creator of the famous Meltdown Festivals Dave Sefton and Cornucopea organiser Liz McCudden come sweeping up.

'That was such a moment, Paul!' says Dave.

'They don't happen very often, and that? That was a moment,' says Liz.

Blimey! Was it? I wished I'd been in the audience to see and hear it. Pouring myself a much-needed large glass of hospitality, I spot Julian near the door. He's the one in the lurid manmade fibres looking like a Medieval jester and MTV-era David Lee Roth gene-splice experiment. Brilliant. Considering he's pulled off a monumental event, he appears a little subdued. Is he pissed off with me? I have no idea. I hope not. Perhaps he'd planned to do more encores. I'm sorry, Copey, but you did ask me.

Four, five-octave keyboards, 103 drawer stops, and 7,866 individual pipes? Even Rick Wakeman would have given that mother a swerve.

IV

DRIVING INTO MORDOR

2000. NORTH WALES. Driving across the Runcorn Bridge at 7am, dawn breaking over a chocolate-coloured Mersey, I'm heading southwest on the A557 for North Wales and the welcoming lights of the Gossamer Dome recording studio in Moelfre, on the island of Anglesey. Coasting through the dead lands, I'm lost in an eerie pre-storm light that turns the sky to negative and the sparse clumps of gorse and hawthorn a surreal shade of radiation green. Across the bay, Hale Head Lighthouse is lost in shadow, and as the ultra-violet gantry lights of the Rocksavage heavy chemical works loom into view, the temperature drops and a vast cloak of rain envelops the M56. It feels like I'm driving into Mordor.

A CD of Agitation Free's *Malesh*, a recent birthday present from my friend, Serpents co-founder and Skyray collaborator Alan Holmes, is weaving its smoky Eastern tapestry on the car stereo, while spheres of orange sodium light slide up the windscreen like wax in a lava lamp. The car's petrol tank is full of unleaded, and the glove compartment is stuffed with music compilations and cheap sweets. I've got the fuel, I've got the drugs—I'm a one-man road movie.

I am heading to Moelfre to record a new Skyray track for *Interface*, a CD compilation of contemporary electronic artists to be released by Space Age Recordings, home of Sonic Boom and the Spacemen 3 back catalogue. The deadline is up and I haven't composed a note, but of course Space Age and my old pal Henry Priestman, co-pilot and producer of this session, don't know this. I may not have a flight plan, but I do have the means to gain altitude: several bottles of Bordeaux, a 35mm film canister of Northern Lights (an indica hybrid), and 'Ornate Flame Terminal'—a song title loaded with kaleidoscopic promise. A characteristic of Northern Lights is its ten-minute slow fuse, just long enough for you to forget that you're trying to get high. You find yourself thinking about something mundane, then *Kaboom!* You're flying.

By Queensferry, I'm driving on autopilot, my mind a swirling soup of abstract thought. The eternal struggle between good and evil, the inevitability of death, and which *Blue Peter* presenter I'd like to have sex with.

So far on this journey, I've annihilated a family-sized bag of mesquite-flavoured kettle chips, two russet apples, six strawberry laces, and half a roll of Lovehearts. I'm in the throws of a major sugar rush and my blood runs thick with warring chemicals. But what's this? Swizzels Matlow, manufacturers of the Loveheart, have decided to update their childhood classic by changing the phrases printed on some of their sweets. The last time I ate these pastel-coloured delights, they had cute 50s-sounding phrases like *Oh Boy!*, *Be Mine*, and *Sweetheart*. Now I'm disgusted to find they also include *Page Me*, *E-mail*, and, bizarrely, *Web-Site*. I'm incensed. Why wasn't I consulted about this? Yes, I know there are bigger problems facing the world than this right now, but to my pot-addled brain, it's just another nail in the coffin of my youth, like Palitoy selling Action Man to Hasbro, the BBC cancelling *Noggin The Nog* and Cadbury's doing away with Lucky Numbers and the Bar Six. If the whiz kid marketing team that works for Lovehearts is so intent on being contemporary, why don't they go the whole hog and print their delicious kinderdrügs with phrases like *Crack*, *Rohypnol*, and *New World Order*?

Swerving to avoid a shredded lorry tyre in the road, I adjust the balance of the car's stereo system to favour the left channel. I'm partially deaf in that ear due to what has to be my earliest sonic experiment. It was during the sweltering summer holidays of 1970 that my father brought home a beech veneered stereo system to replace the Pye mono player that was exhumed every other Sunday to enrich our lives with Ray Charles, Nina

& Frederic, and a fresh-from-Tiger-Bay Shirley Bassey. The moment my parents left the new record player unattended, I lay down on the carpet and positioned my head between its speakers. Then, pulling them to my ears like a pair of giant headphones, I turned the volume dial up as far as it would go, filling my head with a deafening white noise. A slow sucking sensation in my left ear followed by a gentle popping sound, and *Hey Presto!* I've been asking people to repeat themselves ever since.

Pulling off the A55 now and following signs for Penmaenmawr, I'm early, so I look for directions to the Druids' Circle, the ring of ancient granite stones and megaliths that Copey wrote about in his recently published cosmic Yellow Pages, *The Modern Antiquarian*. It's still only 8am, and apart from the village postman there's not a soul on the streets. Slowing to a stop alongside him, I open the passenger window, lean across, and politely ask for directions. Removing his Walkman headphones, he bends down and does a Ben Turpin silent-movie double-take before backing up and speed-walking away. WTF?

'Thanks for your help!' I shout after him.

Checking myself in the rear-view mirror, all becomes clear. I look deranged! If White Noise's *Electric Storm* album issuing from the cassette player and the twelve-pointer stag antlers and bleached rabbit skulls still on the back window shelf from my recent trip to the Highlands weren't enough to spook the postie, my asking for directions to the Druid's Circle through lips and tongue stained a bloody E-number red from the cheap sweet orgy probably clinched it. I'll be the talk of the village pub this lunchtime, and the stuff of local legend by the weekend.

—

When *Mind Lagoons* was released in June of 1999, it sold well and got stellar reviews in both the rock press and the major dance-music magazines, but after my spoken-word album *The Dream Diaries*, the *Ice Rink Music* EP, and *Liquid Crystal Display* all pass by unnoticed, I decide to put Skyray to bed forever.

Knut Hamsun once said that he wrote to kill time; well, I have just murdered nearly a decade of my life on a project that for the most part went unheard. Skyray was never going to be the great ladder of ascent or top the peak orphic moments I had enjoyed with The Wild Swans, but it did allow me a creative outlet in a barren time, and a chance to decompress for a few weeks each year while dealing with the stresses of my father's terminal illness and co-parenting my young son, Ben.

I don't want these Skyray albums to be my last recorded statements. Shelving plans for my *Death Ray* album, I dump the remaining Skyray back catalogue in a skip at the Waste Recycling Centre in Bootle, dropping boxes of a hundred CDs at a time into the recently emptied 'hard plastics' skip. They land with a satisfying, reverberating clang.

V

DEMONISED

2005. SOMEWHERE IN LANCASHIRE. Booking an appointment to talk with a Church of England vicar about demon infestation is harder than you might think. But after two weeks, a dozen phone calls, and a brief 'check he's not a crank' meeting with go-between verger Christine, I've done it. Eleven o'clock Wednesday morning outside the church, and disappointingly Michael, the vicar, has left a note pinned to the door. He won't see me in his church but in the church hall opposite. Well, that's a blow—I wanted the full holy-water Sani-flush exorcism at the font.

The door to the church hall is answered by one of those generic, white-perm old dears whose responsibilities include changing the dirty flower water in the vestry and mopping out after the carnage that is the Country Dancing Society. Ushered into a back room, I'm further disappointed. This is too small! There's nothing in here but stacked chairs. Where is the vicar going to tie me down and brandish his flaming cross?

Offered neither tea nor biscuits, I'm left alone for twenty fucking minutes. I know the vicar is here because I saw him arrive shortly after I did, so what is he doing? Maybe he's back there with a towel around his neck, working out on a punchbag, getting himself match-fit for the great showdown with the antichrist.

When the Reverend Michael eventually enters the room, he won't look at me. Really? Is he scared that something unholy will jump out of my eyes and straight into his? Wishing him a good morning, I extend my hand for him to shake, but he won't take it. Bit rude. I mean, why make this situation even weirder than it already is? He's not Denzel Washington in *Fallen*.

Early fifties, running to fat, greying hair cut by Lancashire County Council, Michael is so physically vague a child given a lump of dirty pink Playdough could fashion a better vicar.

In trying to normalise things, I'm being too friendly and overpolite, but all I'm doing is making him scared. I know he has been pre-briefed by his lovely verger as to why I am here, so why is he exerting so much effort to pretend that he hasn't?

'So, Paul, is it?' He's pacing now. 'What can I do for you?'

'Well,' I reply, desperately trying not to sound mad. 'Thank you for seeing me. I'm sorry to bother you, but I don't have anyone else I can talk to about this.'

He's still not looking at me. He's looking down at his black slip-on vicar shoes, and now I am too. They look like charred pig snouts. Slip-ons. Where do you even buy shoes like that? Is there an ecclesiastical shopping catalogue of these things?

'Go on,' he says.

'I'm having nightmares.'

'Yes?'

'Every night,' I continue. 'Nightmares about demons. It's been going on for months—years, actually. My whole life, in effect. But they are particularly bad right now. I am exhausted with it.'

No reaction. Nothing. I'm waiting for his gently probing questions, his soothing wisdom, his empathy, sympathy, anything, but he's giving me the ecclesiastical permafrost and thereby forcing me into more talk.

'They are all variations of the same nightmare, really,' I continue. 'I'm in a remote location—a house, a church, a ruin.'

His ears prick up at the word *church*, but still no eye contact. Has he never seen the *Omen* trilogy, or *The Exorcist*? The priest has to feed the conversation! We can't both be weird, Michael, or we'll never get this project green-lit.

'Err . . . well,' I continue. 'Last night's nightmare wasn't entirely typical, but it does fit the general template. Last night, I dreamt I was waiting at a dusty, moonlit crossroads—you know like Robert Johnson?'

Okay. That was too much. He doesn't know who Robert Johnson is. Probably doesn't know who David Bowie is.

'When an enormous harpy landed directly before me.'

No reaction.

'You know, the mythological creature? Half-bird, half-woman? Beautiful, actually. Very sexual. Like Halle Berry with feathers. Top half-naked woman, bottom half . . . kestrely. With talons.'

Kestrely? Did I really just say that?

'She was wary of me at first, keeping her distance, pacing back and forth raising dust. I could feel her trying to read me. Somehow I knew that she'd never seen a human before and she was curious, and trying to gauge how powerful I was.'

Still nothing. Michael is still staring at those godawful shoes of his while making a little church steeple with his fingers.

'What happened next is what always happens in these nightmares of mine. She slowly began striding toward me on her scaly hawk legs. I wasn't scared at this point; in fact, I was filled with a sense of righteousness. Feeling invincible, I advanced to meet her. In these dreams I always feel all-powerful, convinced of my authority to subdue these demons. And subdue her I do. Raising my hand, I fill myself with holy light and she reacts, shrinking away, cowering, her hawk eyes blinking in confusion and fear. As I advance, I am willing her into the ground, back to Hell and out of my plane of existence. This is when she attacks. Because, of course, this is not my plane of existence. It's a nightmare, so I'm astral travelling.'

Okay. I know I've gone too far and I'm near babbling at the vicar now, but if I stop I'll lose the most important part of the dream.

'Anyway, she's furious and savagely tearing at me and way more powerful than I ever imagined, and I wake in a cold sweat, flailing and shouting out. My skin crawling. The worst part is, I could feel her horrible presence in the room with me. Like the distillation of her evil has travelled over with me from sleep into our reality.'

Tumbleweed . . . no reaction whatsoever. Nada. Now, mad as I may be, even I know that was the best bit of drama he's witnessed so far this week.

I can't bear the silence. Does Michael simply think some scally baghead has wandered in here?

I cut to the quick.

'I need your help, Vicar. I was wondering if you could give me a blessing or something?'

Eventually, and with a thousand tons per square inch of reluctance, he stands and places his splayed sausage fingers upon my recently washed-for-the-occasion head, and he mutters some words I can barely make out in a voice duller and flatter than Norfolk. I can't hear him, and I'm pretty sure Halle Kestrel and all my residual demons can't either. I was hoping for a bit of liturgical Latin, but he could just be fobbing me off with the tagline in a TV advert:

One thousand and one cleans a big, big carpet, for less than half a crown.
It's the fish that John West reject that makes John West the best.

Whatever he's saying, it takes about fifteen seconds, tops. There's no blinding light, no spiritual transference, no vibrationary cleansing, no epiphany or redemption.

And that is when I know. I know with absolute certainty that this man is entirely without faith. He doesn't believe in God, the Holy Spirit, or the little baby Jesus. He has no power or authority to bless me, pray for me, or even comfort me as a fellow human being.

It took some balls for me to walk in here this morning. Boy, do I feel swizzed! This is not a joke to me. I am desperate. Tears are streaming down my face, but Michael just stands there, looking embarrassed. He knows that I have him sussed. I should have gone to the Catholics—they'd have loved this. I'd be seated in the priest's office, slurping tea and eating the cream of his M&S chocolate assortment now while he telephoned Rome for permission. He'd be rubbing his hands with glee, impatiently waiting to turn me inside out.

Exiting the church hall, I walk back to where I left my old Nissan Micra outside the church. That's when I hear someone whistling in the graveyard. I know that Sinatra tune . . .

I'm half a mile away when, with a shudder, it comes to me.

I've got no defense for it
The heat is too intense for it
What good would common sense for it do
'Cause it's witchcraft, wicked witchcraft

VI
SHUT UP AND KISS ME

2008. Her breath is hot and sweet, and her musky perfume wraps itself about me like an exploratory tentacle. *My God!* I think. *Life has finally found me!* I always suspected that beneath the mundane surface layer of existence lay hidden substrata of magic, where, if one could only tune in to it, the genuinely miraculous happens.

I'm attending the opening of a new restaurant. Uniformed waiters serve canapés, and the champagne is flowing. After chatting to the owner for a few minutes, I decide to explore the lower dining room of the two-storey building.

Descending the staircase, I become aware that I am being stared at by a stunning-looking woman with eyes of the rarest sapphire blue. My gorgeous observer resembles nothing less than Valentina Vostok from the *Doom Patrol* comics, and she may well have trained a sniper's laser sights upon me. Maintaining her gaze, I plough through the crowd toward her, as though we are the only two people in the room.

'You look breathtaking,' I say. 'Who are you?'

Instead of answering my question, she stuns me by slipping her hand into mine and leaning in close to me. With her lips against my ear, she exhales her whispered command.

'Kiss me.'

I'm shot through. Done for. Ended. Only a film star or a real-life spy could be so ridiculously cool. Well, kill me if you must, Valentina. If there is poison on your lips, I don't care; death will be a small price to pay for the unique thrill you have sparked in me. This is by far the most exciting thing that's happened to me in, well . . . ever.

Gently taking her face in my hands, I kiss her full and deep on the lips for far longer than is appropriate in this well-lit and very crowded room. When I let go, she gasps and wobbles a little, shooting out an arm to steady herself upon me.

No longer a spy, she now resembles a fragile Victorian undergoing an attack of the vapours. I'm totally confused, until with eyes wide, she laughs breathlessly.

'I said . . . my name . . . was Kitty.'

VII
MY LIFE WEIGHS A TON

SEPTEMBER 2009. The evening has grown wild about me. Dead leaves swirl in turbulent eddies while wheelie bins topple under driving, *Whistle Down The Wind*, Lancashire rain. I'm sitting on a yellow metal railway station bench where three red fire buckets used to hang, one filled with water and two with sand. In the 1960s, in autumn and winter, a coal fire was kept permanently stoked in the grate of this station's now permanently locked waiting room. If the uniformed station master spotted me swinging my little legs on one of the slatted wooden benches in there, he'd chat with my mum, ruffle my hair, and offer us chocolate biscuits from a tin. Now he's long dead, my mum has early-stage vascular dementia, and a lone Merseyrail operative sits scowling at me behind toughened safety glass while counting the day's takings. Maybe I'm radiating some negative aura tonight? Christ knows I have nothing to be positive about right now. When did the colour drain from my world?

I've had a spectacularly horrible day. It started at 8am this morning, when my Micra finally gave up the ghost outside my home in South Liverpool, necessitating a ten-minute walk in the rain before catching two trains to get to my childhood home to care for my elderly mother. Frustratingly, I missed both trains by just moments and had to wait on a graffiti-covered bench without cover in the rain.

After a forty-five-minute train journey and a fifteen-minute walk, I finally arrived at my mum's house only for the landline to ring the moment I turned the key. It was my old pal Les, informing me that Jake 'Fifth Bunnyman' Drake-Brockman had died after crashing his vintage BSA while circumnavigating the TT track on the Isle of Man. First original Wild Swans bassist Jim Weston was killed in the early 80s when hit by a motorcycle, then Pete de Freitas twelve years ago, and now lovely Jake.

Waking Mum, I gave her her morning medications with a pre-cooled cup of tea. I vacuumed, I cleaned, I cooked, I calmed her many fears.

Never a worrier before my dad died of prostate cancer, now she's scared of everything. Before I knew it, it was 7:38pm and time to walk back through the dark, past Arrowsmith's farm, where I used to play so happily as a kid, only to end up marooned at the railway station in the pouring rain with a thirty-minute wait followed by a twenty-five-minute journey just to catch my connection home to South Liverpool. I've had nothing to eat all day, there's a full moon sucking all the blood to my head, and the shaved pig in the ticket office is giving me the evil eye. God, I feel low.

Poor Jake. He was always so sweet to me and my fellow Wild Swans. One Wednesday night at Plato's Ballroom, back in the day, I tripped on quadruple-strength microdot acid with him and Julian. As the acid was coming up, Jake spied a girl applying smoky eyeshadow using a hand mirror, and Jake asked if she would apply some to him. I was so high while DJing I played the same two Manicured Noise and Pop Group singles on a loop until someone complained. Wondering why that night's band, New Order, looked so soft-focus, I realised I'd forgotten to remove my reading glasses.

Fuck it: the local Spar shop is open for another twenty minutes, so I walk back across the bridge in the rain, up the hill, and I pay over the odds for a screw-top bottle of New World red, and get further soaked in the process of walking back while swigging from the bottle. As a toddler, I stood on top of this cast-iron bridge, nervously holding onto my dad's hand as a steam train passed beneath us; no fear, just a sense of wonder as we were enveloped in a cumulus of warm steam. Then again, riding into Liverpool with my mum to meet Father Christmas at the famous grotto in Blackler's department store, where one of Santa's elves held open an enormous glittering Christmas stocking from which I pulled a mystery gift: a golden toy dagger with three magical jewels in the handle. Years later, on my eighth birthday, sitting on the upholstered maroon carriage seats returning from Liverpool town centre with my first Action Man— the 1966 Palitoy original with facial scar, moulded hair, and no genitals.

It was from here I embarked the morning I lost my virginity to a pretty hippie girl from Huyton; it was from here I left to watch The Clash play at Eric's in 1977; it was from this station Les and I disembarked, again fresh from a later punk gig at Eric's, shaken but victorious after being attacked on the last train home by three denim-clad rock Trogs. I have history here.

When the Liverpool train finally arrives, it's liveried in Peter Saville-like industrial grey and yellow, over-lit, and entirely lacking in poetry. Where are the shelves of knotted brown string for one's bags, and where are the watercolour prints of Scottish lochs that once hung here?

Sitting down, I swig from the bottle and stare out into the relentless diagonal Northern dreich. Is it legal to drink wine from a bottle when travelling on public transport? Just curious, because that's what I'm doing.

Several weeks later, I'm on the London train, reading John Cowper-Powys's *Wolf Solent* while drinking the second of four M&S gin and tonics, when the Nissan Centre call me. A woman with a heavy Warrington accent informs me that after plugging it into their computer diagnostics machine, their engineers have finally diagnosed the problem with my car. It's fucked to the moon and back. So far, it has cost me £230 just to find out that the timing chain is kaput—a fact I was already aware of and told them about when I booked it in with them the day before yesterday. Making my car road-worthy again will cost the eye-watering and Kabbalistic sum of £1,111.00. I tell her to cease work immediately. The car simply isn't worth it.

Back in Liverpool the next morning, Les phones, asking if I will meet him in the Albert on Lark Lane at 11am. Jake's body has finally been released after the accident inquiry in the Isle of Man and is being driven down from Liverpool to Bristol in an unrefrigerated yellow Tonka van by Andy Eastwood and a few of Jake's best friends. The idea being, the boys thought Jake might appreciate a quick mini tour of his former Liverpool haunts, including the old Bunnymen house on Aigburth Drive where Pete, Jake, Les, Will, and Deaf School's drummer, the late Tim Whittaker, lived in the late 1980s. The undertakers are only allowing these highly unusual—and, let's face it, slightly unhygienic—travel arrangements on the strict proviso that the body is taken directly to Bristol with no stops, arriving no later than 5pm.

I drop what I'm doing and head over to the Albert. When the van arrives, there's a sizeable crowd of Jake's friends outside the pub, all smiling sadly. As the side doors are opened, we are greeted with the surreal sight of Jake's coffin lying with stereo speakers at its head, from which issue Van Morrison's *Astral Weeks*. Someone gets the beers in, and we stand around for a few hours, passing around photos of Jake in various exotic locations around the world: Jake on top of a glacier, Jake in a jungle clearing, Jake onstage with the Buns, Jake backstage with the Buns, Jake in a canoe up some Amazonian river, Jake on his bike, Jake drunk at the kitchen table.

Two things occur to me:

1. Jake had a fabulous life, filled with friends and adventure.
2. He is smiling in every single shot, even the ones where he didn't know his picture was being taken.

After a night on the beer and another drink here, Andy is over the limit, so he asks Simon—'The Captain'—to drive the first leg. Simon does a five-point turn outside the pub, and we say our last goodbyes to Jake before the funeral proper. We are all thinking the same thing: there's no way they are going to make it to Bristol by 5pm, and if that van gets stopped by the police en route for any reason and they look in the back, they are not going to believe their fucking eyes.

PART EIGHT

ENCHANTED
2011–2022

I
PHOSPHORESCENCE

OCTOBER 2011. WESTER ROSS. The six-hundred-mile drive from Liverpool to Kyle of Lochalsh on the west coast of Scotland is a killer. Four hours into the journey, with the outskirts of Glasgow in the car's rearview mirror, my accelerator foot begins to ache and my seat feels like it's made from Highland Toffee. Surely our destination must be close by now? As the crow flies, it almost is, but the serpentine roads around the loch and over and between mountain and glen mean that, depending on the weather conditions, I still have another four or five hours of clutch-depressing, gear-changing, high-concentration driving still to go.

I've been doing this road trip in the second week of October with my family for twelve years now, so I should be used to it, yet every year, somewhere around Culloden, the physical and mental toll of such an epic drive, amplified by the psychic weight of the landscape, still manages to catch me unawares. Exhausting as the journey is, the tapestry-coloured hillsides, Victorian train viaducts,1930s wooden telephone posts pitched at expressionist angles, and the sheer Shakespearean drama of it all make it spectacularly worth it. This year, my *Spot The Roadkill* prize winner is found on the A830 near Lochailort: a ten-pointer stag with one entire haunch sawn off by a passing opportunist.

Located on the banks of a secluded bay on the south shore of Loch Carron—one of the most unspoiled and beautiful areas in the British Isles—the two cottages we three families share at autumn half-term are so inaccessible that they can't *quite* be reached by car. Unloading our many bags of supplies on the hillside by a raging burn, we carry them across a railway track and a field of nervously bleating and defecating sheep. Arriving in the late afternoon with perhaps just a half-hour of daylight remaining, our fellow Liverpudlian friends of thirty years—Mike and Jeanette Badger and their kids, Amber and Ray—are already here, and the lovely Walker family, driving up from their home in Manchester, have texted us en route to inform us they'll be late as they are still in Fort William, stocking up on supplies.

I've been itching to get out upon the loch since this time last year, and it's all I've been thinking about for the past hour. A fortnight ago, I drove all the way to the Black Country to collect this Canadian-style kayak, and I'm impatient to try it out. Novice that I am, I've also bought a retro-looking but insubstantial Norwegian life-jacket more suited to aiding someone falling into a canal than a tidal sea loch. Unwilling to wait until morning, and filled with the designated driver's sense of entitlement, I ignore the pleas to relax and have a restorative cuppa and set out for a twenty-minute 'paddle around the island' before it gets dark.

—

Allegedly the inspiration for *Neverland* in J.M. Barrie's Peter Pan, *Eilean na Creag Duibhe*, or Heron Island, is a Scots-pine-covered heron sanctuary that rises out of Loch Carron some one hundred yards in front of the cottage. On spring tides you can walk out to it upon a narrow strand, but right now the tide is on the ebb. Pushing off from the shore, I steer the kayak's nose out through the sweet-smelling, ochre-coloured kelp close to shore and head out into clear water. Jumping in and settled into the seat, the first arc of my paddle startles a cormorant from off his rocky perch on the island's promontory and into panicky, low-level flight.

Paddling with the outgoing tide is easy at first, the water offering little resistance to the blades. Close to shore, the water is so clean that even at a depth of six metres I can look over the side and read the loch bed in detail. Pale cream sand overlaid with saltwater flame shells, starfish, broken coral, and the local grey mussels known as Clappy-Doos. On my first visit to the area in 1996, I nearly choked when one became lodged halfway down my throat.

With *Ulluva*, the small rocky outcrop and seal haven to my back, I paddle anticlockwise around the perimeter of the island and into the deep waters in the centre of the channel. In doing so, I've already passed the point where, in previous years, using a borrowed kayak, I'd felt I'd left my comfort zone; but this being my kayak's maiden voyage, I feel like a modest adventure. With *Kishorn* to starboard, I am now half a mile equidistant from the shore on the narrowest sides of the loch, so I stop paddling and allow the outgoing tide to gently nose the kayak around.

The centre of the loch affords me a 360-degree view of the landscape. From the lunar barrenness of the Isle of Skye to distant tree-covered Applecross, from the castle ruins at Strome to Glenelg, it is all, uniformly, achingly glorious. The beauty is so extreme, the quality of light so remarkable, the wildlife so abundant, it's simply too much information to process. The only way to filter all this magnificence is to stop looking for single 'events' and widen one's focus to envelop the whole.

Autumn on the west coast of the Scottish Highlands is never less than astonishing, particularly during October, when the mercury dips and the shortening days trigger a chemical change in the flora. Nature's grand reveal isn't June or August but now, in its last exhilarating burn before the sleep of winter. This is no electricity-pylons-in-fog, raincoat-and-fag-smoke English autumn of regret; it's celebratory, easily the most exquisite firework in the box. From June to Christmas 1996, my wife and I lived in a remote cottage in a horseshoe-shaped glen not far from here. Formerly owned by the Forestry Commission, the cottage was as damp as it was charming, its whisky-coloured tap water fed by a tumbling burn running straight off the mountain. Marooned alone without a car for the first month, I walked the surrounding forest and found that the landscape awakened something in me—some dormant Celtic, Simpson-forebears thing. We didn't know it until the following spring, back in Liverpool, but my wife become pregnant while here, and that, combined with the warmth of the locals, brought us back with our young son, to rewild here each autumn with friends.

The current is already stronger than I'd anticipated, and although I can't see it yet, I can feel the hull beneath me being gently guided in the direction of Plockton Harbour, famous for its use as a location in *The Wicker Man*. My plan is to potter up and down for a bit, get a feel for the kayak, and then, before the tide gets too strong, I'll break from the current and row toward the shore by Duncraig Station. Once in shallower water, where the pull is weakest, I'll about-face and head back home, slowly hugging the coast.

Before I can attempt this, I become aware of a vast shadow falling across the hillsides. Within seconds, the light fails, and the colour entirely drains from the landscape. An extraordinary cloud formation is developing across the ridge of Precambrian Munros and the mountains that comprise the Five Sisters of Kintail. It's a *downward nimbostratus*; a colossus that spreads vertically at astonishing speed, pouring down the sides of the three-thousand-metre-high Sisters and surrounding braes like dry ice cascading from the lip of a bowl. My God! It's Wagnerian! Gathering mass, it obscures the *Bealach na Bà,* or 'Pass of the Cattle', at over two thousand feet one of the highest roads in the British Isles. Down it tumbles, a roiling ghost avalanche that swallows up hectares of pine forest in moments. Reaching sea level, it haemorrhages out across Loch Carron toward me, soon enveloping me in a John Carpenter-esque fog. It's as if the sky has collapsed.

Floating in a whiteout now, I can just make out the kayak's prow and the blades of the double-ended aluminium paddle laid across my knees. Turning my head, I can see the stern but nothing beyond. This is the stuff of dreams, possibly nightmares. The closest I've come to experiencing something as disorientating as this was back in the mid-1980s when I encountered an 'infinity cove' in the photographic studio of Andy Catlin, while he was shooting images for The Wild Swans' *Bringing Home The Ashes*. The infinity cove is a smooth, white-painted wall that curves out on its top, bottom, and sides. Looking into it, this cyclorama tricks the eye into thinking there is an infinite distance in front of you that you could be facing any way up, even floating in space; whereas, in reality, you can just reach out and touch its walls.

Disorientating and beautiful, the difference out here on this two-mile-deep loch is the risk to life. The North Atlantic water is cold, and my waterproof army poncho runs with atomised mist on the outside and condensation on the inside. Seated in the kayak, hair plastered to my face, my range of vision is down to just a metre in any direction. Lost in fog, drifting on an outgoing tide, am I in actual physical danger here? I think I might be. What is this huge rock outcrop looming to port? It can only be *Sgeir Bhuidhe*, the 'yellow skerry' offshore near Duncraig—but, if it is, then shouldn't I be passing between it and the mainland? It should be on my starboard side, which must mean I've drifted a lot further from shore and safety than I'd realised.

I'm being pulled backwards now, caught in the outgoing tide. This isn't good. If I am lucky, I'll end up somewhere in the outer reaches of Plockton Harbour; if not, I'll be channelled past the decommissioned lighthouse on *Eilean a' Chait* and into the Inner Sound. Beyond that are the measureless depths of *The Minch*—the deepest water on the continental shelf; waters so impossibly deep that the Royal Navy use it to perform their submarine sea trials.

What was I thinking coming out on a sea lock when tired and ill-equipped? And why was I so impatient to get out onto the loch as darkness was falling, rather than waiting for morning? I don't have a phone with me, and even if I did there'd be no signal out here. In October seawater this cold, swimming is not an option. As if this weren't disturbing enough, something large and sleek in the water below skims the fabric of the kayak's hull, causing it to lurch horribly. The inertia turns my stomach. It's too big for an otter, so it can only be a seal, toying with the unfamiliar shape floating above it.

I'm not absolutely sure, but through a gap in the fog, I thought I just glimpsed an area of unstressed water between the running narrows. Paddling carefully, I find it and manoeuvre inside it. Miraculously, my momentum is halted. Why is it here, and how is it possible?

Gasping in panicky lungsful of chilled air, I consider my options.

1. I can row in any random direction, praying that I won't hit a rock and capsize—maybe I'll get lucky, avoid the swift running narrows out to open sea, and make landfall on the opposite shore to Duncraig, or

2. I can sit off here in this miraculously calm pocket of water and wait for the situation to change for good or ill.

The former feels akin to playing Russian roulette, the latter head-in-sand madness. I thought I had experienced fear before, but the reality is, I haven't. I've had to fight my way out of ugly situations before—particularly in the late 1970s and early 80s, when just having a weird haircut or the wrong clothes was enough to get me jumped. In those situations, the fight-or-flight response would kick in, but there's no discernible adrenaline rush now, presumably because my brain knows that it wouldn't serve me in this situation. There is no right choice right now. It's like I've been absolved of any responsibility for my fate.

Against all logic, it's now, suspended inert in this moon-coloured soup, that the fear and desperation I've been battling to suppress this past half-hour or so is overwritten by an ineffable sensation of stillness and calm. It's as though a soft cloak has been draped about me by an unseen hand. I have the sensation that I no longer exist in physical form but in something closer to dream consciousness. Divine experience or divine madness, a subliminal and benign presence is here with me, and it feels better than any drug I've ever tried or had administered. Am I closing down? Experiencing some natural mental and physical anaesthesia before I succumb to hypothermia and eventual drowning? Is this the body's intuitive coping strategy, or am I, as I'm inching toward believing, trespassing in sacred space, floating within some nautical version of R.S. Thomas's 'Bright Field'?

If I *am* dying, I honestly don't care right now, because I'm in the phosphorescent womb—the *aevum*—the sphere of the soul. Is this why Byron swam the Bosporus? Why free divers risk narcosis? To access the holy narcotic? I have no idea how long I've been out, both on the loch and lost in eternity. It could be an hour, it could be ten thousand years.

Like a miracle, just as I feel the sickening inertia of the current's pull upon the hull beneath me, a breeze blows and begins to disperse the fog, skein by gauzy skein. There's a waxing moon up there somewhere, and between the retreating whorls of mist I can see silvered threads of water running off the hills, and, long distant, the glint of wet roof tiles of Duncraig castle. In its way, the fog has protected me. Had I been able to see just how far away from land and safety I've drifted, how close to the Crowlin Islands I am, I'd surely have panicked and possibly made the disastrous mistake of paddling for the closest shore—and thereby meeting the invisible channel that could drag me out to sea.

Paddling against the outgoing tide is hard enough, and my back and arms ache horribly, but having the landmark of the Castle to aim for, I fight for my deliverance. Over the next fifteen to twenty minutes, I make slow but steady progress, the mist retreating into pockets and folds in the hills. Spotting a distant pinprick of warm light, my heart surges. If I am right, it's a lantern burning in the larger of the two cottages' window. But, if so, why is Arnold Bocklin's *The Isle Of The Dead* looming out of the darkness immediately ahead of me?

Quickly reverse-paddling so as not to puncture the kayak's skin on the barnacled rocks ahead, I manoeuvre backwards. Wait! The topography may be unfamiliar, but I recognise those wind-warped Scots pines. This must be the far side of Heron Island, and that means I'm nearly home. All I need to do is turn about and then, once clear of the jagged promontory, steer hard to port.

Close to shore now, I recognise the outline of the conjoined cottages and can even smell the damp wood smoke escaping the chimney. Finally hearing the crunch of the sand beneath the kayak's hull, I exhale with relief and look up to a magnificent sky peppered with stars. I am delivered. Once I get home to Liverpool, I must try to capture and record this perilous voyage. I can't do it in music, I know that. If it eluded Wagner, I am hardly likely to nail it in one of my three-chord wonders. I'm going to paint this experience, or at least attempt to. I've never worked in oil paint before, but that's the medium I'll choose.

Exhausted, I drag the kayak up the beach and upend it onto the grass with the paddle stored beneath it. Pulling off this ridiculous buoyancy aid and soaking cagoule, I tramp up to the door to the cottage, pull off my wet boots, and open the farmhouse door. Inside, it's warm; wood burner roaring, the smell of dinner cooking, kids sprawled on sofas drawing. I haven't even been missed. In the ninety minutes I now realise I've been gone, our friends the Walkers have arrived and are busy unpacking. Apparently, Nick has also brought a kayak up this year.

Mike passes me a bottle of beer.

'Nice time?' Jan asks.

Lost for words, I am a man transformed. Sheepishly, I don't tell Jan or any of them about my experience on the loch until I am back on Merseyside a fortnight later, and even then I disguise the metaphysical stuff as 'lost in fog'. People already think I'm mad.

II
DEATH IN A PENCIL SKIRT

JANUARY 2012. LIVERPOOL. A thin cold rain is falling as I navigate my way through the cobbled Regency backstreets and terraces of Liverpool 7, in the direction of the Nuclear Medicine Department of the Royal Liverpool Hospital, the collar of my naval pea-coat buttoned against the wind. I'm listening to Mahler's 5th Symphony on iPod headphones. Convinced that I am dying, I want to do it with some style. If I've got to go before my allotted three score years and ten, I can't exit to a jazz-funk soundtrack.

In the first weeks of autumn 2011, after a once-in-a-lifetime family holiday in the tropics, I fell ill with a fever that left me breathless, exhausted, and plagued by migraines. Somewhere in the jungles of Sri Lanka, or more likely the petri dish of recycled shower water that is the paradise island resort of Kuramati, I've picked up some larval hitchhikers, the strongest contenders being the parasitic roundworm *strongyloides-stercoralis* or the flatworm *schistosomes*. Roundwound or flatwound, they are causing me breathing difficulties, and the slightest exertion exhausts me.

Today, I'm dropping 'biohazard' bags containing sealed bottles containing stool samples at the School of Tropical Medicine before undergoing further exploratory tests at the Infectious Diseases wing of the Royal. Strange as it might sound, I'm becoming resigned to an early death, and I have almost started to enjoy the idea of myself as a tubercular poet on a protracted slow fade.

Stiletto heels echo down early morning hospital corridors. It's my sexy, woman-of-a-certain-age radiographer, Death In A Pencil Skirt, informing me that I am about to undergo a pulmonary ventilation/perfusion scan. Shivering in a too-short hospital gown, bare feet on disinfectant-smelling linoleum, I feel like I'm climbing the steps to the guillotine. Death, or DIPS as I call her, is one of an incredible NHS team trying to ascertain which if any strain of tropical parasite has undertaken a grand tour of my liver and lungs. Inserting a plastic mouthpiece between my lips, she leans in close, and I close my eyes breathing in her dark perfume. Counting off the nanoseconds onscreen, she squeezes my hand, the signal for me to begin to inhale the radioactive gas. Together, we watch via monitor as my lungs slowly begin to fill with poisonous silver glitter. Incredible! They look like half-deflated Montgolfier air balloons on fire over eighteenth-century Paris.

'I thought I told you not to talk!' she scolds.

Opening a lead-lined metal box, my evil Mary Poppins now removes a chrome syringe and shoots me up with radioactive albumin that goes in warm and lights up my veins and ventricles like flaming chaff on a radar screen. Instructed to extend my arms wide, I lay my chest flat against a large photographic plate.

'Crucifixion pose,' I say. 'My favourite.'

'Don't move,' she scolds. 'And don't talk. You may feel a little dizzy. Now, brace your legs a little wider, and keep as still as possible.'

'We'd make a fortune making fetish films,' I reply.

Beyond dizzy, my head is swimming, and onscreen things are becoming decidedly aquatic. Is that my ribcage? It resembles a resin prop in an aquarium, something for guppies and neon tetras to swim through. Through its spars, I can just make out the wreckage of my old clockwork pilot boat. *Look!* A school of fruit-flavoured fizzy fish! Are those coral branches my lungs? *Battle stations! Anything can happen in the next half hour.* Here come my toy Lone Star frogmen astride their midget submarine. *Marina, Aqua Marina!*

There on the seabed, the key to my Hornby trainset, my Meccano spanner, and the glow-in-the-dark skeleton I got free with Kellogg's Frosti—

'Mr. Simpson! Are you listening?'

Play, Sparky, Play! *I will not play for you, Sparrrrkeeee.*

'Mr. Simpson!'

God. I love it when she's cross with me.

'It appears that you are getting approximately eight percent less oxygen than you should be,' says DIPS. 'This would account for the *brain fog* you mentioned.'

What I've not mentioned to DIPS, my GP, my thoracic consultant, or even my wife, is that I am convinced that there is also something wrong with my eyes. Something John Carpenter-ish swimming around inside my pupils. I know this is probably psychiatric-hospital-grade madness, but just to make sure, once home, I take some close-up photographs of my eyes in the mirror, and I am horrified to see that there really is something near-microscopic swimming around inside the pupils of my eyes.

When a moth lands in my rioja at dinner, I interpret it as a symbol of my impending death. Have I been cursed? Am I really the victim of some kind of *Serpent & The Rainbow*-style scorned-woman hex?

—

After twelve months, thirty-two blood tests, and a physically depleting but nothing-to-lose Malaria treatment, my consultant signs me off.

'We've given it our all,' he says. 'Trying to locate a parasite at the right stage of its life cycle is notoriously difficult. Whatever it was, it's run its course. It's knocked your system for six, might take a year to go, possibly two, but it won't kill you. You need to help yourself now. Work hard, reboot your system with a program of exercise.'

'I'm not dying, then?' I ask. Waves of relief wash over me.

'Oh, no. You are.'

What?! Oh my God! I knew it! Now that he's confirmed it, I realise that don't want to die. How will I break it to Ben? I'm not ready to leave my family and friends yet. So much I haven't done! Have I really listened to Elgar's *Nimrod* for the last time?

Seeing my face drain of colour, the consultant delivers his punchline.

'We all are dying, Paul . . . you included. Just not today.'

'Don't mind me,' the bastard says, laughing. 'Medical humour.'

III

DREAMING WICKED

JULY 2012. CUSHENDALL, COUNTY ANTRIM. Dropped off a little after 10am, we exit the car, shoulder our kitbags, and stare up at the imposing sight of the forty-foot-tall sandstone Curfew Tower rising before us. We look and feel like paranormal investigators about to spend the night in Hell House. Just minutes after dialling the mobile number we've been given, a magical creature appears like Mr Tumnus, the faun from Narnia; it's the tower's keyholder and Bill Drummond's man on the spot, Stephen 'Zippy' Kearney, son of one of the two village butchers, or 'fleshers' as they are called in these parts.

Zippy is aptly named: he's by far the most animated person I've ever met. He walks fast, talks fast, and fizzes like a Mento dropped in Coke. Unlocking the padlock on a sturdy iron gate, our hyperactive new friend leads us through a small unkempt garden, down shallow steps to a door at the back of the tower. 'Prepare to be underwhelmed!' he proclaims, as he throws it wide and flicks a light switch to reveal a modest kitchen illuminated by a strip light diffused by a repurposed thirty-three-year-old Teardrop Explodes/Echo & The Bunnymen gig poster. I'm thinking that it should be in a museum, not used as a coffin for flies.

Here at the invitation of Paul Sullivan, founder of Liverpool's fabulous Static Gallery, I've flown in with my friend, the playwright and author Jeff Young, to stay in a two-hundred-year-old Curfew Tower owned by my friend Bill and his infamous musician pal Mark Manning, aka Zodiac Mindwarp. Commissioned by Irish landlord Francis Turnley in 1808, the four-storey tower was constructed at the crossroads of the village as a means of subduing the 'riotous' locals. Resembling a guardhouse from the Great Wall of China, this enormous, castellated ship's biscuit is to be our home for the next seven days.

Anything situated on a crossroads is magical—everyone knows that— so I'm fully expecting to confront Beelzebub, the Goat of Mendes, or Van

Morrison sooner or later. To qualify for this artist's residency, Jeff and I are each required to write and record an audio piece using the primitive four-track cassette recorder supplied. These recordings should be works that are a *response to the tower, the locality, or the people of Cushendall.* Not a problem—words are what we do, after all—but Jeff and I have an ulterior motive for being here. You see, twice a week for the past twelve months, we've been spending our afternoons in the Little Grapes on Roscoe Street, getting wasted on rum while exchanging ideas and making notes for a psychological horror film script. No ghosts or monsters, *Ornithology* is just three characters in a remote rural location in peril, and where better to write about the dark stuff than here? We know we have a strong idea, and the running joke between us is that when we do sell it to 'the Americans', they retitle it *Claws*, replace our sensitive male lead with an all-American action hero with a gun and dynamite, and we'll never be able to show our faces in literary circles again.

After catching a 6pm flight from Liverpool's John Lennon airport, we were met in the car park of Belfast Airport by our lovely friend Suzanna McBride, sister of the author Frank Cottrell-Boyce and one-time member of my favourite Liverpool band, The Revolutionary Army Of The Infant Jesus. As luck would have it, Suzanna lives in Glenarm, just a twenty-minute drive from the tower. She picked us up, took us to her home, introduced us to her delightful family, fed us like kings, and now, along with her lovely youngest daughter, Esther, has taxied us right to the tower's studded-iron door. Because we've flown cheaply on Ryanair and were only allowed hand luggage on the flight—and despite being more a tweed suit and brogues kind of guy—for the next six days my wardrobe is a battered US Navy flying jacket, military chinos, and a pair of Redwings bought on eBay, and in my bag, there's a heavy knitted cardigan in case it gets cold. To give the project extra gravitas, I've even grown a crap beard. Jeff and I both considered bringing copies of Joyce's *Ulysses* to better help us channel that Stephen Dedalus, Buck Mulligan in the Martello Tower thing—you know, eating devilled kidneys and shaving on the battlements while cursing our beastly dead mothers. Battlements? Check! Dead mothers? Check! Oh, crap, Jeff is a vegetarian.

Zippy informs us that Bill has recently stripped the interior walls of the tower of ten years' worth of artworks created by previous artists staying on residency here. Although starker than we'd imagined, this place feels somehow right for our film project. Living as nakedly as this isn't going to be easy, though—on the one hand, we want to amplify our sense of isolation in the tower and explore that whole 'lighthouse keepers going mad thing' to the max, but we're not as young as we were, and much as we love staring into the abyss, we'd have preferred to do it with central heating.

Peering into the dungeon cell on the ground floor, I'm disappointed to find it empty. Knowing Bill as I do, and Zodiac by reputation, I was at minimum expecting to find the Spear of Destiny, the lost multitrack of Jimi Hendrix's *Black Gold* album, or blueprints for Hitler's UFO.

Suzanne and the adorable Esther bid their farewells, and after explaining the Boolean-Pythagorean mechanics of the hot water boiler and wishing us a good night, Zippy Stardust disappears in multicoloured sparks back to Nutwood, or Neptune, or whatever he appeared from. Locating the linen closet, we pick out the oldest, warmest woollen blankets and carry them up to the incredibly narrow staircases to the bedrooms on the two uppermost floors to make up our beds. A little lanolin itch will make for better writing. After an hour, we realise that comfort isn't going to be an issue here, for Cushendall at night is noisier at night than Heathrow Airport. The cacophony of boy racers revving their cars outside the tower and the roar of suicidal motorcyclists screaming through the crossroads is terrifying. There was I, expecting some sleepier version of Innisfree from John Ford's *The Quiet Man*.

Exorcist cold, bare floorboards, a single bed, a rustic wooden stool, a chamber pot—my bedroom on the fifth and uppermost floor of the tower is austere enough to give a Quaker an erection. Worryingly, the room has a number of small skulls crudely painted on the walls and ceiling using candle soot that are only visible from certain angles. I suspect this is the work of Bill's evil twin and fellow literary arsehole, Mark: a hidden easter egg he's left to disturb the dreams of Bill's puffy Liverpool pop-musician mates. Jeff's bedroom on the floor below, with its chest of draws and cosmetic fireplace, appears positively luxurious by comparison.

In an attempt to beautify this recently stripped-of-art building, I pick flowering weeds from the tower's tiny garden and place them in an empty Hendrick's gin bottle on the kitchen table before retiring to the sitting room on the third floor that we've already christened Base Camp. I've brought my briar pipe and several tobacco blends. I've also brought a Cuban cigar so expensive that I can't bring myself to smoke it. The expectation has become too great, and because the cigar has been the subject of so much discussion since yesterday, it's already become a totemic, unsmokeable thing—a phallic fetish that sits in its cardboard coffin on the mantelpiece, radiating a little Santería here in the Glens of Antrim.

By 1am, Jeff and I are exhausted. We have a long day of writing ahead of us tomorrow, and it's now we make the mistake of having a nightcap. The following morning, our first in the tower, I pad downstairs in bare feet to make a pot of tea and wince to discover that the litre bottle of Bushmills Black Bush we bought at the airport is three-quarters empty. As a consequence, the day, and our writing, goes slower than molasses.

—

Although Jeff and I grew up in the same area of Merseyside, attended the same secondary school, and both spent significant time in Amsterdam in the early-to-mid 80s, we only met for the first time in 2002, when, one bright autumnal day, he stopped me on Liverpool's Bold Street and asked me if I would be interested in composing some music to accompany a BBC radio play he'd been commissioned to write. And so began the first of many such collaborations with my literary chum.

Today, I am watching him with all the wonder of Mungo Park observing the unfamiliar customs of the natives when on his maiden trip to the African interior. Jeff sits motionless at the table by the window in Base Camp, staring into the blank scrying screen of his laptop for an hour solid without writing a word. He gets up and paces before sitting down again to gaze into his digital Palantir. Relocating to a chair on the opposite side of the room, he sits brooding for a while before jumping up and pulling down a tome from Bill's bookshelf, glancing at it momentarily before putting it back. He then disappears from the room, only to reappear like a stage magician a moment later through a different door and start feverishly typing. When, hours later, he reads me a short excerpt from his *Curfew Tower Journal*, I'm surprised at how serious in tone it is. It's like a brilliant but less cheerful Herman Melville.

Jeff has commented that I too am acting strangely. It's fascinating stuff. Perhaps we've entered some *Sapphire & Steel*-like temporal anomaly. In my mid-twenties, while on tour in Lausanne in Switzerland, standing outside the Museum of Art Brut, I stumbled into a temporal jag where the new flushed away and the medieval town was revealed to me. Terrified and unprepared for this thinning of the veils, I ran back to my hotel and hid under the bedcovers.

As Jeff refreshes our whisky glasses, I attempt to explain to him my version of intuitive magic. He's intrigued to learn that at breakfast this morning I did not choose the colour of our tea mugs arbitrarily. Ignoring the many impotent pastel shades on Bill's mug tree, I pulled out the entire contents of the cupboards in order to locate the occult ceramics I knew must be hiding somewhere. An intense blood-red mug for its energy and its potency for Jeff, while I took the blackest, ugliest looking hand-thrown vessel to encourage more dangerous writing. To Jeff's credit, he doesn't scoff. Already au fait with my madness, he gets me. He knows when I'm in the pub I'll spend ages reading the labels on the beer pumps, as if they are a tarot card spread, before making my selection. I'm not looking for specific gravity or hop varieties, I'm searching for symbols, portents, and resonators. And don't get me started on my aftershaves. I have three. The 'safe' one to ensure nothing miraculous occurs, the intermediate one that allows some small potential for magic to manifest, and then there's the one I must never wear as it causes absolute fucking carnage.

My breakfast this morning consists of cinnamon bagels with cream cheese, dates, and banana. This I eat accompanied by a carafe of strong Lavazza coffee, a brand that Jeff reliably informs me is the favourite of the Italian working classes. Really? Then how come we paid nearly a fiver for it in the local minimart? While I clear away the breakfast things, Jeff heads out to find us a very writerly bottle of medium dry sherry or port— something civilised that we can sip until noon without overly fogging our senses. He returns twenty minutes later, empty-handed: he's been told that the local stores don't sell alcohol; apparently, you have to buy your booze from one of the village's three pubs. It's still too early, but seeing a pub's door open for cleaning, Jeff's entered and politely requested in his clearest English if he might perchance purchase a bottle of sherry. How was he to know which bar the local nationalists favour? We'll have to drink coffee for another few hours before trying again.

When the effects of last night's drinking have finally worn off, we both go into another bar and are immediately collared by a feisty local who demands to know why, if we claim to be from Liverpool, we don't have Liverpool accents. We do, we tell him, just not strong ones. 'You sound educated,' the man says accusingly. We apologise for this, and while waiting the agonising ten minutes for our Guinness to settle, we have to fend off a bewildering barrage of invasive questions about what schools we went to, what football teams we support. Clearly, we are regarded as contaminants here.

Realising we've probably made a mistake in coming in here, I sit down, trying to ignore the sports on the humongous flat-screen TV on the wall to my left, but when I do turn around, I am flabbergasted to see a man in what appears to be a log cabin in Alaska wearing my shirt and heavy zip-up cardigan. I'm not talking about a cardigan similar to mine, or even one almost identical to it—I mean he's wearing the very same shirt and hand-knitted garment I am now wearing. My wife, Jan, works in costume on TV, and when filming a Coors-Lite commercial several weeks ago, she borrowed not only this very jumper but the heavy plait shirt I have on beneath it. Not only have I never seen this TV advert until now but neither has she. It's a surreal moment, the first of many to come.

Joining me at my table, Jeff returns with a couple of pints of stout. He's looking pained. We can't even begin to understand the politics of this area, but we owe it to the locals to try. To my mind, the Catholic village of Cushendall, surrounded by Protestant villages, is like a fairy ring of fly agaric mushrooms in the centre of a field of wild edible fungi. The Fly Agaric is rare, hallucinogenic, beautiful, and only dangerous if abused. My maternal grandmother was a Liverpool Catholic who fell in love with a protestant man. Because her local priest refused to marry them, she abandoned the church forever. Her grandmother hit the cobbles of Liverpool from Ireland during the great Drochshaol and settled there. My father's people were Gaelic stock too—tough-assed Simpsons from the Black Isle—so I don't feel any guilt at staying in a curfew tower built to subjugate the locals, although perhaps I should flagellate myself a little as payback for all that WWII garden-party bunting and antique military ephemera I wheeled out last time the Wild Swans played in Liverpool. (In my naivety, I thought projecting Lindsey Anderson's film *If* on a screen behind us would be implicit enough to show our attitude toward the establishment.)

After the pub, Jeff and I go for an exploratory walk around the village. Passing by the window of MacAuliffe's stores I recognise a pair of leather-soled, elastic-sided Banbury boots made by Hogg's of Fyfe cheaper than I've seen them elsewhere, so I grab Jeff and dive in. Jesus! It's like going back in time to 1972—the whole shop is filled with vintage deadstock.

'Is it me or is hotter than Borneo in here?' I ask Jeff.

'It is warm out today, so it is,' says Mrs MacAuliffe. 'Here, sit down.'

'I'm burning up,' I report, while struggling out of my leather jacket.

'Hugh. Get the man here some water. He's unwell.'

Jeff is preoccupied. There's a portable TV on in the corner of the shop, and he's pulled a chair up in front of it and is absorbed in watching the golf. Being an intelligent man, Jeff obviously has zero interest in golf, but it's coming live from Lytham St. Anne's, where Jeff and I have just been working on *The Ghost Telegrams*—a project featuring Ron Moody, the fabulous actor who played Fagin in the film of *Oliver!*—and they are showing footage of the town, and that's got to be better than watching me expiring from heat while trying on dealer boots.

'My word! You're sweating like a pig,' says Mrs MacAuliffe. 'You should probably see a doctor. Hugh, where's that water for the man?'

What's going on? It's like the palm house at Kew in here. It's only when I stand up to get a tissue out of my trouser pocket to wipe my forehead that I see the portable gas heater turned on full, pointed directly at my back.

Relocating the chair to the rear of the shop, I try on the left foot I've been presented with and it's a perfect fit. I'm definitely going to buy them, but before I do, I'd better try on the right foot, as it's a micron smaller. Even with the aid of a shoehorn, and Mrs MacAuliffe pushing it with all her might, I cannot get the right boot on.

'It's a mystery, right enough,' she says.

'Are you sure this is a matching pair?' I ask.

Mr MacAuliffe laughs at this. He thinks it's a hilarious thing to say.

'Winnie! *Is it a matching pair*, he says!' He's shaking his head and rolling his eyes at his wife like I've lost my mind. But there's no getting around the fact that one shoe fits me perfectly while the other won't go anywhere near.

Holding them back-to-back, it's obvious that the right boot is a good inch shorter than the left. I ask again, 'Are you absolutely positive it's a matching pair, Hugh?'

Mrs M takes the right shoe and examines it.

'Hugh! This one's a size 7,' she says, without an apology.

'A size 7, is it?' say Hugh. 'Hmm. How did that get in the box marked 10?'

Twenty minutes later, I'm still sitting here, sweating, and Hugh has near destroyed the shop trying to locate the right 'right' size 10. He's near apoplectic that it's not in the box marked 7. Eventually, after much ado, a matching right shoe is located and presented to me as if it's the Holy Grail.

Desperate to get this over with and get into Johnny Joe's for a pint, I'm losing the will to live, but something's wrong. The right shoe I'm given is as loose as a Wellington boot. It may be a size 10, but unlike the narrow-fitting left shoe, it's an extra-wide fitting.

'This isn't the right boot,' I protest.

'Oh, it's the right boot, all right,' Hugh says. 'Look, you have the left already on your left foot, so. Look beneath it. See? Size 10, stamped right there.'

'Yes,' I say. 'But it's a G fitting—it's huge. It's horribly loose and baggy. See?'

Hugh frowns. 'But it's a size 10!'

'That's as maybe, but the left is a narrow F fitting. The right is a G, wide fitting. The left and the right boot are two completely different fittings.'

Meanwhile, Jeff has tears in his eyes; this is by far the funniest thing he's seen and heard since the gas fire incident a few moments ago. Frustrated to bursting point and apologising profusely to the lovely MacAuliffes, we explode out of the door in giggles into the cool of the street and speed-walk to the pub. I'm near desiccated from the heat and desperate for a drink and a bag of cheese-and-onion-flavour Taytos.

Sitting here sipping my Guinness, I am reflecting on a few idiosyncrasies I have noticed in my fellow light-keeper Jeff's behaviour. In fact, I suspect he may have some mild form of OCD. It's the toilet rolls in the Tower's bathroom, you see—they keep moving. When we arrived a few days back, they were stacked at the side of the toilet in a pleasing sort of three-on-the-bottom, two-in-the-middle, one-on-top mini-ziggurat, probably Zippy's work, but twice today they have been moved into two different architectural formations. I can only think that they must have a ritual significance that Jeff has chosen not to disclose to me, like the four columns in Luc Besson's *The Fifth Element*. Perhaps these rolls of Andrex must be aligned in a specific order in a specific place on a certain date, in order to implement

the eschaton or maintain the psychic equilibrium of the planet. Whatever
it is, I'm considering locking my bedroom door tonight. Jeff's gone rogue.

—

With its working fireplace and a few items of actual furniture, Base Camp
is the cosiest room in the tower. There are powered speakers in here, too,
so I plug them into my laptop and, risking incurring the wrath of Mr 'No
Music Day' Drummond, we listen to music to help or hinder our work.
If it's the film script we are working on, we listen to Pentangle, Mellow
Candle, John Martyn, and Jeff Kelly's *Coffee In Nepal* album. If we are
writing our non-collaborative *Curfew Tower Journals* for Paul Sullivan, we
listen to improvisational trio The Necks, and every night, just before bed,
it has to be Marvin Gaye's late-period masterpiece 'Life's Opera'—a track
so sublime it even survives having its bass line played on what sounds like
a Yamaha DX7 keyboard preset.

There's an antique school map of Africa on the wall here, one of those
canvas-backed roll-up jobs we had in school, which I take it is something
to do with Bill's travels up the Congo for the second of his collaborations
with literary madman/genius Mark Manning. A trip that resulted in *Wild
Highway*, a book so disturbing that the original publisher, Penguin, refused
to publish it.

As the Bushmills begins to take effect, the shape of Africa actually
begins to bleed.

'Jeff, is it just me or is it weird that the corner shop opposite is still
open at five past eleven on a Sunday night when it only sells beach balls
and children's toys?'

Jeff, draining his massive whisky, replies hoarsely, 'Here be dragons.'
For a man who barely drank a year ago, he's caning it tonight. Despite a
striking similarity to Samuel Beckett, with a monster cheroot in his mouth
right now he more closely resembles 'Papa' Hemmingway. We are both
horribly drunk and start doing that shorthand telepathy thing that good
friends do of answering questions the other only asked in their heads.

While I'm sitting smoking my pipe tobacco, thinking about how that cream-coloured wall at the end of the sitting room would look better if it were decorated in Haitian voodoo sigils, Jeff answers me with, 'We should paint something magical on that wall—a mythical Caladrius-something.'

It's raining when I wake the next morning. Jeff is still asleep, so I make coffee and sit in base camp making notes for *Dreaming Wicked*, my official response to the curfew tower. I'm playing the audio narcotic that is Terry Riley's live-in-Paris double-album *Persian Surgery Dervishes*. This is post-psychedelic music, as mystic as Western music gets. With the exception of *If A Baby Had Infinite Power It Would Destroy The Sun* by The Museum Of Witchcraft, I don't do psychedelic music; it's a done-to-death, easily faked genre, and I am bored to my core by it. I've never seen the point of only listening to 60s music when trying to disorder the senses when one has the mystical shortcut to God's eye of Sufi devotional music.

—

Come evening, after a full day's writing, Jeff and I decide to give Johnny Joe's a swerve. We'll only get ourselves in trouble. While I make a peat fire, Jeff finds Bill's copy of *Ulysses* is up on the shelf after all and sits reading. Neither of us can face cooking, so we eat slutty instant noodles, drink whisky, and smoke our pipes and cigars. Everything is cosy until we are disturbed by the relentless beeping of car horns. It doesn't stop, so we are forced from our seats to look out of the window.

What we see below makes our blood run cold. A flatbed van with its hazard lights on is driving very slowly through the crossroads at the head of a small convoy of vehicles. On the back of this truck, a near-naked near man stands bound by his hands and feet in a crucifixion pose to a steel frame that runs behind the cab. He's covered in what looks like white paint. We're too high up so we can't read the man's face, can't tell if this is a joke or not. But the symbolism is terrifying.

The next morning, Zippy pops by to see how we are doing, and we ask him about the crucified man on the truck.

'Sure, that was just a local boy, he's getting married on Saturday. He had a grand old time.'

Jeff and I spend the entire day working on our film script, and by 5pm we relax a bit, knowing that we've made good progress. In the evening we slope off to Johnny Joe's bar with Zippy and his fiancée, Steph. The back room is full of delightfully tipsy women, fresh from something called a 'wallpaper party'. I chat with a pretty girl called Orla who claims she doesn't get my sense of humour and misinterprets my simple question— 'Who are you?'—as a Zen riddle. When I jokingly ask her what wallpaper paste she used at the party, she answers, 'Tikka Masala.' When she asks what I do for a living, I answer, 'Chemistry.'

Orla is delighted. '*Chemistry*, he says! Girls! Look at your man's eyes here. Sure I wouldn't trust him not to blow a big ol' hole in the sky. Quick, run before he tries an experiment on us.'

'What is it you do, Orla?'

'I tickle the grass in the churchyard up on the cliff path, you know?'

'What lawnmower do you use, petrol or electric?'

'*Lawnmower*, he says! Sure, I'm not Richard Branston. I use my wallpaper scissors.'

'It's Branson,' I say. 'Not Branston.'

'Branston! The pickle baron. I know who I mean.'

I can't stop laughing. She's fucking with me, and she's good at it.

'You talk funny,' she says.

'I'm not talking at all. You're telepathic.'

'That'll be it! We've been talking completely different sandwiches.'

After a surreal half-hour discussing my lifelong fear of the scene in *Darby O'Gill & The Little People* where all the horses bolt from the mouth of the cave and hers of anything with either Julia McKenzie or fish in it, she concludes our conversation by telling me she has to go, that I am altogether too dangerous to know, how she should probably call the Garda on me, and how locked up in a curfew tower is probably the best place for me tonight.

I tell her that I've read her case notes; that if she ever learns to read, she should look me up in the phone box.

'Phone box? You mean phone book, ya eejeeit!'

'I should know where I live,' I say.

'Now tell me, Einstein. How do I look you up when you haven't told me your name? Go on, I'm one big enormous, gorgeous ear.'

'Nigel.'

'Feck off. It's not.'

'It is. Nigel Dankworth.'

'Fucking hell! Hardly James Bond, is it?'

'It's the quiet ones you have to watch.'

'What's your pal's name there? The one with the face.'

'Zippy.'

'Not fecking Zippy! I know Zippy right enough, I live here. Your man with the sparkly eyes there, doing all the gesticulating,' she says, nodding in the direction of Jeff.

'That's my half-brother, Nathaniel.'

'You're havin' a laugh now.'

'No. It is, I swear! He's a priest.'

'What? Father Nathanial Dankworth?'

'Yes. He's having a crisis of faith,' I tell her.

'Having you as a brother, I'm not surprised. Anyway, what d'ya mean, it's the quiet ones you have to watch? Sure, you're the opposite of quiet. You've been yakking me *bodhar* since you arrived.'

'I'm sorry. I'm on day release.'

'Ah, listen, Nigel. It's been lovely, really. But I have to go. The girls and I have been here since eight o'clock. We told the men we'd be strippin' the walls until eleven, but we tore through it fast so we could get a few hours in without them. Look!' she says, tapping on her wedding ring. 'It's almost midnight. I'm sorry, but I can't phone ye, I'm a married woman, so I am.'

'That's okay, I am too,' I reply. 'Never mind, we'll always have Paris.'

As Orla and her drunken friends collect their bags and stumble drunkenly out the door, she looks back over at me laughing.

'Hey! Chemist! When you're experimentin' up in your tower tonight, don't let your test tube fizz over.'

—

After breakfast in Arthur's Tea and Coffee Warehouse—Jeff on scrambled eggs, me on an Ulster fry—we walk up to the ruins of Layd Church, where we separate and explore the gravestones. I find one with eleven bodies interred inside it.

Returning by way of the coastal footpath, we marvel at the beautiful hedgerows and the cormorants drying their iridescent wings on the rocks. It's a gorgeous morning, and once back at the tower we assemble the scenes for a read-through of the rough first draft of our script, then we pack, empty the bins, and give the tables a wipe.

At 2pm, Suzanna runs us to the airport past the Union flags and bunting of the protestant villages. The plane accelerates and we are borne up into the clouds.

—

CURFEW TOWER NOTES

Like a village from an Alan Garner story, Cushendall in the Glens of Antrim is a place of barely concealed magick. Impossible to contain, this supernatural concentrate seeps from the ground like Radon gas, half as dense but twice as dangerous. In McAlister's café, the ghosts of Iron Age bog men enter through the cold taps, swirl molecular in teacups while overhead rooks patrol the skies overhead cawing trespass like the agents of Sauron. With its pastel-painted houses and garish gable-end frieze celebrating a hundred years of the local hurling team, one could be forgiven for thinking that this rural community on the ruggedly beautiful northeast coast of Northern Ireland is just a pretty but inconsequential leftover, a faded picture postcard of the old country, but beneath the surface layer of Cushendall lies a preternatural undertone often perceptible to sensitive outsider 'blow-ins' yet seemingly invisible to the locals. The veils between the gross, the subtle, and the subtlest expressions of reality are thin here. Struggle against this concept and it will retreat before you, but surrender to it and the façade of consensus reality will flake away to reveal a region as enchanted and perilous as anything depicted in a Richard Dadd painting yet as raw as the meat in Kearney the Flesher's window. The Welsh have a name for it, Annwn, the domain of magick; the Irish call it Fae. For Northern Antrim falls into a woolly and unmapped area the local press has christened 'the wild west', a lawless zone where, just fifteen kilometres away, two hundred sheep go missing from a farmer's field in a single night. Jägermeister girls in five-inch heels, wobbly as newborn foals pour from the bars of the Central and the Lurig and queue for takeaways while their drunken matador boyfriends fight cars unaware that Oisin, Warrior King of Tir-Na-Nog, rides through and between them on the back of a giant Irish elk. It's a Celtic Khumb Mela, a tribal gathering that predates organised religion by thousands of years. In an age where the young have lost the ability to engage with their surroundings, the youth of Cushendall bathe in their village's pre-history unawares, and like plants they draw their nutrients from their roots. Swollen with rainfall from Laurigithen mountain, the River Dall roils beneath the bridge on Glenariffe Road, a turbulent liquid diary bisecting the village, churning dark with peat and blood, amber beads, and particles of iron from the Neolithic. The Dall channels the past; fresh water to salt, ashes to ashes, dawn till dusk, before discharging its blue specific energy into Cushendall Bay, the Sea of Moyle. In the ruins of twelfth century Layd churchyard, lichen-covered gravestones jut like broken molars. From its clifftop edge, the haunted come to stare out to the Mull of Kintyre fifteen miles distant and the Isle of Arran that rises like a mythic kingdom through a tracing paper mist. On Friday and Saturday nights, in the back room of Johnny Joe's bar when the borans rumble to the blind girl's penny whistle, the air is charged with an 'otherness'—an invisible etheric ribbon that affects the listener on a sub-atomic level. Harmless to the short-term visitor but amassing in dangerous levels in the 1700 local inhabitants, the residents of

Bun Abhaan Dalla live work and procreate in this Shamanic spirit dimension, as if this were all perfectly normal. Meanwhile, Van Morrison's asking, 'Did ye get healed?'

IV
SEMI-PRECIOUS METAL

OCTOBER 2019. After a gap of eight years, I am back in the Philippines, and this time I'm headlining a prestigious new-wave festival in the Okada Resort, a forty-two-hectare, eight-billion-dollar entertainment complex overlooking Manila Bay. Tonight, for the first time in my life, I will be performing under my own name—and, unlike my last visit here, so far nothing at all (touch Carrera marble) has gone wrong. Even the weather is behaving itself.

This is the fittest, healthiest, and sanest I have been in twenty years— not bad, considering my high mileage. In an effort to prepare, I've been running along the dunes on Crosby Beach near my home in Liverpool these past nine months and exercising in my local gym. I've also been practising more of those ludicrous Chester Cheetah singing exercises. For tonight's show, I've ditched the tasteful Roxy suits of 2011 and I'm flirting with a sartorial cliché: black jeans and fitted shirt, the Mexican silver skull ring I bought when my father died, wrist chain, necklace, three-tier studded belt, and boots. I'm stopping just short of heavy metal, but more Josh Homme than Rob Halford. This is *semi-precious metal.*

This *meta* image is entirely predicated on the assumption that my audience knows that I'm normally the tweed suit and brogues guy. In dressing this way, I am only *pretending* to be a rock star. But in the pretending I believe that I may finally locate the authentic artist in me.

Back in the early 80s, the greatest crime a post-punk frontman could commit was to be seen to be trying too hard. Dressing in cheesy 'rock star' clothes, 'working' the stage, attempting to charm the crowd—all were perceived by my Liverpool circle as being akin to prostitution. All that 'Good evening, Merthyr Tydfil! Are you ready to rock? I can't hear you! I said, are you ready to . . .' Fuck that shit. Right?

Thing is, in rejecting those showbiz tropes, I threw Axl Rose's ugly baby out with the bathwater. I forgot that the frontman holds the reins to the entire show. My reluctance to play the game even slightly may have been 'post-punk', but it hobbled the career of many an ex-bandmate. No wonder that, immediately after working with me, almost to a man they found fame and success.

For the first time in my life, I am preparing to give my audience the performance it actually wants—and, let's face it, paid for. Earlier tonight, Jesse advised me to just 'play the hits'. But 1983 Top 50 single 'Flaming Sword' aside, I have no 'Killing Moon', no 'Reward', no 'Lucky You' in my set. Housewives have never sung along to anything I've had a hand in, and cigarette lighters are never held aloft at my gigs. On my last trip out here with The Wild Swans, I ignored Jesse's advice, and Ricky, Rich, Les, Mike, Stuart, and I peppered our setlist with songs from our just-released album, *Coldest Winter For 100 Years*. Just released in the UK, that is—not just released in the Philippines. Cue a thousand Filipino fans all checking into Facebook and Twitter at the same instant.

The Wild Swans haven't had any 'hits' per se, but all of the songs on our two late-80s Sire Records albums are massively popular here.

'Okay, Jesse. I'll play *the hits*,' I tell him. Leaning in, I add, 'But I'm getting old, I might forget the words.'

Handing me my Jack Daniels, Jesse smiles. 'You might forget them, brother, but your audience won't. If you go blank, just hold out your microphone to the crowd.'

My brilliant band of Filipino musicians, The Silver Swans, are pre-rehearsed, excited, and revving their engines backstage. As my intro music plays over the PA, I'm chatting with my friend Owen Vyce, who has flown over from his home in Bangkok just to attend the show and hang out with me for a few days. Owen fronted the short-lived 90s rock band Starclub, and he has rock'n'roll stories that would make Mötley Crüe blush. He's just about to land the punchline to one when an excessively loud male voice shouts over the tall, black-draped security barriers that separate the auditorium from the musician's holding area.

'Paul! Paul, over here! Let me backstage!'

Err . . . no. That's not going to happen.

'Paul! Paul! You don't know me, but I am your brother!'

Yeah, yeah, I think. *We are all brothers on this planet, but now is not the time my fanatical, possibly unhinged friend.*

'Paul! Paul!' It continues. 'Your dad got my mother pregnant when he was here in the 1960s!'

WTF?!

My bandmates—Ryan, Japo, Dax, Levy, and Japs—are now onstage, tuning up, and I am just thirty seconds away from joining them. I so don't need this.

'Paul! Paul! Let me in. I'm your broth—'

Appalled at what he sees as a major lapse in event security, Owen appoints himself as my private Vin Diesel. Incredulous that this delusional fan has been allowed to get within haranguing distance of his skinny Scouse pal, he's itching to engage. With biceps thicker than undersea fibreoptic cable, Owen is up for steaming into the crowd, ripping the guy's head off, and using his skull to drink protein shakes from, but no, I tell him. It's fine. Probably just a hotel guest who's had a few too many in the casino bar and got lost trying to find the toilets. Keyboard player Japo is frantically giving me the nod to join the band onstage, and as I climb the steps, a vast, organic cheer rises from the crowd. I'm just paces from the microphone stand when I spot my noisy doppelganger in the crowd. Over six foot tall and the only *Kanô* or Western-looking man in the room, he's hard to miss. Waving maniacally as if he's applying screen wash to the windshield of a lorry, he's determined to get my attention.

'Paul! I . . . am . . . your . . . brother! Your dad got my mother preg—'

My glittering musician friends Julian, Ian McCulloch, and Ian Broudie have all encountered the occasional 'unglued' mega-fan over the years, so I suppose it was only a matter of time before I attracted a Rupert Pupkin of my own. I'd rather wear a crown of thorns than the baseball cap my *alleged* brother-from-another-mother is wearing tonight, but I have to admit, there is a family resemblance. He will definitely look like Peter Cushing when he's old.

Fuck! Is this weird? It's definitely weird. I wouldn't normally give credence to a stranger's fantasy like this but for the fact that this one is privy to a piece of information that no one else on the planet could possibly know, which is that my late father, Captain Roy Andrew Simpson, who was never late for anything in his life, voyaged here many times in the 1960s with the Merchant Navy. My mother, Doris, who was late for her own funeral, always suspected that Dad had a girl in every port. This guy *could* be my sibling.

My magical cousin Kevin Wright, who passed away a few years ago, was the closest I ever had to a brother, and that spot is very much taken in my heart. I don't need another. My very much alive sister Val, eight hours behind us in the UK and asleep right now, is going to freak out when I tell her the news.

—

The New Wave All Stars, LVNA, Skarlet Brown and Wency Cornejo, and The Edralins have all performed and put on an incredible show tonight, but considering we are several hours into a new-wave festival, the audience is suffering from a collective slow puncture. Fatigue has set in and energy levels are dipping. It's a seated venue, and I suspect that the front rows have been assigned to wealthy hotel guests, gratis, and local dignitaries. As headliner, I feel compelled to take action. I want this evening to be a blood transfusion, not just a swig of Haliborange. As such, I've frontloaded the setlist with The Wild Swans' most popular songs out here, and I'm holding back two of the three Care singles for the encore. During the intro to 'Whirlpool Heart', I advance to the lip of the stage, remove the microphone from its stand, take up a 'Ziggy Stardust doing archery' stance, and glare over the heads of the front rows, psychically willing those seated further back to rise up and walk to me.

These beautiful, generous people grew up on the music of The Wild Swans. Tickets to this event were not cheap—they wanted to come. All they need to really come alive tonight is for me to give them permission to do so. Naturally shy, beyond singing I rarely give anything of myself onstage, but tonight I give it all. When I go blank on a lyric during the song 'Immaculate', I follow Jesse's advice and thrust the microphone out as if it's a magic wand, and—*abracadabra!*—the missing line is sung back to me by the entire room. Touching the outstretched hands of those nearest the stage brings a human tsunami rushing down to the front. *Voila!* The blue touchpaper is lit. Kick out the jams, Brutherfuckerrrrr!

Courting crowd participation may be normal practice for your Tim Booths and Liam Gallaghers, but it's a new one on me, and it's joyous. Who knew? Well, everyone who has ever climbed onto a stage before but me, obviously. It's not the great selling out I always believed it be but rather just—as my teen idol Bill Nelson sang—a fair exchange.

Seventy minutes later, high on post-show adrenalin, I'm backstage, peeking through a door crack into the venue, scanning the long queue forming for photos and autographs. There's no sign of 'our kid' anywhere. He's vapourised. Did I dream him? Asking around, security tell me that they know nothing about any missing brother, but they did have to eject one crazy *puti satanas* from the venue just two songs into my set. Apparently, his flailing arms were seriously infringing upon the concert photographer's personal space, and his endless yelling was ruining the audio recording of the gig. Bit harsh. This was hardly Dylan at the Budokan.

Midnight in my ultra-luxurious suite atop the Okada, I'm eating sushi washed down with Lakan coconut liqueur while trying to process the evening's remarkable turn of events. God, this place is insane. Adjacent to my bedroom is a walk-in wardrobe larger than the footprint of my entire house in Liverpool, three double bathrooms with showers, four high-tech Japanese-style talking toilets, an eight-person hot tub, a cinema and karaoke room, a homeopathic massage room, a kitchen/dining room with seating for twenty, and a balcony overlooking the bay. Okay, whatever you are now imagining, quadruple it, then dip it all in twenty-four-carat gold.

—

5:49am. Dawn is breaking over the bay, but despite having a bed the size of the Ark Royal and swallowing enough sleeping pills to fell an Aberdeen Angus, I haven't slept a wink. Why? Ask long-dead 70s TV comedy icon Terry Scott, who, drunk on ninety percent proof coconut liqueur and dressed in semi-precious metal fashion, locked himself in the karaoke room all night singing:

Who put jam in Mother's shoe?
Who made real caterpillar stew?
Who locked Grandad in the loo?
My brother.

V
PAINT THE DEVIL

NOVEMBER 2019. ELEVATOR STUDIOS, LIVERPOOL. The professional recording studio I have hired to record the new Wild Swans album may be located on Cheapside, but that's the only cheap thing about it. I'm using the bulk of my fee from last month's solo concerts in the Philippines to fund this project, and despite the studio's owner, Tim, giving me 'mate's rates', financially this fortnight is still going to stretch me like a Slinky.

In the eight years since drummer Stuart and I last saw each other, he has trained and qualified as a GP; guitarist Ricky has had a son and toured the world several times over with the BJM, while also producing bands and promoting gigs in China; Les 'Bunnyman' Pattinson has emigrated to Australia; and the keyboard player and the engineer of our last album, Richard Turvey, has become a successful record producer, working with bands including Blossoms and The Coral. Conspicuous by his absence, Michael 'Mooneye' Mooney is *Missing, Presumed Groovy*.

Me? I've sat drinking rum in the Little Grapes on Roscoe Street with my friend Jeff, about as productive as a Gonk. Ok, I've not been completely idle: I've written a short story called 'The Life And Adventures Of Lord Biro', inspired by a young Liverpool eccentric I knew in the late 80s who dressed like a Poundland John Keats, wrote poetry using a feather sticky taped to a ballpoint pen, and tragically died of a heroin overdose after moving to London. That story led to a theatre commission to write a play that I set in my late-70s bedsit on Rodney Street, concerning a man who, for reasons revealed only in the final moment of the last act, believes that snow is falling from his ceiling, his carpet is a minefield, and that upon waking each morning the guard towers and barbed-wire and around his bed draw ever closer. A second play I drafted was a two-hander fantasy set in a one-room temporal anomaly in which Thomas de Quincy, high on opium in his rooms in 1830s Everton, reclines upon a double chaise longue conversing with his 1980s Liverpool stoner counterpart, each of them believing the other a phantasm—an idea that was openly stolen from me on the very same day that I naively blogged its central conceit on social media.

With Les out of the country, I have engaged Edgar Jones, formerly of The Stairs and an old friend of The Wild Swans, to sit in on bass. Having just arrived back in the 'pool after a long string of European dates, Ed is at the top of his game right now. Somehow, with just MP3s of my home demos of the album to listen to on the flight home, between endless cups of tea and 'rollies', he is pulling off something miraculous on his beautiful Gibson Ripper. Like James Jamerson on Marvin's *What's Goin' On*, Edgar is supplying consistently cool parts to these wildly diverse songs of mine while also linking them all into a cohesive and soulful whole. On a break from touring, Enrique 'Ricky' Maymi is back on board and is next door right now, layering drones into a sonic mille-feuille on a baritone Fender Six.

Incredibly, Marty Willson-Piper, formerly of neo-psychedelic Australian janglers The Church, has agreed to play guitar on the album and has driven up from Cornwall with his elegant musician wife, Olivia, and a few of his favourite guitars. Nineteen of them, to be precise—beautiful, rare models by Rickenbacker, Gretch, Gibson, Vox, Burns, and Fender. I'm scared to tell him that the only six-string that gives me the post-punk glow I crave is my ten-bob Japanese Kasuga.

Henry Priestman, a regular on all of my records from 1996 onwards, drops in to say hello and immediately gets drafted in to play piano, and when my good friend Russ Sanders calls in, he presents each of us with a beautiful Zippo lighter engraved with the Wild Swans logo.

The session is being engineered by tousle-haired wunderkind Tom Roach. He may only look about twelve years old but I instinctively trust his sonic judgment from day one. Every time Tom gets up to stretch, I slide into his padded chair, hoping some of his tranquillity will rub off on me.

Breaking for roll-ups every twenty minutes, Ricky and Edgar are the smokers; drummer Stuart and I are the drinkers, so we begin each day by nipping out for a few bottles of red, and at the slightest pause or technical hitch during recording, we escape to the nearby Irish pub to decompress over snatched pints of stout. Being progressive rock fans, Marty and I bond by playing virtual prog Top Trumps. There are no rules; the game consists of us simply naming vinyl obscurities, hoping to find one the other doesn't know. *Stained Glass Stories* by Cathedral, *Caverns Of Your Brain* by Lift, *An Invisible World Revealed* by Krokodil. Frustratingly, he not only owns first pressings of everything I name but also the Japanese or Italian variants. I hold my own, but only by making up ludicrous band names and album titles while keeping a poker face. My winning hand is a Cold War-era Russian bootleg of Kriegsmarine's *Toltec* pressed onto an X-ray of a child's fractured femur.

Juliette Binoche and chocolate-covered Tunnock's wafers aside, nothing is perfect, so although no punches are thrown during the recording session, by the end of week two, nerves, as well as guitars, have been jangled. On the very last day of recording, Marty, normally as serene as a zen master, explodes when pushed too far by a misjudged comment, and Stuart storms off temporarily without a goodbye. But, in our fucked-up musicians-of-a-certain-age defence, one can't split the atom without a massive release of energy. Volatile materials require careful handling.

Ludicrously, the 'soft metal' look I premiered in Manila has now become my default wardrobe, and all things sulphurous and infernal have seeped into my recent writing. There is a German saying, *Paint the devil on the wall, and he will come*, and it's true: dwell too long in the underworld and you'll end up shunning the light. With Jung's *Red Book* and Rogan P. Taylor's *The Death And Resurrection Show* in my reading pile, lyrically the whole album has darkened significantly.

This is particularly noticeable in the album's epic opening song, 'Lucifer's Childhood', for which I've imagined a scenario where the creator chances upon his old favourite, the Morning Star, while out on patrol one day, finding him in reduced circumstances and begging for change. Appalled at how far the mighty are fallen, he sings, 'You look rough, my old friend. Do you still run with the bad crowd? Where are you dwelling now?' 'Three Lions' it's not.

Perhaps it's an age thing, but of late I am increasingly beginning to dwell on the possibility of my experiencing an early death. As far as I know, I'm not ill—not seriously, anyway—but fear nibbles at me like a rodent trying to gnaw through a skirting board. As Dylan at his most visionary sang, 'It's not dark yet, but it's getting there.'

One morning, in the late 90s, when my son was still just a toddler, I awoke in the early hours disturbed by a terrifying lucid dream. Tiptoeing out of bed so as not to wake anyone, I rifled through cupboard drawers in search of a pen and paper and meticulously wrote it down in as much detail as I could while shivering on the hallways stairs.

Battalions of angels walk broken and ruined from battle. Thousands upon thousands returning to the marble courts of paradise from a multi-dimensional war in heaven. I am horrified to see that their wings, a symbol of their purified and expanded auras are coated and dripping with a black tar-like substance that appears to swallow light. Inconsolable with grief, this tide of light-bearers limp past me like seabirds caught in a tanker spill. Ashamed by their lowly state, the angels weep uncontrollably because the unthinkable has happened—the side of goodness and love and positivity is losing. To me, that scenario is a spiritual impossibility. Gently smiling, I try to reason with them, telling them that as long as just one photon of light remains housed inside any one of us, we can use it to command the negative entities back to a lower, denser plane of existence, and once contained there, we will triumph over the forces of darkness for all eternity. But, infected from their proximity to their demonic counterpart while fighting, my brother angels have literally become 'dispirited'. They are not listening. As the implications of losing this war in heaven begin to sink in, the fear spreads telepathically, despair snowballing into a communal loss of faith. The ensuing vacuum allows the void to rush in. Panicking, one senior angel runs into a recessed chamber, a holy of holies, where he picks up and holds aloft an inscribed stone tablet, and smashes it upon the point of a marble obelisk at the room's centre. As he does this, I know that the last of the sacred seals protecting the heavens and the Earth are broken, the last spark of light within me—the very last photon in existence is extinguished, and the darkness engulfs us all. The end times are come.

'Tea, anyone?' asks Tom.

'Nah, I'm still on the wine,' replies Stuart, who I've just noticed is wearing some ridiculous star-shaped Bootsy Collins sunglasses. Reading from my lyric book, he asks me what my song 'Pleasure Receptors' is about.

'I don't know yet,' I reply honestly. 'I have no idea what any of my songs are about until years after the event, but maybe it's about when your own sexual fantasies surprise you?'

'Okaaay,' he replies. 'What about "Cooling Towers"? No, wait! "The Pinnacle Of Western Art", and . . . I can't read your writing . . . "Sacred-something"?'

'Sacred Hours'? Okay, that is one song where I do know what it is about. It's the one I've envisaged as closing the album. It's a co-write with one-time member of The Teardrop Explodes, co-founder of The Wild Swans, and renowned fine artist Ged Quinn. Just last month, I'd driven down to his farm in Cornwall to hang out for a few days, to see his new paintings, get fucked up on his wine, and enjoy whatever other mischief was on offer. As the day turned to evening and the empty bottles stacked up, we grew a little maudlin at how little we get to see each other these days and how time appears to speed up as we get older, and just how little of it we have left. When discussing the betrayal and collapse of The Wild Swans mk1 and that whole Lotus Eaters mess, Ged told me his side of the story of our split for the first time and expressed his regret at the small part he found himself playing in ending what was the first and purest incarnation of the group.

After dinner, while he played a mournful chord progression on his piano, I sat nearby, playing a naïve-on-purpose four-note guitar motif and improvising a vocal melody.

If we had our time over again,
If we could peel the years back,
What then?

The words just poured out, sad as Christmas.

Sacred hours with you.
Holy moments with you.

To our drunk and drugged ears, it sounded rarefied, like something Sandy Denny might have ended her live set with. I detest Dumont and Vaucaire's classic 'Non, je ne regrette rien', but only because I regret nearly everything I've ever done. Don't we all? And Paul Anka's 'My Way'? What arrogant codswallop. *I may have killed your cat and given you a black eye, Margret, but at least I did it my waaaaaay.*

'Sacred Hours' is a song about remorse; about how Ged, Jeremy Kelly, and I have spent our lives pining for a grail that we held in our hands at the age of twenty-one, then casually tossed in a skip.

When I left The Teardrop Explodes in the spring of 1979 in order to front my own band, I wasted a few months perfecting my look before answering a *Musician's Wanted* advert sticky taped to a pillar in Probe Records on Button Street.

> Bass player and drummer seek singer. Into Japan and Siouxsie & The Banshees.

Drummer Budgie aside, I wasn't fussed about either of those bands, but in phoning the number on the card, I'd finally entered the stream where magic can happen. If we don't focus our will and act, we can't complain that life has passed us by. Ged and I had conversed by mail about forming a band, but he was away studying art up in Edinburgh. If this was ever going to happen, it was going to be down to me.

Prior to all this, I'd seen Jeremy playing in local band Psychomesh. They were good, but Jeremy was ASTONISHING. He and I spoke after the gig, swapped numbers, and subsequently had a few half-baked jams in a freezing room in the local Hindu Centre, but, unlike him, I couldn't really play the white Strat I'd borrowed from Julian's brother Joss. I didn't even know if I could sing, but I had a strong image.

When Ged returned from college that August, I had the engine of a group. Justin Stavely on drums. James Weston on bass. Inviting Jeremy down to rehearse with us was the spark to the tinder I'd laid. An hour after plugging in, we had a song. Ged's verse chords, my chorus chords. It just needed words. I'd never sung a note before, and when I did open my mouth, something emaciated and horrible escaped.

What blessed thing, stirs me from my slumber?

Jesus! I thought. *Where did he come from? Slumber! Who says that? I'm from Huyton! What a cunt.*

—

During a lunch break from recording at Elevator, I bump into Ian Broudie, who invites me to accompany him back to a large rehearsal space nearby, where he and his fellow Lightning Seeds are doing the technical run-throughs for their upcoming Jollification Anniversary Tour. As we arrive, Ian's eyes go wide and his mouth hangs open. While he's been out getting coffee, an enormous fibreglass strawberry has been delivered, winched up to the lighting gantry, and secured by a heavy-duty chain. Some Spinal Tap-style metric/imperial miscalculation must have been made, as it's fucking ENORMOUS, leaving barely any room beneath it for the musicians to stand. It's a wondrous thing, and we can't stop laughing.

Before I leave, Ian blindsides me by inviting me to sing with him onstage at the Philharmonic Hall tomorrow night. I'm incredibly moved and have to fight back a genuine urge to cry. I've been carrying the guilt of my walking out on him and our Care project for thirty-five years. Back in 1984, blinded by a doomed infatuation, I'd abandoned my girlfriend, my home, and my band in the same instant, all for a season in Hell in London. Despite Ian's subsequent success with The Lightning Seeds, I know how damaging my actions must have been for him at the time. He and I mimed to our records on TV back in the day, but although we recruited a bass player and drummer, Care split up before we got ever got the opportunity to perform live. Ian asking me to join him onstage tomorrow at his hometown gig is a huge gesture, and I am temporarily winded by this kindness.

Walking back to Elevator, my mind is reeling. So much has happened since Ian and I hung out together when he produced my 1990 album *Space Flower*. In 2015, my decades-long marriage collapsed in a sudden and painful fireball. Jan was just eighteen and I was twenty-one when we met and fell in love. She liked my non-conformity and I liked her Aquarian calm. We married in 1991, and six years later we had a beautiful son together whom we adored. Entirely coincidentally, but as if it were scripted, the week he turned eighteen, time bent, reality collapsed, and before either of us had had a chance to even talk about the implications, I moved out of the family home. I can only blame myself for the derailment; Jan only ever tried to keep us on track. I just regret hurting her so badly, and the collateral damage to our families, and circle of friends. Never marry a rock musician. Seriously. We are selfish, ungrateful children walking into traffic while following brightly coloured balloons.

The following afternoon, I leave the Wild Swans session early and head over to the Philharmonic Hall, where Ian, his son Riley, and backing singers Niamh and Fiona of The Sundowners are waiting for me to catch a twice-through-the-song acoustic rehearsal in the green room. Later that evening, while waiting backstage to be introduced as a surprise guest to a packed house, I become jellified with nerves. Singing the high notes on the bridge of 'Flaming Sword' was hard enough when I was a young man, never mind now. Typically, at that very moment onstage, I almost forget to sing it at all, but Ian, being a pro, leans in as a cue to remind me. He and the band sound fantastic tonight, but it's a below-par performance from me. I can live with that, though, as from where I was standing, it was something infinitely better: a healing, a cure.

—

With the backing tracks for the album completed, The Wild Swans go our separate ways for the Christmas holidays. The plan is for me to return to Elevator in the new year to record the vocals and mix the album when schedules allow, but, come spring, Britain is hurled into suspended animation. COVID-19 has arrived, uninvited and about as welcome as a drugs raid. When my friend Hambi Haralambous dies while on a respirator in Liverpool's Royal Hospital from complications arising after contracting the virus, my friends and I are rocked. With its near-deserted streets and faces hidden by PPE masks, Merseyside looks like the set of *12 Monkeys*.

With the UK on lockdown, I spend the bulk of 2020 in my study, creating elaborate collages of eminent Victorian gentlemen transformed through scissors and glue into psychedelic Love Dragoons. When I post a particularly dark mycological collage online, Will Sergeant insists on buying it from me. It's Will—I can't take his money! But he won't take no for an answer, rides over on his motorbike, and stuffs a bunch of cash in my hand.

From 1977 onward, when Will and I made music together under the name Industrial Domestic, he has only ever been supportive of everything I've ever attempted. He's played on my Skyray records, joined The Wild Swans onstage, and even when he's been away on long international tours with the Bunnymen, he's always made a point of staying in touch. In the days before email, I would receive postcards, records, and souvenirs—once even from behind the Iron Curtain. Will is writing a memoir himself right now, and judging from the excerpts he's sent me, it's brilliant. None of my pretentious, over-ornamented fuckery.

When Preston punk band Ginnel see photos of my artwork online, they ask me to create a cover for their debut single. Spurred on, I use an earlier piece for the sleeve of *Death Must Be Beautiful*, a previously unreleased 2004 solo album of mine to be released on ex-Shack member Pete Wilkinson and Nick Graff's AV8 Records. Written and recorded while I was suffering from particularly bad depression after the recent death of my father, I considered the collection too lyrically bleak and too sonically raw for release at the time.

When award-winning documentary team Grant McPhee and Angela Slaven of *Big Gold Dream* and *Teenage Superstars* fame get in touch to discuss my involvement in their projected film about Zoo Records-era Liverpool, it would appear that I am not quite as invisible as I thought—not completely erased. According to Grant, I am the 'missing thread' running through the tapestry of the Liverpool music scene. I don't know about that, but being unwell with the slight return of my Sri Lankan virus when on camera, with crazy lockdown hair and beard, I certainly resemble a medieval wizard.

'Oh, God,' I say. 'I look like a tramp. I should have got my hair cut.'

Grant disagrees. 'No, you look like a rock star.' Bless him. If I do, it's not Ziggy Stardust but a member of Hawkwind.

After asking me to bring some period photos and Zoo Records ephemera to the shoot, Grant is appalled when I dump a binbag on his hotel bed and the actual copy of the *Daredevil* comic I found the name for The Teardrop Explodes in over forty years ago tumbles out, along with the first draft lyrics to 'Revolutionary Spirit.

'These should be in a museum!' he exclaims.

—

One afternoon, while drinking with my son in the Ship & Mitre on Dale Street, I am approached by a stranger. 'Paul Simpson? I thought it was you! Sorry to bother you. I just wondered when your book is coming out?'

'Next year,' I say.

'I can't wait,' he replies. 'It's about time someone documented the Liverpool scene in the 80s. All those clubs, all those fantastic bands.'

'Thank you,' I say. But mentally, I've fallen down a lift shaft. Is that really what is expected of me? Surely those Eric's-era band-origin stories have already been told, albeit with little peripheral vision or sense of what Brian Eno calls *scenius*. I have zero interest in chronicling my musical journey like that, let alone that of Merseyside's entire post-punk scene. That story needs to be told by a more impartial writer than me. Anyone in my wider music circle flipping through my paperback hoping to find their band's histories written for them is going to be horribly disappointed. I'm writing a memoir, not an autobiography—the clue is in the name. Cheesier, and containing more holes than a block of Emmental, mine, if I do ever get it written, will be a trojan horse built to conceal photons, a patched and sewn Frankenstein's monster of psychotherapy and analysis. Somewhere near the end of my book, I'd also like to reveal the secret global plan to reduce the Earth's population through a series of—

Ben is appalled.

'What the fuck, Dad? Don't tell your publishers that, for God's sake.'

My son knows I'm eccentric, but he's okay with it. He knows it's not destructive but a creative Dalinian, Blakean, John Cowper Powys, Richard Dadd kind of shallow madness. Anyway, he can't talk. The Discordian apple doesn't fall far from the tree.

—

When the CEO of a swishy new record company messages me, writing that he considers me an 'enigma' and wants to sign me to his label as their heritage act, and how he's adamant that he can get the next Wild Swans album into the charts, I am ecstatic. I haven't cared about the charts since I was fourteen years old, and I still don't, if I am honest, but this is HUGE, and I phone Gemma, my partner of six years, to tell her the news. Christmas is back on! When a month goes by without hearing anything further from him, I call his city-centre offices, only to be told that after examining sales figures for my last record, he's changed his mind.

Really? Am I going mad? I mean, either I am an enigma or I'm not. I later discover that he's found and signed another heritage act, and, just to add lemon juice to the wound, it's an old friend of mine—one I helped get started in music back in the late 70s. You can't throw a rock in this town without concussing an enigma, apparently.

Fuck it. I'm becoming inured. Just another harpoon scar on the back of a fifty-two-hertz whale.

Meanwhile, Gemma, the artistic director of Liverpool's Everyman & Playhouse Theatres for these past eighteen years, is considering a new professional adventure. An East End Londoner by birth, she loves Liverpool even more than I do, but opportunities for theatre directors on Merseyside are limited. She's being actively headhunted right now for jobs outside of the area, and I'm encouraging her. The truth is, I've been feeling a little unloved in my own city of late. I'd miss seeing my son and my friends so often, but how long can you wait in the cold for the last bus home before you have to start walking?

'Wouldn't you miss Liverpool?' Gemma asks.

'God, yes,' I say, 'but I can work from anywhere.'

Gemma knows that, by work, I don't mean *work*, I mean that I have a memoir to finish, an album to complete, record sleeve commissions to create, and the kernel of my first novel.

'Fortune favours the bold,' I say. 'We must be fluid. We can't expect magical things to happen if we don't enter the stream.'

'Where's all this water coming from?' she laughs. 'Are you on drugs?'

'Not anymore,' I reply.

Something is coming. I can feel it.

EPILOGUE

*I have no money, no resources, no
hopes. I am the happiest man alive.*

HENRY MILLER

Fold back wings to full extent.

MILK CARTON OPENING INSTRUCTIONS

In the autumn of 2019, when a police marksman shoots dead a rare white stag running wild through the terraced backstreets and industrial estates of Bootle, just two miles from my home, I read it as a sign that it is time for me to leave Merseyside.

Whatever the deputy chief constable's excuses to the press, killing a messenger from the otherworld cannot auger well; one doesn't hunt the fabled white buck when it appears, one follows it. Meanwhile, my own magic had been haemorrhaging for years, the radical counterculture of my Liverpool adolescence long gone, in a commercial reconstruction of the city that I couldn't locate the heart of. Rootbound and devitalised, I needed to force a change.

In January 2022, my partner and I board a train bound for Glasgow. With just one suitcase apiece, we feel like excited teenagers running away from home. Hell-bent on re-enchantment, while Gemma finds her feet in her new appointment, I map the city on foot, searching for a permanent home and any residual magic hiding between the tenements.

In February, we awake to snow and the news that Russia has invaded Ukraine and that Nobel prizewinning physicist Roger Penfold has declared that the Big Bang wasn't the birth of our universe at all but the death of the previous one.

Whether it's some *I Know Where I'm Going*-style, Simpsons-returning-to-Scotland-after-a-hundred-years thing, or simply having fresh soil to root into, the energy of Glasgow swirls positively, and we expand into it. Come autumn, after a gap of forty years, The Wild Swans' debut single, 'Revolutionary Spirit', is re-released, and the Queen of England dies, right on cue.

PAUL SIMPSON. GLASGOW. SEPTEMBER 2023.

AUTHOR'S NOTE

Writing in the historical present tense denies one any reflection. I wrote it as I remember feeling it in the moment. As such, I hope any friends mentioned in the text can forgive any seemingly hard tackles and oversharing. It was a hard call, but out of respect for their privacy, some fundamental companions in my story were omitted.

—

Love and thank you to the multi-camera-angle brain that is my partner Gemma Bodinetz, and to my son Ben for lovingly haranguing me to finish this book.

Sincere gratitude to my editor Tom Seabrook for his tact, skills, and patience, all at Jawbone Press, and to my agent Matthew Hamilton for the positive booster shots.

To my sister Val, and lifelong friends: Will Sergeant, Les Pattinson, Ged Quinn, David Palmer, Henry Priestman, John Montgomery, Jeff Young, Mike Badger, Mick Finkler, Ian Broudie, Bill Drummond, Ian McCulloch, Rolo McGinty, Julian Cope, Mick Houghton, Dave Balfe, John Hollingsworth, Jem Kelly, Ricky Mayme, Mike Mooney, Rich Turvey, Steve Beswick, Stuart Mann, Edgar Jones, Marty Willson-Piper, Joe Fearon, and all past members of The Teardrop Explodes, The Wild Swans, Care, and Echo & The Bunnymen. Love to Doreen Allen, Jayne Casey, Roy White, Deaf School, and the Liverpool Eric's posse. Jeff Davis and all at Probe Records, Justin Stavely, Gary Lornie, Dave Pickett, Paul Green, Martyn Muscatelli, Phil and David Hynes, John McEvoy, Michael Head, Jon Savage, Courtney Love, Robin Barbur, Chris Sharrock, Peter

Coyle, Suzanna Boyce, Stephen 'Zippy' Kearney Ian McNabb, Hilary Steele, Penny Kiley, Francesco Milena, Suzanna McBride, Peasy Gordon, Pete Wylie, Rachel Furness, Owen Vyce, Luc Vergier, Marcus Russell, Mike Stoddart, Richard Hermitage, and Andy Catlin.

For offering me torches when light was failing: Russ Sanders, Mitch Poole, Colin Fallows, Dave Battersby, and Nick Halliwell.

Serpent love to Mike Ward, Mike Cross, Kev Fox, Ant Walker, David Wrench Alan Holmes, Zoe Skoulding, Ant Walker, Emyr Glyn Williams, Laurie Gane, Julie McGrail, and members of The Serpents living or dead (a stand-alone book).

Recent love to The Voices Of The Galloverse, John Fleming, Nick Graff and Pete Wilkinson at AV8, Neil Tilly, Ian Allcock at Optic Nerve, Stuart Gould, Dom Martin, Richie at 1 of 100, Grant McPhee, Angela Slaven, Douglas MacIntyre, Gorbalz, Ian and Julia Smith, Chris Thompson, Graeme Skinner, Bobby Bluebell, and the LNFG all stars.

Long distance hugs to my Filipino brothers: Jesse Cambossa Sr, Arnold Toledo, Japo, Dax, Ryan, Levy, Japs, and Zairel.

'Miss you's to my dad Roy Andrew Simpson, Kevin Wright, Andrew Billington, Alan Wills, James Weston, Hambi Haralambous, Pat Bellis, Janice Long, John Hodgkinson, Rommel Avenido, Rio Parr, Seymour Stein, Jake Brockman, Andrew Billington, and the incomparable and incandescent Peter Louis Vincent deFreitas. Be seeing you. x

ALSO AVAILABLE
FROM JAWBONE PRESS

The Yacht Rock Book: The Oral History Of The Soft, Smooth Sounds Of The 70s And 80s Greg Prato

What's Big And Purple And Lives In The Ocean? The Moby Grape Story Cam Cobb

Swans: Sacrifice And Transcendence: The Oral History Nick Soulsby

Small Victories: The True Story Of Faith No More Adrian Harte

AC/DC 1973–1980: The Bon Scott Years Jeff Apter

King's X: The Oral History Greg Prato

Keep Music Evil: The Brian Jonestown Massacre Story Jesse Valencia

Lunch With The Wild Frontiers: A History Of Britpop And Excess In 13½ Chapters Phill Savidge

Wilcopedia: A Comprehensive Guide To The Music Of America's Best Band Daniel Cook Johnson

Lydia Lunch: The War Is Never Over: A Companion To The Film By Beth B. Nick Soulsby

Zeppelin Over Dayton: Guided By Voices Album By Album Jeff Gomez

What Makes The Monkey Dance: The Life And Music Of Chuck Prophet And Green On Red Stevie Simkin

So Much For The 30 Year Plan: Therapy? The Authorised Biography Simon Young

She Bop: The Definitive History Of Women In Popular Music Lucy O'Brien

Relax Baby Be Cool: The Artistry And Audacity Of Serge Gainsbourg Jeremy Allen

Seeing Sideways: A Memoir Of Music And Motherhood Kristin Hersh

Two Steps Forward, One Step Back: My Life In The Music Business Miles A. Copeland III

It Ain't Retro: Daptone Records & The 21st-Century Soul Revolution Jessica Lipsky

All I Ever Wanted: A Rock 'n' Roll Memoir Kathy Valentine

Southern Man: Music And Mayhem In The American South Alan Walden with S.E. Feinberg

Renegade Snares: The Resistance & Resilience Of Drum & Bass Ben Murphy and Carl Loben

Frank & Co: Conversations With Frank Zappa 1977–1993 Co de Kloet

Here They Come With Their Make-Up On: Suede, Coming Up ... And More Adventures Beyond The Wild Frontiers Jane Savidge

This Band Has No Past: How Cheap Trick Became Cheap Trick Brian J. Kramp

Gary Moore: The Official Biography Harry Shapiro

Holy Ghost: The Life & Death Of Free Jazz Pioneer Albert Ayler Richard Koloda

Conform To Deform: The Weird & Wonderful World Of Some Bizzare Wesley Doyle

Happy Forever: My Musical Adventures With The Turtles, Frank Zappa, T. Rex, Flo & Eddie, And More Mark Volman with John Cody

Johnny Thunders: In Cold Blood—The Official Biography (Revised & Updated) Nina Antonia

Absolute Beginner: Memoirs Of The World's Best Least-Known Guitarist Kevin Armstrong

Turn It Up: My Time Making Hit Records In The Golden Age Of Rock Music Tom Werman

ALSO AVAILABLE
FROM JAWBONE PRESS

The Yacht Rock Book: The Oral History Of The Soft, Smooth Sounds Of The 70s And 80s Greg Prato

What's Big And Purple And Lives In The Ocean? The Moby Grape Story Cam Cobb

Swans: Sacrifice And Transcendence: The Oral History Nick Soulsby

Small Victories: The True Story Of Faith No More Adrian Harte

AC/DC 1973–1980: The Bon Scott Years Jeff Apter

King's X: The Oral History Greg Prato

Keep Music Evil: The Brian Jonestown Massacre Story Jesse Valencia

Lunch With The Wild Frontiers: A History Of Britpop And Excess In 13½ Chapters Phill Savidge

Wilcopedia: A Comprehensive Guide To The Music Of America's Best Band Daniel Cook Johnson

Lydia Lunch: The War Is Never Over: A Companion To The Film By Beth B. Nick Soulsby

Zeppelin Over Dayton: Guided By Voices Album By Album Jeff Gomez

What Makes The Monkey Dance: The Life And Music Of Chuck Prophet And Green On Red Stevie Simkin

So Much For The 30 Year Plan: Therapy? The Authorised Biography Simon Young

She Bop: The Definitive History Of Women In Popular Music Lucy O'Brien

Relax Baby Be Cool: The Artistry And Audacity Of Serge Gainsbourg Jeremy Allen

Seeing Sideways: A Memoir Of Music And Motherhood Kristin Hersh

Two Steps Forward, One Step Back: My Life In The Music Business Miles A. Copeland III

It Ain't Retro: Daptone Records & The 21st-Century Soul Revolution Jessica Lipsky

All I Ever Wanted: A Rock 'n' Roll Memoir Kathy Valentine

Southern Man: Music And Mayhem In The American South Alan Walden with S.E. Feinberg

Renegade Snares: The Resistance & Resilience Of Drum & Bass Ben Murphy and Carl Loben

Frank & Co: Conversations With Frank Zappa 1977–1993 Co de Kloet

Here They Come With Their Make-Up On: Suede, Coming Up ... And More Adventures Beyond The Wild Frontiers Jane Savidge

This Band Has No Past: How Cheap Trick Became Cheap Trick Brian J. Kramp

Gary Moore: The Official Biography Harry Shapiro

Holy Ghost: The Life & Death Of Free Jazz Pioneer Albert Ayler Richard Koloda

Conform To Deform: The Weird & Wonderful World Of Some Bizzare Wesley Doyle

Happy Forever: My Musical Adventures With The Turtles, Frank Zappa, T. Rex, Flo & Eddie, And More Mark Volman with John Cody

Johnny Thunders: In Cold Blood—The Official Biography (Revised & Updated) Nina Antonia

Absolute Beginner: Memoirs Of The World's Best Least-Known Guitarist Kevin Armstrong

Turn It Up: My Time Making Hit Records In The Golden Age Of Rock Music Tom Werman